PRAISE FOR **THE LAST RIDGE**

"The story is a good one . . . [Jenkins] is intent on describing the grim realities of battle."　　　　　　　　　　　　　**—The New York Times Book Review**

"Researched thoroughly, written clearly and dramatized with aplomb, this presentation of the U.S. 10th Mountain Division's WWII exploits increases our knowledge of the war's Italian theater—and of the postwar American outdoor recreation industry."　　　　　　　　　　**—Publishers Weekly**

"Ambrose is gone, but journalist-historian McKay Jenkins capably works the same territory in *The Last Ridge*, exploring individual and group heroism in a little-known corner of WWII history. . . . A roaring good story, with requisite run-ins with pesky brass and plenty of villainous foes to dispatch."　　　　　　　　　　　　　　　　　**—The Hollywood Reporter**

"Compelling."　　　　　　　　　　　　　　　　　　**—The Denver Post**

"[A] gripping war story . . . brutal and amazing . . . riveting . . . Jenkins brilliantly blends the nuts-and-bolts battle history with the view from the front in the words of soldiers and their commanders."　　　　　　　　　　　**—Omaha World-Herald**

"Like *The White Death*, Jenkins' new book portrays the drama and heartache that can result when people are pitted against the environment, in this case, during wartime."　　　　　　　　　　　　　　　**—Naples Daily News**

"Jenkins' direct descriptions of combat leave no room for euphemisms. . . . [A] competent composition."　　　　　　　　　　　　　　**—Booklist**

"Engaging . . . a fine acccount, for WWII and outdoor adventure buffs alike."　　　　　　　　　　　　　　　　　　　　**—Kirkus Reviews**

"*The Last Ridge* tells a great, untold story of mountaineering and war. It's a terrific read, sharp with characters, full of real drama, and, best of all, it's true. I can almost see the movie." —RICHARD PRESTON, **author of** *The Hot Zone*

"Stymied by army bureaucrats, forced to climb snowfields without ice axes or crampons, trained in skills that were never properly exploited, the soldiers of the 10th Mountain Division nonetheless became the stuff of myth. Without McKay Jenkins' meticulous research, the achievements and eccentricities of this remarkable group of men could easily have been forgotten. Instead, they have been brought to life."

—ANNE FADIMAN, **author of** *The Spirit Catches You and You Fall Down*

"The 10th Mountain Division was the only American Alpine unit to fight during World War II, and its heroic and daring exploits during the final months of the Italian campaign are fully documented by McKay Jenkins in this stirring, first-rate account of men at war."

—CARLO D'ESTE, **author of** *Eisenhower: A Soldier's Life*

"Few have written about the Army's elite 10th Mountain Division, and no one has done so as dramatically and with such passion and insight as McKay Jenkins. The perfect war story has, at long last, found the perfect storyteller." —ANDREW CARROLL, **editor of** *War Letters: Extraordinary Correspondence from American Wars*

"*The Last Ridge* is one of the very best books yet written about any part of the World War II story. My friend the late Stephen Ambrose would be proud of this work about one of the most fascinating, yet little-known records of the mountain ski patrols—both in war and in the peacetime that followed."

—SENATOR GEORGE MCGOVERN

"*The Last Ridge*, based on skillful interviews with the survivors, is a fine account of a great story, long overdue in the telling, and very well told."

—PETER MATTHIESSEN, **author of** *The Snow Leopard*

MCKAY JENKINS is the author of *The White Death: Tragedy and Heroism in an Avalanche Zone* and *The South in Black and White: Race, Sex, and Literature in the 1940s*, and the editor of *The Peter Matthiessen Reader*. He holds degrees from Amherst, Columbia's Graduate School of Journalism, and Princeton, where he received a Ph.D. in English. A former staff writer for *The Atlanta Constitution*, he is currently Professor of English and a member of the Program in Journalism at the University of Delaware. Jenkins lives in Baltimore with his family.

THE LAST RIDGE

RANDOM HOUSE TRADE PAPERBACKS

NEW YORK

THE **LAST RIDGE**

THE EPIC STORY OF AMERICA'S

FIRST MOUNTAIN SOLDIERS AND

THE ASSAULT ON HITLER'S EUROPE

M^cKAY JENKINS

2004 RANDOM HOUSE TRADE PAPERBACK EDITION

COPYRIGHT © 2003 BY McKAY JENKINS

This work was originally published in hardcover by Random
House, an imprint of The Random House Publishing Group,
a division of Random House, Inc., in 2003.

LIBRARY OF CONGRESS CATALOGING-IN-PUBLICATION DATA

Jenkins, McKay.
    The last ridge: the epic story of America's first mountain
        soldiers and the assault on Hitler's Europe / McKay Jenkins.
        p.   cm.
    Includes bibliographical references and index.
    ISBN 0-375-75951-4
        1. United States. Army. Mountain Division, 10th—
    History—20th century.   2. World War, 1939–1945—
    Regimental histories—United States.   3. World War,
    1939–1945—Campaigns—Italy.   I. Title.
D769.310th .J46   2003
940.54'215'09143—dc21   2003041419

Random House website address: www.atrandom.com

Printed in the United States of America

246897531

Book design by Barbara M. Bachman

For my parents, Donald and Carla Jenkins,

and my son, Steedman McKay Jenkins

The untrained mountain soldier has two foes—the enemy and the mountain. But he can make a friend and ally of the mountain by learning to know it. The mountain can give him cover and concealment, points of vantage and control, even, at times, food, water, and shelter.

—"Proposed Manual for Mountain Troops," Mountain Training Center, October 1943

CONTENTS

LIST OF MAPS

HIGH IN THE COLORADO ROCKIES, nearly two miles above sea level and a good three-hour drive from Denver, the cracked foundations of sixty-year-old army barracks lie along the Pando valley floor like ancestral bones. Walking these grounds and the sharp valleys that rise above them, one cannot but feel the presence of the remarkable experiment that gave birth to this country's first unit of mountain soldiers.

Like anyone who has spent time in the mountains of the American West, I have long been aware of the legacy the men of the 10th Mountain Division left after World War II. All over the Rockies, ski resorts from Aspen to Vail to Sun Valley were founded or operated, or had their ski schools directed, by division veterans returning from Europe. Paul Petzoldt, known as "the highest man in the world" after climbing to 26,000 feet on K2 in 1938, served the division as a mountain rescue instructor and later founded the National Outdoor Leadership School. After returning from the front in Italy, David Brower would go on to become the executive director of the Sierra Club. In the course of my own recent research, I met an inspiring division veteran named Bob Frauson, now a retired park ranger and wilderness rescue expert. The more I learned of these men, the more interested I became in what had moved them to lead such dignified lives working in and protecting our native wilderness; to me, the work so many veterans did after the war has been every bit as honorable as anything they did on the battlefield—perhaps more so, in that it provides us with an alternative vision of what excellent physical training and wilderness experience can mean to the national character. What these men learned during their astonishing years of mountain training made them far more than elite soldiers; it made them worthy of the great American landscape. Though this book is entirely about the 10th Mountain Division's foundation, training, and wartime experience, its imaginative origins are in a postwar legacy that has gilded virtually every mountain range in the country.

The 10th Mountain Division was officially disbanded soon after the war. In 1948, the 10th Infantry Division was reactivated at Fort Riley, Kansas; it played a role in training soldiers for the Korean War and supporting NATO in Europe. In 1958, the division was once again disbanded. In 1985, it was reactivated and moved to Fort Drum in upstate New York, becoming the first division formed since 1975 and the first based in the Northeast since World War II. Units from the division have served in the Persian Gulf during Operation Desert Storm in 1991; in Somalia during Operation Restore Hope in 1994; in Haiti a year after that; and in Bosnia in 1997. As of this writing, mountain troops have recently returned from six months on the front lines in the war against the Taliban and the Al Qaeda network, most dramatically during Operation Anaconda on Afghanistan's mountainous border with Pakistan. Three weeks into the war against Iraq, units from the division were beginning to move north into Iraq from Kuwait, initially to help upgrade roads and airfields.

But this book is concerned with the division's origins and its original members. It is based primarily on more than a thousand pages of personal letters written by soldiers during their training and battle experiences, and many hundreds of pages of military and extramilitary documents written during the division's years of training and months of fighting. All of this material is meticulously catalogued and lovingly cared for by the remarkable staff of the 10th Mountain Division Resource Center, part of the Western History and Genealogy Department of the Denver Public Library. It is to this staff that I owe my greatest debt. Debbie Gemar and Barbara Walton assisted my research in ways that are truly beyond measure; their patience, diligence, and meticulous knowledge of the division's history made this project not only possible but a real pleasure. Bruce Hanson and others at the center, both staff and volunteer, were also helpful, guiding me through files and copying box upon box of documents.

I also wish to thank in the deepest way possible two division veterans, Conrad Brown and Edward "Nick" Nickerson, who not only contributed hours of interview time but scoured this manuscript from top to bottom. Brown, a retired editor, and Nickerson, a retired journalism professor from my own department at the University of Delaware, represent what Nickerson wryly calls "the Writing Tenth," a remarkably talented collection of scholars, writers, and professors from within the division's ranks whose postwar numbers sometimes seem to challenge their wartime reputation as "the Skiing Tenth."

The vast majority of the letters quoted and paraphrased in this book were taken from the collections of Denis Nunan, Stuart Abbott, Hugh Evans, and Dick Wilson, for reasons that will become apparent to anyone who reads them. All four were not only remarkably prolific but vivid and passionate writers. I was fortunate enough to interview Evans and Wilson in Boulder, Colorado, and Grantham, New Hampshire, respectively; Abbott and Nunan I also came to know through their families. My thanks in this regard to Timothy Nunan, Denis Nunan's son, and Abbie Kealy, Stuart Abbott's niece.

John Imbrie, who has become the division's unofficial majordomo of research, has been an invaluable resource; his assistance, both personal and through his meticulously updated database, helped keep facts straight. There were times during the researching of this book that he—and through him, his wife, Barbara—answered a half dozen of my inquiries a day. Newc Eldredge, the division's film archivist, also helped solve a number of perplexing problems.

I also wish to thank the veterans who gave so generously of their time during dozens of hours of personal interviews, particularly Bob Frauson, John Litchfield, Arthur Delaney, Gene Hames, Dick Wilson, Hugh Evans, Earl Clark, Howard Koch, and Harry Reinig. In Exeter, New Hampshire, Bob Bates, one of our pioneering mountaineers (and a member of the team that got Petzoldt to 26,000 feet) became, through his equipment-testing expertise, one of the cornerstones on which the division was built. Bates remains, in his nineties, an inspiration and elder statesman for those dedicated to exploring wilderness worldwide.

Dan Kennerly, whose taped oral histories provide what has to be the most vivid recollection of the division's wartime experience ever recorded, deserves thanks not only from me but from anyone interested in the division's history, or in World War II history broadly conceived. Listening to nearly two dozen hours of Kennerly's recollections was one of the most pleasurable experiences I have had as a writer; his skill, humor, and understated pathos as a storyteller place him firmly in the greatest southern tradition. For other details and anecdotes, I have also relied on a number of memoirs published by division veterans, including those written by Bill Putnam, Robert Ellis, Hal Burton, and Harris Dusenbery. Division histories, particularly Flint Whitlock's *Soldiers on Skis*, were also of great value, as was, for details on the Aleutian campaign, Brian Garfield's *The Thousand Mile War.*

In Denver, Chips and Gail Barry offered room and board during my frequent trips west, even during months when they were themselves nearly incapacitated. Ingrid Hinckley's place in Vail made my field research around Camp Hale rather less than onerous. Bruno Bartolomei, innkeeper at the Hotel Monte Grande in Vidiciatico, Italy, not only served as generous host and field guide, he taught my son, Steedman, to climb stairs.

Once again, the staff at the University of Delaware's interlibrary loan office proved themselves invaluable in locating out-of-print material from all over the country. My research assistant, Stacey Carlough, contributed not only hours of research and copyediting but a cheerfulness that made working with her a delight. Wes Davis and Chris Sheldrick, looking over sections of the manuscript, offered their usual mix of intelligence and wit; their friendship remains very dear. At Random House, Elena Schneider, Lee Boudreaux, Laura Ford, Sybil Pincus, and Lynn Anderson all helped move this book through the pipeline, and to them I am grateful. Both my editor, Scott Moyers, and my agent, Neil Olson, proved themselves remarkably able readers of military history. I owe them both deep thanks not only for their depths of knowledge but for their unwavering encouragement and support.

My wife, Katherine, and my son, Steedman, were by my side at Camp Hale, on top of Riva Ridge, and on the shores of Lake Garda. They are my tribe.

PART ONE

THE MOUNTAIN

THE NORTHERN APENNINES,
WINTER 1944

B Y DECEMBER 1944, the eighteen-month Allied effort to slit the soft underbelly of Europe had banged up against the last hard bone of the northern Apennine Mountains, a rugged line of peaks belting the width of northern Italy below the Po River valley. What had been conceived as a way to drive a knife into the Axis had instead turned into a bloody and ambivalent slog up a jagged peninsula against an enemy that had proven far more ferocious and resilient than Allied strategists had predicted. The fact was that Europe's underbelly had never been soft; Winston Churchill, who had coined the term, had gotten it tragically wrong. Italy was mountains from south to north. At best, the campaign had become a drain on Hitler's army, a third front. At worst, it was a cursed and forgotten war, where tens of thousands of men from both sides died fighting over a piece of ground that seemed to have nothing to do with the rest of the campaign in Europe.

After a great triumph in Sicily, even the Allied victories in Italy had gradually faded from view. The grim battles of Salerno, Cassino, and Anzio had given way to General Mark Clark's triumphant taking of Rome in June, but only two days later, the world's eyes had turned to the beaches of Normandy. Every week since then, it seemed, divisions had been pulled from the staggering campaign to support the push in France. The defensive genius of German Field Marshal Albert Kesselring had turned even the Allied successes into a chain of Pyrrhic victories. The advancing troops staggered north not with aplomb but with despair, news photographs capturing men's faces pulled down by months of incessant carnage.

Although the steadfastness of the Allied push up the Apennine chain had its admirers, the campaign's slow, costly progress—covering just 315 miles in 365 days—gave rise to voices critical of the entire Italian strategy. "Why should we not be frank about Italy and admit that Kesselring, on a very small budget, has done a masterful job in making a primary Allied force pay bitterly for every dubious mile of a secondary battlefield," Eric Sevareid wrote in *The Nation* in December 1944, "that no matter what heroism our superb fighters showed, the monstrously difficult terrain of the peninsula, with its few roads winding through precipitous mountains, made encirclement and destruction of a retreating enemy impossible at any stage; that the terrain was not an unknown quantity when the original plans were made? The Allied peoples—and history—may well ask whether the bloody Italian campaign has been a 'victory,' whether, indeed, it has accomplished anything of a decisive nature."[1]

If Italy were ever again to matter, General Mark Clark's Fifteenth Army Group, which oversaw the American Fifth and British Eighth Armies, would have to break the German grip on the Apennine Mountains running between Florence and Bologna, chase the retreating troops through the Po River valley, and cut them off before they escaped through the Brenner Pass into the Alps. Throughout the summer and autumn of 1944, Allied troops had attacked the mountain fortifications with a strategy one German general compared to "jabbing a thick cloth with a sharp spear." Built on the backs of forced Italian labor, the final German defensive barrier had been dubbed the *Gotenstellung,* or "Gothic Line," by Kesselring, an unshakable optimist who hoped to invoke the heroic Italian kingdoms ruled by Germanic tribes in the sixth century.

Finally, in late September 1944, the American Fifth Army broke through the Futa and Il Giogo Passes; to the east, the British Eighth Army pushed through Rimini and had begun making its way north along the Adriatic. "Nothing that the Fifth Army had done since it landed at Salerno has been harder than this breakthrough of the strongest defensive works in Italy, which the Germans thought impregnable," *The New York Times* reported on September 25. "The much vaunted Gothic Line now lies a shattered mass of rubble and battered fortifications still littered with the bodies of the enemy."[2]

The trouble was, the Apennines to the north of the Gothic Line would not crack. "Jerry's retreating, all right," a frontline joke went, "but he's taking the last ridge back with him." Twice the Americans tried to punch through the German fortifications on a round hump of a mountain called Mount Belvedere, and twice they were rebuffed. Just fifteen miles southwest of Bologna, Belvedere was the German linchpin, the most heavily fortified position in a strategically crucial series of mountain ridges. It offered German artillery positions a clear sight line onto any movement along the only north–south route in the region, Highway 64. In addition to leading to Bologna, the road was also a trunk line into the densely populated Po River valley, one of the most important industrial regions under German control and a critical source of food for the German war effort. A century and a half earlier, Napoleon had called the Po River valley "Europe's granary."

With winter fast approaching, Allied strategists grew increasingly anxious, and not simply for strategic reasons. Despite General Dwight Eisenhower's triumphs in France, and despite broad doubts about the wisdom of prolonging the fight in Italy, General Clark continued to push northward, hoping to reclaim some of the glory lost so soon after the capture of Rome. Hammering the Germans into the Alps by the end of autumn, he thought, might just also end the war in Europe.

But as had been the case since the beginning in Italy, the cliffs still facing the Allies were like a stiff palm. The Germans, taking advantage of a comparatively gentle slope on their side of the range, had spent months placing heavy weapons all along the ridgelines. Under the technical direction of the Todt Organization (founded by Dr. Fritz Todt, who had designed the German autobahns before the war), engineers had sunk into the hillsides hundreds of concrete machine-gun pillboxes and turrets of tanks equipped with 88-mm guns, and strewn landmines on every flatland approach. They had more than eighty large guns covering Highway 64 alone. Worse, the Germans had such a panoramic view that they could see not only every lone soldier walking down a dusty road but everything *behind* the Allied lines. It was, it seemed, a perfect defensive stronghold. Journalists looking in from outside the military command—and not a few soldiers looking up from below it, bled white by their seemingly unending march through Italy—began to wonder about the wisdom of continuing the quixotic drive northward. Attacking such a mountain range seemed more and more like suicide. "It is awful to die when you know that the war is won anyhow," Martha Gellhorn wrote in *Collier's* on October 28. "It is awful, and one would have to be a liar or a fool not to see this and not to feel it like a mystery, so that these days every man dead is a greater sorrow because the end of all this tragic dying is so near." The effectiveness of the German defensive position, Gellhorn wrote, made her physically ill.[3]

After eighteen months of continuous fighting, followed by weeks of bitter paralysis in which twenty-seven exhausted Allied divisions could do little more than stare up at the positions held by thirty-three Axis divisions, an American general by the name of George P. Hays flew from Washington to Naples. On January 8, in the midst of a hard freeze and a blanketing snowfall, Hays made his way to the town of Traversa, where he met with General Lucian Truscott, recently named the commander of the Fifth Army. Truscott laid out his maps and described his army's frustrations. The mountains, he said, had become too daunting, the German positions too formidable. It was like looking up at a series of castle turrets and seeing sentries waiting with cauldrons of boiling oil.

General Hays replied that every defensive position in the mountains had a keystone. Knock out the keystone, and the entire position would collapse. While soldiers firing down from mountaintops are as secure as soldiers can be, Hays argued, a ridge-top defense, once broken, crumbles as fast as any other. Or faster. A hundred years before the war in Italy, Carl von Clausewitz had written that mountain defenses can quickly become as pitiless to retreating soldiers as they had been to those on the attack.

After scanning aerial maps and poring over intelligence reports, Hays decided—as other strategists had before him—that the one remaining keystone in the Apennines was the heavily fortified Mount Belvedere, the southwestern butt of a four-mile ridge that also included, farther north, Mount Gorgolesco and Mount della Torraccia, with a series of smaller rises filling in the ridge between. Belvedere was the key.

The trouble with Mount Belvedere was that it was completely protected laterally by a dramatic five-and-a-half-mile escarpment, a series of nearly 5,000-foot peaks rising above the Dardagna River. The ridgeline looked over the lump of Mount Belvedere like a panther stalking a sow; the deeply gouged flanks facing the Allies were all sinew and coiled muscle. Running from Mount Spigolino to the mountain town of Rocca Corneta, the ridge was banded and broken by fractured limestone cliffs, a geologic formation that gave the escarpment its name: Riva Ridge, for its prehistoric position at the edge of the sea. Marine fossils could still be found all along the summit ridgeline. The ridge provided an easy position of defense and a clear line of sight for artillery observers watching over Mount Belvedere. Through aerial reconnaissance, Hays could see another reason the line had proven so attractive to the Germans: the western slope of the ridge, a rolling series of hills and plateaus, offered easy access for German resupply trucks from the towns of Sestola and Fanano.

An attack on Mount Belvedere, Hays decided, would be successful only if German artillery observers could first be knocked off Riva Ridge. Once Riva Ridge was taken, Americans could more easily direct fire on the rest of Mount Belvedere, covering an assault from the valley floor.[4]

Impossible, Truscott said. The Fifth Army had been working this line for months. Riva Ridge could not be climbed. Reconnaissance reports indicated that the German defenses were manned by soldiers from the 1044th Grenadier Regiment and the 232nd Fusilier Battalion; hundreds of reinforcements remained below, in Fanano and Sestola, where the 4th Mountain Regiment had its headquarters. How many men might be on the ridge itself was hard to estimate. Some thought 50; others thought it was closer to 170. However many there were, they all had bunkered down in well-fortified positions, with clear views over all angles of approach. With the mountain slopes behind them so gradual, the men on top could also easily be reinforced; after all, they had the entire German army in Italy to their rear. The German positions had been exceedingly well laid out along the series of the ridge's promontories, each one overseeing the other and all able to fire straight down onto any enemy attacks. So clear was the view from the top that a handful of machine gunners could fend off most attacks; indeed, the Germans were so certain of the invincibility of their position that they made no secret of their weapon emplacements. Just for kicks, it seemed, they would peer over the lip of the ridge and send down a volley or two from their burp guns just to remind the Americans of the superiority of their position.

Worse, the flanks of the mountains were locked up in ice and snow by one of the coldest winters in recent memory. What were friable, crumbling cliffs in summer were impossibly slick now. After so many months at the front lines, Truscott's men were too exhausted to fight on flatland, let alone on steep, frozen mountain slopes.[5]

To these cautions, General Hays had an audacious answer: The Germans can't shoot us if they can't see us. We'll climb the ridge at night. I've got just the men to do it. They're fresh, they're exceedingly well trained, and they know a thing or two about high country. They have just completed three long years of the most rugged training in U.S. military history, on some of the continent's highest and most forbidding terrain. Though they have yet to see a single enemy bullet, they are among the most famous soldiers in the American army. They are the 10th Mountain Division, and within a few weeks they will be right here, camped out beneath Riva Ridge.

CHAPTER ONE

SKIERS

N JULY 1942, THIRTY MONTHS before General Hays first cast his eyes on Riva Ridge, a strong-minded Irishman named Denis Nunan boarded a troop train at California's Camp Roberts and headed north to join an experimental training center at Fort Lewis, near Washington's Mount Rainier. Soldiers on the train slept in four Pullman cars and were fed in a baggage car outfitted with a wood-burning field stove bolted to the floor. Nunan had grown up in Short Hills, New Jersey, just outside New York City, and had never before seen the great mountain ranges of the West. As the train clicked north through the mountains and vast forests of the Pacific Northwest—past Mount Shasta, past Klamath Falls, and into the Cascades—Nunan found himself overcome with delight. The majesty of the landscape so transfixed him that he amended his brimming eagerness to join the fight overseas. He had thought of himself as training to liberate Europe from the Germans, he told a companion. Now, he declared, he was training to protect his own beautiful country.[1]

Immediately after Pearl Harbor, Nunan had left a desk job at IBM, and he was already well into his basic training at the infantry replacement center at Camp Roberts. Upon his arrival on the West Coast, Nunan had instantly noticed a dramatic difference in the sense both soldiers and civilians had about the war. San Francisco Bay was full of warships; military planes cruised along the Marin headlands; armed guards were ubiquitous in the city streets. "You really know there's a war on out here," he wrote home. "Too bad the East isn't as awake as they are here." When he told his military superiors about his business experience, they automatically pushed him to run the base's IBM machines, but Nunan begged off. Although he was thirty-two, much older than the average enlisted man, he was determined to fight on the front lines as a private. War was a grave business, and he was unwilling to take refuge behind the boys with their necks on the line. Indeed, Nunan's relative maturity inoculated him from the unbridled bravado native to the typical nineteen-year-old soldier. Already an adult with an established career, Nunan had no illusions about establishing his manhood on the battlefield. He signed up not with bloodlust or pride but soberly, a citizen offering to risk his own death in a war he considered unambiguously just.

Yet Nunan's seriousness of purpose was always leavened by a twinkling sense of irony and playfulness. For months he had been reading about a remarkable collection of world-class skiers and mountaineers being trained as the country's first mountain troops, and though he hardly fit the mold, he knew instantly that he wanted in. The soldiers dressed in winter camouflage, white hoods pulled over faces painted with white grease, their eyes protected from high-altitude snow blindness by glacier goggles. They rappelled over cliffs, marched over glaciers, and learned to ski in military formation. Nunan wanted to join them, even though, by his own admission, the highest he had ever climbed was "to the top of a Fifth Avenue bus."

If nothing else, Nunan figured, the training he would receive as a mountain soldier would serve him well at the front. Mountaineering and combat were alike in that the physical dangers native to each—be they avalanches and rockfalls or sniper fire and land mines—required learning to live with extreme psychological stress. Training at high altitude, under the tutelage of experienced mountain men, would be a good way to prepare for the terrors of war, wherever his unit was sent. Mountain training also offered a chance to develop capacities that would be useful long after the war ended: superior physical conditioning, high-altitude navigation and rescue skills, intimacy with the great mysteries of the wilderness. All things a young man would be unlikely to learn in an office job in New Jersey. Indeed, from everything Nunan could gather from the newspaper coverage trumpeting their arrival, the mountain troops were a kind of mythical brotherhood, its members descending like gods from mountaintops all over Europe and North America to save the world from the advancing shadows of evil dictatorship.

By the time Nunan arrived in the Cascades, the training at Fort Lewis had been under way for just six months, but already the camp had attracted dozens of the best skiers in the world. The first man to appear at Fort Lewis had been the former captain of the Dartmouth College ski team, Charles McLane. When he showed up wearing his ski team sweater, McLane asked a guard at the main gate where the mountain troops were. After calling headquarters and checking McLane's papers again, the guard looked McLane over and said, "Lad, you *are* the Mountain Infantry. You're a one-man regiment!"[2]

McLane was not lonely for long. As word began to spread that the army was forming its first-ever mountain units, Fort Lewis began to seem more like an Olympic ski lodge than an army base. Hard-eyed European mountaineers—many having barely escaped Nazi imprisonment in Austria and Norway—had been recruited to turn mostly teenaged Americans into skilled Alpine soldiers. What the Europeans brought to the fledgling troops, in addition to the technical skills necessary for survival in the high mountains, was a tradition of warfare entirely unknown to an American military establishment. Fighting in the mountains required not only specialized equipment and practice, none of which American soldiers possessed, it required an entirely different degree of psychological preparation. American soldiers were used to training at warm, flatland bases in California and the Deep South, and that alone, regardless of how well the men learned their trade, would be a decided disadvantage against an army with centuries of mountain and cold-weather fighting in its history. This history was well known to General Frido von Senger und Etterlin, the commander of the Germans the American mountain troops would eventually face. When it came to fighting in the mountains, physical preparation and military training were only part of the equation, Senger would write. Far more important was for soldiers to overcome the natural dread of dying alone on an exposed slab of Alpine rock. For soldiers accustomed to fighting only in flat country, he wrote, mountains "intensify all fears."[3]

THE FIRST CHALLENGE in training elite American mountain soldiers was finding men who knew how to make use of the mountains. Fortunately, given the number of expatriate Austrians, Swiss, and Norwegians eager to return to Europe to fight Hitler's armies, the continent's finest skiers began pouring in from the very beginning. You couldn't swing a ski pole, it seemed, without hitting a gold medalist. Among the most admired was Walter Prager, the elegant thirty-three-year-old Swiss coach of Dartmouth's team, who had grown up skiing the glaciers around Davos, Switzerland, and later became a two-time winner of Europe's Gold Kandahar ski race and, in 1931, world champion. From New Hampshire's Cannon Mountain came Peter Gabriel, an expatriate Swiss ski instructor and mountaineering guide who had led noteworthy expeditions in the Alps and Alaska. From Sun Valley came the future U.S. Olympic coach and Aspen ski resort founder Friedl Pfeiffer.

Among the best known of the Europeans were Austrian and Norwegian expatriates who had joined up with the express purpose of liberating their countries from German occupation. They included the Austrian Ludwig "Luggi" Foeger, an internationally known ski jumper and the director of the Yosemite Ski School, and Ernst Engel, the former ski coach at Cornell, who had escaped from Austria four months after the German invasion. Perhaps the most famous was Torger Tokle, a small, chunky Norwegian ski jumper who had fled to Brooklyn in 1939. Within three years, he had won forty-two ski-jumping championships, broken records on twenty-four hills, and set the world record of 282 feet in front of twenty thousand spectators at Michigan's Pine Mountain. In camp, Tokle became something of a legend for his astonishing leg strength. To impress his bunkmates, he would strap a sixty-pound pack on his back, walk over to a coal bin or the tailgate of a truck, and, from a standstill, spring the three vertical feet like a cat.[4]

The presence of this many glamorous figures in one outfit was irresistible to the army's public affairs office. In the early years of the war, long before most of them had seen a minute of action, the men pitched to the world variously as "the Ski Troops" or "the Mountain Fighters" had already become one of the most celebrated units in the U.S. Army. Reporters and photographers churned out giddy articles celebrating these young men as if they were explorers training for an expedition rather than recruits preparing for war. "When the time comes to climb the Caucuses or pack a gun over the mountains of Norway or plant the Stars and Stripes on the button of Fujiyama, Uncle Sam's new mountain troopers will be ready," ran an article in *Popular Mechanics* over photographs of soldiers in training, dressed in all-white camouflage gear, storming a forest near the Canadian border. "They are getting in trim by leaps and bounds—leaps from paratroop transport planes into ten-foot snow banks and bounds up the rocky facades of some of our best western mountains. To these lean, hard, bronzed mountaineers, a polar expedition would be little more than a weekend holiday. They'll scout miles through forests and across treacherous ice fields, often with thousand-foot cliffs falling away at the one side of the trail, and then turn in at night to slumber snug in a two-pound sleeping bag at 50 degrees below zero."[5]

A headline over a January 1943 article in *The Denver Post* gushed that "None but Real He-Men Need Apply." The article told how reporters had been "shown how the ski and mountain troops are trained to live out in the open in the high, snow-capped mountains; how they must ski under full pack; the mountain command's method of lowering men over cliffs in toboggans; the method of loading and sledding of mountain artillery, as well as packing howitzers and travel by muleback."

"In short," the article concluded, "this is no 'sissy's life'—it's a military job for only real men of the great outdoors."[6]

From its very first months, the mountain troops represented something distinct to the American public, something that transcended the general fever and anxiety of war. In the face of a still largely mysterious Japanese army to the west and a terrifyingly mechanized German army to the east, the country was encouraged to fall in love with a group of young men training for war in the most anachronistic manner possible: on snowshoes, on skis, on muleback. In the hands of the nation's newspapers and filmmakers, the mountain troops were used to reassure a frightened nation that old-fashioned, even virtuous, soldiering would stand up to the Axis threat.

The country was told that the men filling these ranks were cut from an entirely different cloth than other men pressed into service. These men were a combination of European panache, Rocky Mountain muscle, and East Coast intelligence: lumberjacks, alpine guides, college skiers, forest rangers, trappers. They formed a remarkably self-assured group of men that took its pride not from a region, such as the famed 36th (Texas) Infantry Division, but from a distinct subculture of outdoorsmen that to the public at large seemed to represent a kind of masculine ideal. Rumors circulated that the ski troops had the highest collective IQ of any division ever recorded; stories abounded about soldiers discoursing in the barracks about Schopenhauer and on training hikes on the subtleties of astronomy. Some two thirds of the men were qualified for Officer Candidate School, better than twice the army average. Even while still in training, the mountain troops reached a kind of hero status as a romantic substitute for the millions of Americans who would never see the front lines themselves. Attention so focused on the men's physical prowess and athletic skills that newspaper coverage of their military training seemed as appropriate for the sports pages as for the sections devoted to war preparations. In this way, the mountain troops allowed Americans to imagine something besides the relentless death and fear that the war had begun dropping on their doorstep. They represented the perfect blend of self-confidence and spirited patriotism that a nation that had never lost a war expected from its soldiers. This was an army unit the country could believe in.

Yet beneath the mythmaking was a bitter irony that within a couple of years would become all too tragically apparent: the men training to become elite mountain troops would one day be slaughtered like any other soldiers. As part of a unit training to lead an assault's "sharp end" (a term that also applies to someone leading a climb up a dangerous rock face), the mountain troops could expect—and would indeed experience—dramatically higher than typical rates of violent casualties and deaths. As remarkable as their skills, as competent as they were in surviving the worst a high-altitude wilderness could throw at them, the world's finest skiers and mountaineers were as vulnerable as anyone else to the brutality of shrapnel and machine-gun fire. If there was something magical about imagining men training in the high mountains, there would be something equally ugly about contemplating, and eventually tabulating, their deaths and dismemberments, like imagining Thoroughbred horses being ground into dog meat. None of the fame cloaking these men, in other words, could protect them from war.

Not that any of this was on the minds of the men rushing to sign up. The media blitz served not only to make heroes of the men before they ever left their training camp, it also served as the finest possible recruiting tool. As rumors spread about this unprecedented gathering, applications began to pour into a small recruiting office located not in the bowels of the War Department but in a building at 415 Lexington Avenue in New York City. It was the only time in U.S. history that military recruiting had been entrusted to a civilian organization, and for good reason: when it came to skiing and mountain safety, the cumulative knowledge of the entire military establishment could have fit into the zippered pocket of a relentlessly cheerful amateur skier named Minnie Dole.

ON A SATURDAY NIGHT in February 1940, Charles Minot Dole sat by a log fire at the Orvis Inn in Manchester, Vermont, having drinks and talking about the war in Europe with Bob Livermore, Roger Langley, and Alex Bright, three of the most prominent skiers in the country. The talk quickly turned to the remarkable battle the Finns were fighting against the Soviets on the Karelian Isthmus, a frozen quagmire that provided the Finns with one of their only advantages over the vastly larger Soviet army: landscape and the specialized training to take advantage of it.

As columns of khaki-clad Russian soldiers, tanks, and armored cars advanced down country roads—never having bothered to send out patrols or investigate the forests on either side—Finnish soldiers, dressed head to ski boots in white, attacked on cross-country skis with rifles and bottles of gasoline to make Molotov cocktails. After the attacks, they sped away on skis or, when near frozen canals, on ice skates. The effectiveness of the attacks left the Russian troops not only wounded by gunfire but freezing to death; they were described as living "like Arctic foxes that had not developed a winter coat." Red Army officers figured they had greatly underestimated the size of their foe, when in fact the Finns were vastly outnumbered; their success resulted only from their training, equipment, and the ingenuity born of familiarity with the frozen terrain. While the

Russians stuck stubbornly to the main roads, the Finns built parallel trails in the woods that would accommodate their mechanized vehicles. They camped in log-roofed dugouts and used stoves rather than campfires to eliminate the columns of smoke that gave away the positions of the huddled and terrified Russians. The Finns jammed birch saplings into the treads of Russian tanks. When Russian commanders demanded more ski troops, help arrived from the Siberian ski brigade, but these men too were doomed. Trained to ski only on open plains, they were flummoxed by the thick forests. Whenever possible, they would try to cross frozen lakes, often to be slaughtered by Finns waiting in the woods.

By the end of the second week of fighting, some 36,000 Russians had been killed, two and a half times the number of Finns. Finally, the infuriated Russian army set up a frontal attack on the Karelian Isthmus and a concurrent attack from the Gulf of Finland to force a concession from the overwhelmed Finns. For the men in white, the war was over.[7]

As it happened, a former Dartmouth ski racer named David Bradley had served as a military observer during the Russian invasion of Finland, and when he returned from the front he provided Minnie Dole with a detailed report. Within a few months, virtually everything he advised found its way, through the efforts of Dole, to Army Chief of Staff George Marshall and Secretary of War Henry Stimson.

"No one can say when or where this plague will reach our shores," Bradley wrote in his report, "and so there is no sense in predicting the absolute function of ski troops—any more than the unfortunate Norwegians could have predicted it—but it does seem more than likely that our Alaska territory, Canada and Greenland may have to be held by shock troops of one kind or another, and that necessitates a good deal of familiarity with skis and mountain conditions. The strength of the ski troop is not so much in its concentrated organization, but rather in the unpredictable initiative of each member. The Finnish skiers were their own armies, their own general staffs, and many is the boy who tackled and downed a tank with no more weapon than a log of wood or a gasoline bottle tied to a hand grenade."

American ski troops, Bradley advised, should organize themselves accordingly. Rather than force traditional military discipline on its expert skiers and mountaineers, ranking officers should encourage the natural ingenuity and self-reliance its recruits already possessed. "I would have every member able to take care of himself alone, if need be," he wrote. "All should be able to handle an ax, pack a mule, light a fire in the rain, and know the very special technique of survival in winter conditions. Their training ought to include all of these things in addition to the technique of handling skis, and rock climbing and camping."

Bradley provided detailed descriptions and simple drawings of the equipment the Finns had relied upon, from mittens with trigger fingers to the proper bindings for military skis. He ended his report with the recommendation that any American ski troops should build on a foundation of top civilian skiers, both native and foreign-born—including his former coach and teammates at Dartmouth—who were currently running the country's brand-new ski schools. "There is little use wasting all the time and energy teaching a bunch of southerners how to ski. I should think the army would call in the thousands of experienced skiers, send them to a good training place in Colorado, and from them build the nucleus of an expanding winter defense force."[8]

In the Vermont ski lodge, Dole reminded his friends that winter warfare was not unknown on the North American continent. During the French and Indian Wars, colonial troops had used snowshoes to fight Native Americans in the snowy Champlain Valley. But compared to virtually all the other countries fighting or threatened in Europe, the United States was woefully underprepared to fight in the mountains or in winter conditions. On the flatland bases where American soldiers trained in California, Georgia, and Louisiana, the coldest thing in town was the beer the men drank on Saturday nights. The United States had never been forced to invade or defend a mountain range, at home or abroad, and until very recently had had barely a handful of citizens interested even in playing in the mountains, let alone fighting in them.

Given the current saber rattling in central Europe and the anxiety over American involvement, the inadequacy of warm-weather military training should have seemed increasingly obvious. By the late 1930s, the German army had three mountain divisions and one mountain corps headquarters; by the end, it would have fourteen divisions and eight headquarters. The United States had none. Europeans had been fighting in one another's mountains for centuries and had deep and honored traditions of skiing and mountaineering to draw on for specialized training. Until the early 1930s, skiing and mountaineering in the United States were sports practiced largely by a handful of New England college students—and by smaller pockets of adventurers in the Rockies, Tetons, and Sierras—who had picked them up during trips to Europe. In the late 1930s, though, interest in skiing had begun to boom. Lodges began popping up in Vermont, New Hampshire, and Sun Valley, Idaho, to accommodate well-to-do skiers arriving on well-appointed tourist trains. New England was far and away the most popular region for skiing, and if the United States was looking for mountain troops, its mountains would be the place to begin recruiting.

Dole knew the mountains of New England, and the people who played in them, as well as anyone alive. He had grown up in Andover, Massachusetts, the son of a wealthy paper manufacturer and the grandson of a man who had, in 1849, steamed around Cape Horn to California and become president of the 49ers Association. Dole entered Phillips Andover Academy at thirteen and taught himself to ski. After the United States entered the First World War, Dole enlisted in the army as soon as he was old enough. He arrived at Camp Lee, Virginia, the day the armistice was announced. "What meant life and a new day for Europe, I could only interpret as a personal tragedy," he later moaned in his memoir *Adventures in Skiing*. Left to find some way other than soldiering to prove himself as a young man, Dole managed to convince camp administrators to let him stay on and go through some basic training. If the experience didn't turn him into a soldier, it did leave one lasting mark: his nickname. Still so fresh-faced that a razor had never touched his cheek, Dole found himself, one morning, staring into the face of an angry sergeant. "Candidate, why didn't you shave this morning?"

"I didn't think I needed to, sir."

"You don't say. What's your name?"

"Charles Minot Dole, sir."

"Well, from now on, Candidate, we're going to make it Minnie, not Minot. Minnie Dole, got that?"

"Yes sir."[9]

The moniker could have stuck only to a man with a fully developed sense of humor. Although he had been a three-sport athlete at Andover,

Dole's slight 130-pound frame did not impress the coaches at Yale, where he enrolled after the army. So, like his father, he decided to sing instead. He joined Yale's elite a capella group, the Whiffenpoofs, and some years later he would turn down a professional recording contract that would subsequently be offered to Rudy Vallee. Soon after graduation, Dole quit a dull job in the wool business to join a millionaire Princeton friend on a grand tour of Europe. In Italy in 1926, the two declined an invitation to back the development of a string of earthquake-proof apartment buildings in Rome. The offer had come from "a bald-headed bullfrog of a man" named Benito Mussolini.[10]

By the early 1930s, Dole had begun to devote himself to his true love, skiing, which was becoming increasingly popular among the moneyed set in New England. The Boston and Maine Railroad had dispatched the first "snow train" from Boston's North Station to the sheep meadows of Warner, New Hampshire, in 1931. Within a decade, close to a hundred thousand skiers had used trains from Boston and New Haven to get to the mountains. Over the New Year's holiday in 1936, Dole went skiing at Stowe with a friend named Frank Edson and his wife. During a downhill run early in the trip, Dole fell badly and severely injured his ankle. Lying on the soaking-wet ski slope as two companions went to look for help, he went into shock. Those few who did ski by offered little help; at one point, a young man from Maine zipped by, sniffing that "anybody fool enough to hurt himself on this dumb trail deserves what he gets." Finally two men arrived with a sheet of tin roofing long enough to immobilize Dole's leg, but as they slid him down the mountain Dole's backside dragged in the snow. An uncomfortable trip and ten miles later, Dole finally made it to the hospital, where he was told that the break was too complex for the local doctor to treat. He was outfitted with a temporary aluminum splint and sent on his way. With the pain in his leg too acute for the nine-hour drive back to Greenwich, Dole and his wife climbed aboard the Vermont Railroad's Washingtonian, which left Waterbury at midnight; the trip was made bearable only by a bottle of scotch and a handful of codeine.

As traumatic as Dole's injury was, it took another, far worse moment two months later to cement his ideas about the need for organized ski patrols. In February 1937, Frank Edson, who had been with Dole during his accident, told his friend that he was thinking of entering a race near

Pittsfield, Massachusetts, sponsored by an organization called the Amateur Ski Club. The race was to be held on a course known as "The Ghost Trail." Dole knew the trail, and he felt sure his friend was not an accomplished enough skier to enter the race safely, let alone competitively. When he called to find out how the race had gone, Dole learned that his friend had taken a terrible fall and crashed into a tree. He had broken both his legs and shattered three ribs, fragments of which had apparently punctured his lungs. Once again, the untrained ski patrol had been unable to care for such a traumatic injury, and although Edson made it to a hospital, he soon died.

"Frank's death, the first that most of us had ever heard about in skiing, shook me badly," Dole would write. "It was a shock to us all. We were not only shocked, but we could feel the shock reverberating in the very body of the sport of skiing."

Edson's death forced the officers of the Amateur Ski Club to figure out how to provide emergency medical service both at the club's sanctioned events and for the rapidly expanding recreational ski industry as a whole. For research into ski safety and as a gesture of respect to their fellow skiers, the officers turned to Frank Edson's best friend, Minnie Dole. Dole's first act was to circulate among the region's ski resorts a questionnaire about skiing accidents and the best ways to prevent them. To say the least, it did not receive a universally positive response. One came back saying that the ski club's worries were the product of "sissies, spoilsports, and frighteners of mothers."[11]

Dole persevered. He asked two of the country's best skiers, Alex Bright and Bob Livermore, the latter a member of the 1936 Olympic team, to help get ski clubs to organize and train their own safety patrols. When the National Downhill and Slalom Races were awarded to Stowe in 1938, with entrants from France, Germany, and Austria as well as the United States, Dole was asked to run the ski patrol for the races. During the preparations for the races, Dole met Roger Langley, a Massachusetts schoolteacher and president of the National Ski Association, and Dick Durrance, an Olympic skier from Dartmouth. Looking over the mountain's trails, the three men decided the notorious Nose Dive Trail should be divided into three sections, with patrols equipped at each station with toboggans, blankets, splints, bandages, and thermoses of coffee. Each station would be within sight and hailing distance of the stations above and below; no matter where an accident might happen, a fallen skier would be instantly attended to and, if necessary, triaged, taken off the mountain, and transported to a hospital. Rescue would be systematic and intricately planned.

So impressive was Dole's system that Langley asked him to apply it on a larger scale as head of the brand-new National Ski Patrol. With Dole's leadership, Langley hoped to establish—and, more important, professionalize—ski patrols at all the resorts beginning to pop up in the mountains of New England. Dole agreed and immediately asked a Red Cross doctor named L. M. Thompson to be his medical director. Thompson had recently published the first *Winter First Aid Manual,* a book that helped dispel some foolish myths about winter rescue techniques, such as drinking liquor to warm up or rubbing patches of frostbite with snow. Under Dole's and Thompson's direction, the ground rules of mountain rescue became scientific and codified. Injured people, for example, were not to be moved from where they fell except by trained patrolmen. Dole convinced Harold Hirsch, a clothing maker, to create ski parkas in a color—rust—that he would sell to no one but a certified ski patroller. He divided the ski patrol into five divisions covering the mountains across the country and started recruiting top skiers to run each division's patrols, with Bob Livermore agreeing to oversee the busy eastern division. Even the best skiers agreed to take first-aid training from the Red Cross. Alex Bright took his training so seriously that during a lesson on the body's pressure points, he held his thumb beneath his "patient's" jaw so long that the man became faint, wandered outside, and fell and broke his leg—an accident that led to Bright's first real lesson in traction splinting.[12]

By the spring of 1940, the year the organization officially changed its name to the National Ski Patrol System, Dole had set up a remarkable web of the country's best skiers that in the next decade and a half alone would care for forty-nine thousand people hurt in skiing accidents. It would save at least sixty-six lives. With U.S. involvement in the war brewing in Europe, Dole felt there must be some way to put all this training and manpower to the nation's service. On June 10, Dole sent a letter to the members of the National Ski Patrol System, asking for permission to offer their services to the War Department. The response was overwhelming: 90 percent were in favor.

Dole and Langley wrote Secretary of War Henry Stimson with the offer. The response, from the army's adjutant general, was curt; it thanked the ski club for its "patriotic motive." Army Chief of Staff George Marshall wrote that the offer of "informal advice and assistance in the technique of skiing and the purchase of equipment is appreciated" and seemed to hope the eccentrics from New England would go away. Plainly, the War Department did not know Minnie Dole.[13]

CHAPTER TWO

MOUNTAINEERS

N THE FALL OF 1942, a secretary at her desk in the War Department looked out her window and saw a man dangling from a rope. Convinced that the stress of the young war had finally gotten to someone in the Quartermaster's Office upstairs, the woman let out a scream that brought most of the military bureaucracy running to the windows. Among those peering out was the secretary's boss, Quartermaster General Edmund Gregory, and his assistant, Brigadier General Georges Doriot. Doriot's expression made it plain that this was no suicide. "Bub! Bub!" Doriot shouted in a thick French accent. "Come show the quartermaster your leetle trick!"

The man on the end of the rope could hardly have been less like the typical military bureaucrat. He was, for one thing, a quiet prep school English teacher from New Hampshire's Phillips Exeter Academy, whose slight frame and gentle demeanor hardly distinguished him in a building full of warriors gearing up for battle. He was, for another thing, brand-new to the army, although he had, and would, travel farther and to more remote and dangerous places than virtually any man alive. The man on the end of the rope was Bob Bates, a self-effacing but mischievous man who happened to be one of the world's premier mountaineers, and he was just doing what any climber would have done upon the arrival in the mail of a new coil of climbing rope: he was testing it out.

Bates had been waiting weeks for the rope to arrive from the Plymouth Cordage Company. Since the Philippines had fallen to the Japanese, the world's supply of Manila rope had dried up, and Bates and his climbing companion Bill House—who had also come to work for the quartermaster—had been working with American companies to come up with a synthetic substitute similar to the German fiber known as Perlon. When the new rope, made of a DuPont product known as nylon, finally arrived, Bates pulled the coil from the box, wrapped one end around his desk, and rappelled out his office window. Bates had far more serious things on his mind than how this stunt might appear to a group of gawking desk jockeys. He needed to know how much the rope would stretch. Word was that nylon was more elastic and held far more reliably than the Manila rope that mountaineers had been using for years. Sure enough, as Bates dropped over the window ledge, putting his full weight on the line, the rope stretched a full foot. He had been able to dangle for only a few moments, calmly admiring the rope's elasticity, when the secretary's scream broke his reverie.[1]

What Bates was doing in the War Department—or dangling outside it, depending on the day—was something few in the department would have known about, much less understood. With far more experience with winter weather and equipment than anyone in the Quartermaster's Office, Bates never shied from telling the military bureaucrats about the inadequacies of their standard-issue gear. There was a saying in the office that the army was well prepared to fight in Maine in the summer and Florida in the winter; fighting in the mountains, particularly in winter, would require gear of an entirely different order. More than anyone else, mountaineers knew that when navigating forbidding terrain—be it a mountaintop or a battlefield, or both at once—proper gear and proper training often made the difference between life and death. In this, as in many other things, mountaineers shared the elite soldier's sober acknowledgment of risk and, through intensive practice, the reduction of risk. Mountaineers, like soldiers, knew the shadow of death as a constant companion.

For men like Bob Bates, the parallels between navigating high mountains and soldiering successfully were hard to miss. Not only did both require rigorous training to overcome the extreme physical demands of cliff faces or battlefields, they required a strength of mind to overcome the equally dangerous psychological risks, what an early mountain training manual called "subjective dangers." Training taught climbers and soldiers alike to respond instinctively and spontaneously to situations that for the untrained would lead to swift breakdown. Like mountains, battlefields merely mirror the courage and fear that men project upon them. Soldiers, like mountaineers, live day to day with the tensions between exultation and panic, clarity and confusion, control and chaos. Shooting another man between the eyes or gutting him with a bayonet is no more natural to a man than dangling from a cliff by a slim thread of nylon. It is only through the relentless repetition of these acts under controlled circumstances that men are able to perform them when their lives are in fact at stake.

If Bates's War Department stunt had terrified the secretary downstairs, it was surely one of the easier climbing maneuvers he had pulled off in his young but extraordinary career. Along with his close friend Bradford Washburn, Bates had been climbing for years in New Hampshire's White Mountains and in Alaska, a region that would become the centerpiece of Washburn's renowned career as a mountain photographer. Over the course of several summer trips, the Washburn-Bates teams—often including other top mountaineers such as Charles Houston, Adams Carter, Walter Wood, and Ome Daiber—would explore, among others, Mounts Crillon and Steele and make the first ascent of 17,150-foot Mount Lucania, at the time the highest unclimbed mountain in North America and one of the most inaccessible. In 1935, they conducted a three-month mapping expedition, by dogsled, of the Yukon and the Saint Elias Mountains for the National Geographic Society. The trips were rugged in ways such major undertakings would not, in a sense, ever be again.

In 1938, just a few years before he began working for the War Department, Bates had taken part in one of the boldest mountaineering expeditions in history, an attempt on K2, at 28,250 feet the second highest—and by most accounts the most beautiful—mountain in the world. A team that included some of the country's most accomplished pioneer climbers got one member, Paul Petzoldt, to 26,000 feet; though shy of the summit, this was still higher than anyone had ever climbed. Fifteen years later, Bates would return to K2 with another team and would once again come to appreciate the merits of nylon rope when he and four others were miraculously saved from tumbling into a frozen abyss at 25,000 feet by a single man holding the other end of the line.

In July 1939, the summer after his first year of teaching prep school English, Bates and Adams Carter, a master at Boston's Milton Academy, sailed for Europe for a month of climbing in the Kandersteg region of the Bernese Oberlund in Switzerland. After long days of climbing, Carter and Bates would retire to a mountain hut where climbers from all over Europe bunked down and swapped stories. The buzz that summer had little to do with mountaineering. The Swiss climbers particularly were agitated by the aggressiveness Germany had been exhibiting toward Poland; grim tales circulated about German soldiers strangling Polish nurses and throwing their bodies into a river. Swiss troops were practicing maneuvers all through the Alps, preparing to fight on terrain that offered them their greatest advantage over a flatland enemy: the mountains. In the minds of Bates and Carter, an idea was born.[2]

Bates continued to climb, sometimes with a student named Jim Conant and his father, Harvard president James Bryant Conant. During a climb of the "Pinnacle" on Mount Washington, Bates spoke about his anxieties about the new war in Europe and how alpine countries such as Switzerland had trained their armies to take full advantage of their natural homeland defenses. Given the mountainous terrain on both coasts of North America, much of which Bates knew firsthand, training an elite unit of American mountain soldiers seemed to make a lot of sense. As it happened, the elder Conant had a meeting planned a few days later with George Marshall, the army chief of staff, and promised to bring up the idea. Unbeknown to Bates, Marshall was already under assault from another flank, by the irrepressible Minnie Dole.

BY THE SPRING OF 1940, Minnie Dole had set up shop in a Manhattan insurance office that was just a short ferry ride to Governors Island, training ground of the First Army. Dole wrote to the base commander, offering to use the coming winter months to train soldiers to ski and survive in the mountains. A letter came back stating that the army had already decided to train in the South and had no interest in cold-weather training that year. Undeterred, Dole wrote right back and continued to dog the army bureaucracy from New York to Washington. In an effort to overwhelm the military establishment with evidence of its own inadequacies, Dole and John Morgan of the National Ski Patrol compiled every scrap of information they could find—from magazines, instruction books, and skiing and mountaineering guides—on the German, French, and Italian alpine troops. The British, too, had mountain troops; even the Scots had ski patrols to carry rations and other supplies to snowbound antiaircraft searchlight positions. Dole's determination made it clear to the army brass that they were not dealing with a dilettante. Dole was beginning to seem more like a Revolutionary War patriot, offering to round up the farmers and teach them how to use their squirrel guns to fight the British.[3]

Finally, using introductions from a general sympathetic to his plan, Dole wheedled an interview with George Marshall himself. For this meeting, Dole devised a different strategy. Rather than simply showing Marshall his research on European troops and the ways American troops might be used in a European campaign, he would argue that American mountain troops could prove vital in a defense of our own country. If the Germans ever attacked the northeastern United States, Dole planned to say, they would likely follow the British route of 1779—down the Saint Lawrence River and into the Champlain Valley. The best way to stop them would be to occupy the high ground above the valley, in New York's Adirondack Mountains.

On September 12, Dole and Morgan were ushered into Marshall's office. When the general gruffly asked why it was so important for them to see him personally, they described how quickly the army had brushed them off the last time they were in town. After fifteen minutes, Marshall turned to his visitors. "You have raised an interesting question, gentlemen," he said. "Thank you for coming. You will hear from me one way or another."[4]

THREE MONTHS AFTER Dole's meeting with General Marshall, Bob Bates and his friends at the American Alpine Club, now led by Charles Houston, organized a meeting in December 1940 to explore the ways the club might help the army test gear and organize troops for mountain warfare. The mountaineers discovered, as Dole had, that the War Department knew next to nothing about mountain fighting, and what little intelligence it had from European sources had been translated incorrectly. Pitons were called "nails." Downhill skiers were "off-walking snowshoers." Plainly, the American military establishment was profoundly ignorant about mountain warfare, and ignorance in the mountains, club members knew, meant serious trouble for individuals and armies alike. In the First World War, the Italian army had lost 200,000 men in poorly planned mountain campaigns alone. Yet proper winter training also offered great military possibilities. So far in the new European war, the only effective resistance to German soldiers had taken place in Narvik, Norway, where Norwegians had been joined by French *chasseurs alpins* and specially trained winter troops from Britain and Poland.[5]

To bring the army up to date, the Alpine Club's Adams Carter, a talented translator as well as a veteran mountaineer, offered to conduct a yearlong research project in which he would gather every European mountaineering manual he could find from private collections and military archives. For months Carter translated articles from French, Italian, Swiss, and German sources and interviewed veteran European mountain soldiers. In addition to cataloguing equipment and training techniques, Carter's report also pointed out the differences in the way Europeans and Americans might defend their mountains. The Alps were studded with huts and villages that could be used to shelter troops; American ranges, particularly the Cascades and the Alaska Range, were not only much higher and more dangerous but far more remote. Largely roadless, they would be inaccessible to even the hardiest military vehicles. Since no effective motorized snow machines had ever been developed, the only way to move through these ranges was with mules or dogsleds. In Finland, soldiers transported gear on horse-drawn sleds and slept in heavy, eighteen-man conical tents; they kept warm by sleeping close and sharing body heat. The Swiss army, by comparison, had mastered the art of building caves in glaciers. Neither of these practices would work in the soft, powdery snow of most American mountain ranges. Carter felt reasonably certain his suggestions would reach the appropriate ears; Secretary of War Henry Stimson was a longtime member of the Alpine Club.

Carter's first concern, as it is for most mountaineers, was taking care of the feet. Soldiers left in the field with wet feet often developed trench foot, a debilitating condition that could lead quickly from minor infections to gangrene if left untreated. In the American army, only elite troops were given waterproof footgear; standard-issue American army boots would not suffice in the demanding conditions of high-altitude maneuvers. But preparing the right equipment was nothing compared to the challenge of formulating the proper training. Like Minnie Dole, Carter and Bates saw that the first alpine troops would have to be drawn from experienced mountaineers, who could then set up a training sequence suitable for regular recruits. Getting men comfortable with living at arctic temperatures would take special organization. To date, explorers like Bates and Carter had figured out how to outfit and move small teams of highly skilled mountaineers, but no one in the United States had ever tried to organize, let alone outfit or mobilize, a large group of men in the wilderness.

Veterans of the American Alpine Club had already experimented with dehydrated foods—climbers, they discovered, could survive handsomely on one or two pounds of food per day—as well as lightweight mountain equipment and cooking gear. Advances had been made in sleeping bags and winter clothing next to which standard-issue military gear seemed obsolete, even dangerous, in high country.[6]

The extreme temperatures of Bates's K2 trip had reinforced for him the notion that multiple layers of wool clothing, especially when covered by a windproof shell, sandwiched and preserved body heat more effectively than a single thick winter jacket. Mountain troops fighting in severe winter conditions would need thick wool clothing from head to toe: a wool balaclava; one or two wool sweaters; a parka; a wool shirt; windproof trousers with canvas gaiters to keep out the snow; light wool underwear; and two layers of thick wool socks. Boots would need to be one of two types: heavy, three-ply leather boots or Barker boots, known as "shoepacs," which had thick rubber soles and leather uppers. In either case, to prevent trench foot, the boots should be outfitted with removable insoles and sewn with as few seams as possible to prevent leaking. Boots should also be fitted to each soldier, since blisters could debilitate a man in the mountains as effectively as a broken leg.

Some gear, such as crampons—toothy steel cleats that fasten to boots for travel over ice—and ice axes were very hard to find in the United States and required extensive practice before their use could be mastered. Long, wood-handled ice axes would serve as walking sticks, offering a third point of balance on icy slopes. On more treacherous climbs, axes could be used to cut steps, to knock on snow bridges to listen for hidden crevasses, and to help in belaying climbers. Tapered sleeping bags, fitted with hoods and liners, were far superior to standard military-issue wool blankets. Gas-burning cook sets, high-mountain tents, even sunscreen (made of 4 percent tannic acid, 46 percent alcohol, and 50 percent distilled water)—every item in the mountaineer's pack received an official endorsement or was discarded as useless. If nothing else, America's mountain soldiers would know that the gear they relied upon had been blessed by a higher authority than the standard military bureaucracy.[7]

In the summer of 1941, Bates and Walter Wood led a major expedition to the Yukon and the Saint Elias Mountains in Alaska to help field-test some of the gear. Eager to see its equipment in action, army officials agreed to send a pair of B-15 bombers to drop supplies for the trip. Such a luxury forced Bates to concoct a way to find wooden supply crates before they disappeared into the snow; he rigged each box's sides with steel-spring rat traps attached to poles with strips of bright red cloth nailed to one end. When the traps were sprung, at least one flag would stick straight into the air. Another problem had to do with separating the crate from the parachute once the load had landed, to keep everything from blowing into a crevasse or over a cliff. Bates solved this by fixing a fuse and dynamite cap to the lines connecting the chute to the crate; lit in the plane, the fuse would burn through and cut the chute loose once the load had landed.[8]

This early test run proved so effective that a few months later, the army's quartermaster general wrote Exeter's principal requesting that Bates be given a leave of absence to begin testing mountain equipment full-time. In the War Department, Bates would soon be joined by a remarkable group of some of the country's most experienced outdoorsmen, including Adams Carter; Paul Siple, a weather researcher who had gone to Antarctica with the Richard Byrd expedition and had coined the term *windchill*; Bestor Robinson, a veteran outdoorsman from the Sierra Club; and Sir Hubert Wilkins, the famous Arctic and Antarctic explorer.

Searching for a warmer alternative to the standard shearling winter jacket, Bates and his team gathered up different models of winter jackets and traveled to a cold chamber operated by the Department of Agriculture. With a team of "volunteers" from Fort Myer, they rigged the cold chamber with a fan to simulate a winter wind and sent each man in wearing a different coat to withstand the cold for thirty minutes. Although hardly scientific, the test quickly established one thing: no matter what material was used, thicker coats were always warmer, but only if they were fitted with a windproof shell. Pile was just as warm as shearling and dried much faster; it also didn't require the killing of untold thousands of sheep. Just like that, the army had a new standard for winter jackets. Later tests at an Eskimo Pie Company freezer would establish standards for wool underwear, mittens, and survival suits. Sir Hubert, disappointed that the freezer could get down only to zero, resorted to eating Popsicles to further decrease his body's core temperature.[9]

Now that the army had funded so much research into mountaineering equipment, the question became what to do with all the gear. The Alpine Club and the National Ski Patrol had argued all along that cutting-edge equipment would be worthless in the hands of inexperienced soldiers. What was needed was not a group of flatland soldiers with fancy skis and backpacks but a specially trained, elite unit of mountain soldiers who could use the new gear in just the way skiers and sport climbers did: to enter into and survive in the world's most challenging regions, in the most inhospitable climates.[10]

The man who needed convincing was Lieutenant General Leslie James McNair, soon to be put in charge of all ground troops in the continental United States. A number of senior officers supported the idea, including a lieutenant colonel named Mark Clark, who wrote to McNair that the worst that would happen was that the army would add another division—and one that could be light on its feet and easy to move around.

On August 5, McNair made his feelings emphatically known. There would be no mountain troops. Army personnel and equipment had already been stretched thin, McNair argued; all this talk about a unit that would rely on pack mules for transportation seemed almost quaint in an era of highly mechanized German units.

That same day, a report arrived from the American military attaché in Italy. The previous summer, the Italian army had invaded the Balkans but had fled in confusion before a Greek counterattack that had driven them into the mountains of Albania. The Italian soldiers had been poorly organized, inadequately equipped, and utterly unprepared for either winter or mountain fighting. The result was disaster. Twenty-five thousand had been killed; ten thousand more had frozen to death; and many others had been taken prisoner. The loss in prestige and morale to the Italian army was incalculable, and the military lesson was plain: putting on a uniform does not make a man a mountain soldier. Training and equipment for mountain warfare could not be improvised or faked. Soldiers needed to be provided with special cold-weather equipment and learn techniques far more familiar to mountaineers than to warriors.

Despite the report, most U.S. Army strategists still argued that what was needed for America's defense was not special units that were overly trained for narrow purposes but more standard divisions that could fight anywhere. If regular troops were asked to fight in the mountains, they would fight in the mountains. Soldiers were soldiers, no matter what the National Ski Patrol or the American Alpine Club said.

On hearing this news, Minnie Dole redoubled his lobbying. On October 8, 1941, he posted a manifesto to General Marshall and sent copies to President Franklin Roosevelt and Secretary of War Stimson. Written in the "Whereas" and "Be it resolved" language of government bureaucracy, the memo offered the ski association's most distilled argument yet for the establishment of American mountain troops. The short paragraphs proceeded simply and logically: More than half of continental North America, including the upper third of the United States, was blanketed by snow every winter. Regions in which war had raged over the last few decades or seemed likely to rage soon—places such as Russia, Finland, Norway, and Alaska—were snowbound for much of the year. American troops were largely trained on bases in the Deep South, where they were never exposed to mountainous terrain, cold weather, or snow. Despite a year and a half of lobbying by skiers and mountaineers, the military establishment seemed no closer to expanding its vision of the army. During the past four years, the German army, by comparison, had developed and equipped the finest mountain soldiers in the world.

On behalf of the ski association, which he considered "representative of a great mass of citizens living in the northern and snow-bound sections of the United States," Dole urged the War Department to form a specialized unit of winter-ready soldiers immediately. With another winter on the way, the army could not afford to waste another season of training men and testing equipment.[11]

At long last, the War Department was persuaded. Two weeks later, on October 22, Dole received letters from Secretary Stimson and General Marshall announcing that on November 15, 1941, the 1st Battalion (Reinforced) of the 87th Mountain Infantry Regiment would be activated at Fort Meriwether Lewis, Washington, in the shadow of one of the country's great peaks, Mount Rainier. Moreover, for the first time in history, the army would rely on a civilian organization—the National Ski Patrol—to recruit soldiers to fill the regiment's ranks. Minnie Dole would lead the effort.

Twenty-two days later the Japanese bombed Pearl Harbor, and the United States entered the war.[12]

CHAPTER THREE

CASCADES AND ICE FIELDS

F AN AIR ATTACK in the Pacific brought the United States into the war, it was the rise and fall of the German advance on Moscow that showed the world just how brutal cold-weather warfare could be. The German strategy was to kick down the Soviet door so violently that Stalin's regime would collapse in on itself. Launched on June 22, 1941, Operation Barbarossa knocked out twelve hundred Soviet aircraft in its first day. Within a month, three million German soldiers had spread out along a front two thousand miles wide. By October, the Germans had marched to within fifteen miles of Moscow. Determined to exterminate "the repulse of Jewish Bolshevism," German units claimed to have captured nearly four million prisoners; two months later, slightly more than one million of them were still alive, and 90 percent of these would be dead by the end of the war.

Though Hitler was aware of the fate of Napoleon's army, his armies were likewise destined to be defeated by landscape and weather as much as by a human enemy. As summer turned to autumn, Soviet general Georgy Zhukov, in charge of Moscow's defense, cobbled together sufficient replacements from Siberia— many of them with specialized winter gear and skis—to hold the line until winter weather could arrive.

For their part, German commanders prayed for six weeks without snow to complete their job. Their luck did not hold. November's blizzards and freezing temperatures caught the Germans without proper clothing, food, or supplies. Temperatures dropped so precipitously that German vehicles, without lightweight motor oil, became useless; troops had to light gasoline fires under tanks just to get their engines to turn over.

On the Soviet side, defensive maneuvers also grew desperate as the winter set in. Tanks arrived in such a rush that no one bothered to paint them white. Packhorses dropped dead from the cold. Arriving soldiers, forced to sleep in their greatcoats because they had been given no blankets, were so exhausted that their faces were "black with fatigue," the journalist Larry Leseur wrote. "Several times we saw men stumble as they plodded forward and fall unconscious in the snow. The columns never stopped moving, but I saw fellow soldiers pick up their companions and place them, senseless, on passing sleds loaded with hay. . . . I watched the living soldiers pass by the dead at the roadside without a glance, and the dead looked scarcely human. They resembled wax mannequins thrown from a show-window, lying about in grotesque, inhuman postures, arms pointing toward the sky, legs frozen as though they were running. Their faces were bloodless, waxy white. The clean, cold air carried no taint of decomposition."[1]

On December 4, 1941, the mercury dropped to −25 degrees Fahrenheit. In one German regiment alone, three hundred men succumbed to frostbite. The next day, the winter now firmly on his side, Zhukov switched from a defensive posture to a major counteroffensive that would push the Germans eighty miles from Moscow. A year later, in Stalingrad, freezing weather, inadequate winter clothing, and mass starvation would prove equally decisive. If the Allies learned anything from the eastern front, it was that winter weather could be as deadly as any army.[2]

BACK IN NEW YORK, now that the countless months he'd spent lobbying the military bureaucracy had paid off, Minnie Dole began working his network of skiers as never before. The War Department had agreed to give him money to open a recruiting office in New York City. When a visiting colonel asked Dole and John Morgan how much they thought they would need for start-up costs, Morgan scribbled "$3,500" on a scrap of paper and slid it to Dole. "Sixty-five hundred," Dole said. He got it. He set up shop in the

Graybar Building, near Manhattan's Grand Central Station, and drew up a questionnaire for recruits to fill out. Anyone who wanted to join the ski troops, he decided, would have to provide three letters of recommendation, preferably from people who could testify not just to their intelligence and physical strength but to their experience on skis or with a climbing rope.

In a May 5, 1942, notice to the National Ski Patrol, Dole urged members to help him recruit "men accustomed to living and working in the high mountains—packers, prospectors, trappers, Forest Service men, timber cruisers, guides, and men who have mountaineering as an avocation *whether or not they can ski.*" Over the next two years, Dole and a small group of assistants would recruit more than seven thousand men—including, in addition to dozens of European and American skiing celebrities, hundreds of college-bound and college-educated boys from New England and other cold-weather regions. Recruits began pouring into Fort Lewis from Dartmouth, Cornell, Bowdoin, Yale, Williams, Brown, and the Universities of Michigan, Minnesota, Vermont, and New Hampshire. The third man to appear—shortly after Charles McLane arrived in his Dartmouth sweater—was a lawyer named John Oberlin, whose application had included a recommendation from a sterling source: Bob Bates, who just happened to be married to Oberlin's sister. Among the best known of the Americans was John Jay, a Rhodes scholar from Williams College and a descendant of the country's first chief justice. Jay was already an accomplished producer of military skiing films; after the war, he would become one of the world's foremost ski-film makers.[3]

Three weeks after Dole's letter to the National Ski Patrol, the army's adjutant general, J. A. Ulio, called on Bates and the Alpine Club for help recruiting men as well. "There are only a very few experienced mountaineers in our country," Ulio would later write. "Candidates must have had actual experience with Alpine equipment, know Alpine technique, and be capable of instructing troops in rock climbing, ice climbing, and snowfield climbing. In general, candidates either must have participated in a major mountain climbing expedition or have been trained under a competent mountaineer. It is emphasized that mere hiking or climbing on mountain trails is not a sufficient qualification to justify application." After three months of basic training, Ulio wrote, the recruits would be sent "with the least practical delay" to Officer Candidate School (OCS), where they would be made second lieutenants. Men under thirty would be assigned to combat units; men over thirty would become instructors. Ulio asked club officers to mail applications directly to prospective candidates and to vet the responses themselves. "Since only a very few individuals have the necessary qualifications, it will obviate a mass of useless correspondence if the plan is given no publicity."[4]

As scores of skiers began to arrive in camp, a noticeable tension arose between them and the military bureaucrats nominally in charge of the training. It quickly became clear that many of the officers knew far less about skiing and mountaineering than the enlisted men, and virtually none had any experience training soldiers to operate in winter weather or at high altitude. To some veteran officers, the new crop was full of prima donnas determined to undermine the standards of military authority. Even Minnie Dole recognized the risks involved in admitting so many famous people. Writing of Friedl Pfeiffer, the Austrian ski instructor at Sun Valley who would go on to become a founder of Aspen, Dole wrote that he was "delighted that Friedl has turned out to be such a good soldier. I am sure that that is a further indication that he has been handled correctly, as you know what a pain in the neck these big shots can be if they want to be."[5]

Others were more charitable. "You will undoubtedly be pleased to know that some of our oldest and most hard-bitten Regular Army Personnel are now frankly admitting that the best men we are receiving are the men that have been endorsed through the offices of the National Ski Patrol System," Captain (later Colonel) Paul Lafferty, one of the earliest members of the 87th, wrote to Dole. Indeed, Lafferty said, most of the disciplinary cases in the troops arose among men transferred in from other units, not from the skiers.[6]

As it happened, this great pantheon of skiers was commanded by a man who had spent little time in the mountains; Lieutenant Colonel Onslow Rolfe had learned to ski just the year before. Even Rolfe seemed a little perplexed about his appointment. Perhaps, he thought, he had been given the position because he had been born in New Hampshire, a "mountain state." What the War Department apparently didn't know was that Rolfe had left New Hampshire when he was six.

Rolfe had graduated from West Point as a second lieutenant in 1917 and gone immediately to France, where he served with the 7th Infantry,

3rd Division, until he was wounded. Decorated with the Distinguished Service Cross and a Purple Heart, he returned to the United States and became an ROTC instructor at Rutgers College before stints at the Schofield Barracks in Hawaii, Fort Slocum in New York, and the Wisconsin National Guard. In 1935, he began a two-year course at the command and general staff school at Fort Leavenworth, Kansas, and later became a field artillery instructor at Fort Sill, Oklahoma. The best the army could do to justify his appointment as the head of mountain troops was to tell reporters that on summer leaves in 1937 and 1938 he had gone hiking in the mountains of Guatemala and Mexico.[7]

At first Rolfe was suspicious of all these college boys and ski snobs, who to him seemed to see military training as some kind of extended vacation. In addition to the rugged ones at Fort Lewis, there were also a few of the pampered, including heirs to the Glidden paint fortune and the Funk & Wagnalls publishing empire. Baron George von Franckenstein, nephew of the former Austrian ambassador to the Court of Saint James's, arrived with his wife, the author Kay Boyle. A private named Dyson Duncan, the son of the president of Lea & Perrins, decided upon his arrival that he wanted his wife and children to move in as well. Money being no object, Duncan leased one of the nicest houses in town—right out from under the nose of Rolfe himself, who got the bad news from his real estate agent: "Sorry, General, but Private First Class Duncan has already leased the house."[8]

To be sure, Rolfe had a difficult task. The 87th drew an older, more intelligent, and far more accomplished group of recruits than most army units, and it was not at all clear, in the beginning, what these men were supposed to be training *for.* The War Department had committed itself to training men and testing gear, but to what end? The United States had never trained mountain troops, let alone deployed them, and putting a nonskiing nonmountaineer at the head of the group was something of an inevitability. Inside the military establishment, what other kind of officer was there? "I have heard quite a few good men express their unhappy attitudes in regard to seemingly blundering training, meaning of course the mountaineering exercises at large," a corporal named Jim Briggs, who had helped train soldiers in rock climbing on Mount Rainier and in New Hampshire and Wisconsin wrote to Minnie Dole. Briggs considered it "very bad for the morale of an experienced mountain man to come across a lieutenant leading a platoon of men with eighty pound packs up a moderately steep slope at eleven thousand feet in a *herringbone step*. This is fact, *not fiction*, and there are dozens of examples of a similar nature going on constantly."[9]

In the meantime, however, Rolfe had his ways of showing his men the limits of their own skills. At Fort Lewis, all officers were forced to take lessons in horse riding. Some of the men considered this a form of revenge dreamed up by Rolfe, himself an old cavalryman, as payback for his own bungling on skis. Sure enough, some of the regiment's best skiers found themselves uneasy on horseback and were thrown constantly. Once, explaining a particularly public tossing, a good-natured John Jay told his fellow skiers that he had "caught an edge."

Jay got back at Rolfe a short time later. After walking out on a ski slope with a visiting Minnie Dole, Rolfe had asked Jay to show off his skiing techniques. Jay hiked up the hill, kick-turned, and proceeded to carve a gorgeous set of christie turns. Turning toward the group watching him, Jay pointed his tips directly at Rolfe. Just as it seemed that Fort Lewis's commanding officer was about to be sent reeling into an early retirement, Jay cut a razor-sharp turn and covered the colonel with a shower of snow.[10]

The repartee between Dole and Rolfe—a kind of pas de deux that stood in for the tension between the skiers and soldiers generally—continued at a dinner banquet just hours after Jay's antics on the ski slope. Speaking before a lecture hall full of the men he had recruited, Dole described the fireside conversations that had started the idea for the ski troops rolling. He told of the endless red tape he and Morgan had navigated to get their ideas through to Secretary Stimson and General Marshall. When he was done, Rolfe took over and paid Dole a compliment that seemed to perfectly reflect his ambivalence about the whole project.

"You men seem to have the idea that you're ski troops," he said. "Well, you aren't. You're mountain troops, and anyone who knows anything about the mountains knows that we have to have mules to carry equipment and mountain artillery. And mules won't go anywhere without a little bell mare to lead them. We will have a little bell mare any day now, and I propose we name her 'Minnie.' "

Dole wondered if he was somehow being compared to the rear end of a mule, but he accepted graciously and told Rolfe he was happy to be associated with the outfit in any way he could. Then, in one more turn of the endless dance between skier and soldier, he repaid Rolfe's gesture by handing him a gift that, he seemed to say, Rolfe would have to master if he ever wanted to earn the respect of his men: a pair of skis.[11]

BY THE SPRING OF 1942, a second and third battalion had been added to the 87th Regiment, opening the door for some physically able but less experienced recruits—men such as Denis Nunan, the IBM desk jockey from New Jersey. Although he had done some skiing as a youngster, Nunan was no mountain man. Remarking on all the birds living near California's Camp Roberts, where he had done his early training, Nunan admitted that he couldn't tell one species from another. He took particular note of one long-tailed bird, most likely a magpie, that he would have been unlikely to see in New Jersey. Impressed by the bird's stoicism even in the face of artillery fire, Nunan described it as looking "like a crow, only with a white body and white tipped wings." Nunan's indifference to the subtleties of natural history did not prevent him from becoming a recognized expert on the subject. When fellow soldier Hal Burton, who had worked for the New York *Daily News* before signing up, decided to launch a sheet called "The Fourth Platoon Bulletin," he named Nunan the "wildlife editor." This title probably had less to do with Nunan's ornithological acumen than his antics during weekend leaves.[12]

While other recruits brought more physical strength and wilderness experience to the army, Nunan brought a glowing charisma that charmed not only the men with whom he trained but a fair number of women he met off base. From the moment he arrived at Fort Lewis, outside Tacoma, he became a favorite with some of the most eligible girls in the Northwest. In a single weekend, he might be found on American Lake, at the country home of the timber-magnate Weyerhaeusers one evening, while the next he might be hobnobbing with the timber-magnate Murrays on Gravely Lake, where their giant estate had a driveway a mile long, a pool, and terraced rhododendron gardens. Or maybe he would be wooing one of the Ingram daughters—the family, Nunan wrote home, "had plenty of do-ray-me."[13]

Nunan moved into Paradise Lodge, one of two civilian buildings the

87th would take over for its training on Mount Rainier. It seemed to him more like a ski school or Boy Scout camp than a training ground. Early on, Nunan's courage on the slopes was not matched by his aptitude, and his spectacular falls contributed to his reputation as a cheerful daredevil. So often, and so conspicuously, did Nunan fall that his compatriots attached his name to their calls of condolence whenever anyone fell during a training run. All over Paradise Valley, where the men did their ski training, whenever a soldier went down in a cloud of snow, up would rise the chorus "Nunan, you okay?"[14]

Military ski school lasted six hours a day, six days a week, for eight weeks. Early classes were held in snowplowing, with rows and rows of troopers moving down the slopes like centipedes. After a day's drill, some of the men would get out guitars and have a sing-along; Charlie McLane, John Jay, Richard Whittemore, and Ralph Bromaghin, a Sun Valley ski instructor, got together and formed the 87th Mountain Infantry Glee Club. Their songs became a central part of the division's character. One of the earliest songs was an arrangement of an old western ballad, rewritten to tell how a trooper named Sven and his heavy-weapons company trained on snowshoes and thus spent "two months in Paradise and never learned to ski." Another, called "System and Theories of Skiing," went

> There are systems and theories of skiing
> But one thing I surely have found
> While skiing's confined to the winter time
> The drinking's good all year round.

In early spring, as the snow began to melt in the mountains, attention shifted from ski training to mountaineering. To get the men ready for work on cliff faces, engineers threw up three thirty-foot climbing walls in an old sand-and-gravel pit near the mule stables, where the men could practice belays and rappelling.

Once field training started in earnest, all the soldiers went through a five-day mountaineering school, where they learned everything from navigation skills and map reading to the safest way to haul dead bodies down a mountain slope. If the early training in the mountains around Fort Lewis had sharpened the men's military skills, it also sharpened their sense of humor. Lieutenant Charles Bradley perfected a prank that never failed to impress his trainees: demonstrating a rappelling maneuver on the lip of a sharp cliff, he would suddenly lose hold of his partner and scream to the heavens as the man fell to his death. As his horrified recruits watched from below, Bradley would reveal his partner to have been made of straw.[15]

Mountain safety, the men learned, required as much common sense as it did advanced rope technique. Just picking the appropriate route across a slope or up a face could prevent all sorts of problems. Keeping the body vertical to the slope and maintaining three points of contact with the ground—with a hand or an ice ax providing the third point of the plane—maximized stability. Rock faces were best navigated using the strength of the legs rather than of the hands and arms, which tired far more rapidly. Men learned to climb in groups and alone, up chimneys, under overhangs, and along cracks and ribs. They learned to stop short falls, their own or their partners'. They learned to use pitons for belays and how to run a Tyrolean traverse, a harrowing move requiring them to slide along a line suspended between two pinnacles using carabiners (oval rings with hinged snap gates) as pulleys. They learned how to haul heavy loads of gear—both mountaineering equipment and military hardware, including weapons—up cliffs that seemed impossibly steep from both above and below.

This last technique seemed the most subtly tailored to military climbing. If traditional mountaineers knew well the technique of moving heavy bags of equipment, they had little reason to drag bulky, odd-shaped objects such as weapons up vertical walls. But getting weapons as well as soldiers up rugged rock faces was in large part what the mountain soldiers most needed to know about. It was, after all, the one thing traditional infantry units could not do. If the army ever needed a unit to take a ridge that could not be approached merely by walking, it was to the mountain soldiers that it would turn.

As the general level of mountaineering skills within the regiment began to rise, some of the unit's finest climbers began pushing themselves, and their gear. By late spring, the Office of the Quartermaster decided that the time had come to test, and then purchase, an array of winter mountaineering gear for the new troops. An expedition was launched on Mount Rainier, followed immediately by a far more challenging climb up Alaska's

Mount McKinley (now Denali), the highest peak in North America. The McKinley trip in particular provided all the ingredients the army needed to put its new mountain gear to the ultimate test: tundra, glaciers, arctic cold, and severe wind. Given the severity of the climate, the expedition was turned over to three old friends who by now had as much experience with this kind of work as anyone in the world: Walter Wood from the Alpine Club; Brad Washburn, now working for the Army Air Corps; and Bob Bates from the Office of the Quartermaster.

The expedition included sixteen climbers, all with Alaska experience and many already world-famous adventurers. Setting out in the spring, the team reached its base camp at the top of McGonigall Pass on June 10 and began testing gear on Muldrow and Harper Glaciers. With far too much experimental gear to carry themselves, the team had the Air Corps drop more than a ton of equipment on the snowfields between 15,000 and 20,000 feet.

The group camped at 15,000 feet or higher for three full weeks, and discomfort was welcomed. Sleeping bags failed at −24 degrees Fahrenheit; an experimental pressure cooker exploded. Men let themselves be soaked to the skin to prove the integrity of water-resistant materials; let their body temperatures drop to test the warmth of climbing boots, sleeping bags, and jackets; and at one point worked their boots so hard that two team members were unable to walk for five days.

Just going about their business, they accomplished some spectacular and unexpected things. A mail drop at 17,000 feet became the highest-altitude mail delivery in U.S. history. Brad Washburn found and ate a cache of food—canned chicken, sausages, and pemmican (hard, fist-sized biscuits typically made of flour, dried beef, molasses, and lard)—that was as fresh as the day it had been left by another climbing party ten years before. On July 23 and 24, seven members, including Bates, Washburn, and Albert Jackman, became only the third team—and the first in ten years—to make it to the mountain's summit. Although they found it impossible to develop an absolute standard for some gear, such as how much eiderdown was required to make a sleeping bag perform well at subzero temperatures, by the end of the summer the equipment committee had conducted enough field tests that the quartermaster general approved specifications for virtually everything the mountain troops would need to perform effectively at high altitude: rucksacks, sleeping bags, parkas, ski pants, gaiters, mukluks (later nicknamed "bunny boots"), headbands, felt insoles, boot toe protectors, mittens, ski tents, ski caps, white camouflage trousers, a ski repair kit, snowshoes, poles, ski boots, stoves, and ski waxes.

As patriotic as their duty was, the men never for a moment lost their sense of an entirely different project: finding exciting routes up challenging mountains. "Give it a high priority after the war," Bates wrote to fellow climbers. "You won't regret it."[16]

NINE MONTHS AFTER the first men arrived at Fort Lewis, some soldiers were beginning to wonder just how all this mountain soldiering was going to contribute to the war. There seemed to be no end to the training in sight. Rumors had begun swirling that rather than being deployed overseas, the entire regiment would soon be moved to the Colorado Rockies. For Denis Nunan, "mountain training" had begun to mean idiotic drills such as day-long hikes on which the pace would be sped up on the way home. "These young blokes with bars on their shoulders have *no idea* on handling men," he wrote home. "The morale seems to be getting lower daily and it is in my mind and that of others the fault of management. The way everything is run makes a number of us wonder how in blazes we are going to win this war. Colorado! That is almost becoming a joke around here—when we go nobody knows."[17]

Making matters worse for Nunan was the constant influx of a new crop of soldiers, an entirely different lot from the northeasterners who until this point had figured Fort Lewis for a subsidized ski lodge. The "mule skinners," as they were affectionately known, had been recruited to train and care for a vast herd of mules the army had begun importing to carry the regiment's collapsible field artillery pieces. Typically brawny southern boys trained to saddle and load mules with pack howitzers—some bragged about being from "West By-God Virginia"—mule skinners brought with them a set of skills, such as trail riding and blacksmithing, that the boys from the Northeast knew nothing about. To Nunan, mule skinners were unruly country boys; they were "a tough lot and make more noise than an 'El' train during a bombing raid."[18]

Mules themselves, a cross between a jackass father and a mare mother, were highly intelligent, large—some stood sixteen hands high—and remarkably strong and surefooted; a fully loaded mule could carry enormously heavy loads over terrain and in conditions that would stymie the sturdiest jeep. Mules could climb faster than men but descended more slowly, placing their feet carefully and lessening the impact on their legs by taking small steps. The mules' thickness of skin also made them ideal for military use. They could carry hundreds of pounds of gear loaded atop a saddle that itself weighed a hundred pounds. They could also move through areas of intense shelling without batting an eye; horses, if faster afoot, were much more skittish and unusable the minute the going got heavy. A line of mules was most effectively led by a "bell mare"—the gentle creature Rolfe had promised to name after Minnie Dole—outfitted with a jingle bell tied to her neck.[19]

So taken with the mules was the old cavalryman Rolfe that he had a sign installed over the camp's expansive corrals that played on the sign Sherman Billingsley had installed at the Stork Club: "Through these portals pass the most beautiful mules in the world."[20]

To the skiers, most of whom had seen fewer mules than the southern boys had snowflakes, the animals were a horror. Army field manuals recommended walking beside mules' heads on the downhill side of a slope or along the edge of a cliff because mules have an instinctive tendency to walk on the inside edge of the path, as far from the downhill side as possible. To some men, this behavior demonstrated a mule's determination to make soldiers walk along a path's riskiest edge. If mules felt overloaded, they would simply lie down. If they were feeling ill, they would puff out their bellies, making it impossible to lash a saddle on. If they had it in for a particularly belligerent handler, they would wait for days for the man to walk too close, then lash out with a kick that could end the soldier's military career in a moment.

The men who trained the mules were known to swear so poisonously that even the mules would blink. Once Colonel Rolfe, on a standard swing inspecting stables, saw a blacksmith haul off and punch a mule so hard between the eyes that the animal reeled. "Son, that's no way to treat an animal!" Rolfe shouted. "Maybe so, Colonel," the blacksmith shouted back, "but the son of a bitch is standing on my foot."[21]

The mules became one emblem of the mountain troops, and another, less ornery vehicle became another. In July, with little fanfare or advance notice, Nunan and four dozen other men were herded onto a bus and began making their way north and east to the Canadian Rockies for an assignment they found unfathomable. For men already training on a mountain with enough snow and altitude to suit anyone's taste, the move to the Canadian Rockies seemed odd. What could they possibly offer a mountain soldier that the Cascades could not? The answer, it turned out, had less to do with terrain than it did with secrecy. Rumors had begun circulating among Allied commanders that Germany was planning to use a heavy-water plant in rural Norway to build atomic weapons, and knocking the plant out had suddenly become a high priority. But how to do it? Even in the frozen North, the German army seemed invulnerable to traditional military attack; the Allies did not have the technological ability to move sufficient troops to make an attack profitable.

British prime minister Winston Churchill, never one to turn his back on inventive ideas for prosecuting a war, had conceived an audacious plan to attack the Germans from a place they least expected it: the north. In the winter of 1943, the plan went, the Allies would mount an attack using paratroopers and mechanized oversnow vehicles that could be dropped from the bays of B-17 bombers. The trouble was, no vehicle had proven sturdy enough to transport men and equipment across frozen, snowbound ground. A number of experimental vehicles had been tested—aerosleighs, motorized toboggans, motorized sleds—and discarded. For a truck to be useful in such a demanding operation, it would have to be light enough to be transported by air, tough enough to withstand the air drop, and quick enough to outpace the only enemies they were likely to encounter: Germans on skis. The designers in the Office of Scientific Research and Development settled on a Caterpillar-type vehicle with wide rubber tracks. Among the forces behind the oversnow vehicles was a scientist and inventor named Geoffrey Pyke, who wanted the oversnow vehicles to be airdropped into Norway in November 1942.

Before any attack could be launched in Norway, prototype snowmobiles, commissioned from the Studebaker Company, would have to be tested in the most rigorous manner possible. And when it came to men used to testing equipment, none surpassed the mountain troops. Moving the trials to the Canadian Rockies and trusting them to a tiny unit of just two officers and fifty enlisted men, rather than an entire training camp, would ensure the test program's secrecy. If any word of the trials slipped out, nervous Allied commanders figured, it could jeopardize the entire Norwegian operation.[22]

The remoteness of the Columbia ice fields did much to determine who got to go on the mission: among the men were Norwegians, Swedes, a Pole, a Frenchman, Finns, even a Laplander. Nunan, it seemed, was the only member of the team who was not an expert skier. Nunan guessed that his success during rock-climbing drills had gotten him in, but the truth probably lay more in his sheer gusto. This, after all, was not a skiing expedition, and Nunan had another set of skills that was as useful as any man's: he was an expert driver.

Over the next several weeks, the team of thirty-one civilian mechanical engineers and machinists tested nine vehicles, finally settling on one that came to be known as the Weasel. As it turned out, the vehicle was not needed for the attack on the heavy-water plant. In February 1943, a half-dozen Norwegian commandos, in one of the most daring clandestine operations in the war, parachuted into the wilderness near the town of Vermork, then scaled a 3,000-foot mountain to reach the castle in which the plant had been constructed. Slipping inside unnoticed, they detonated a series of explosives that effectively crippled the German plans for making atomic weapons. A massive American air raid several months later completed the job.[23]

As for the men in the Canadian Rockies, no sooner did they return to Fort Lewis than the whole 87th Mountain Infantry Regiment departed for a stretch of training that would make their days in the Cascades seem blissful by comparison. At long last they—and thousands more men over the next two years—were headed for a brand-new training camp in the mountains of Colorado.

CHAPTER FOUR

THE LAND OF THE BLACK SNOW

W

HEN A SKINNY NEW ENGLAND teenager named Dick Wilson arrived at Denver's Union Station on Christmas Eve 1942, he found the concourse festooned in red and green, a giant evergreen towering over the bustling holiday travelers. The festive decorations helped take the edge off his loneliness. Wilson, who had grown up in Rochester and learned to ski in the Adirondacks, had never been west of Buffalo, and he still had eight hours to wait for the bus to Camp Hale. Unlike Denis Nunan, who had done little skiing before joining up, Wilson was a young veteran of the slopes and arrived in Colorado with his imagination fully engaged. He could hardly believe he would be getting paid to ski all day long, and with the world's finest instructors to boot. Military ski training, for Wilson, was a dream come true, a fantasy right out of *Boy's Life.*

Perhaps given his youth—Wilson was just nineteen—he also had an easier time than Nunan compartmentalizing what he had signed up to do. Sure, there was a war on, but it seemed farther and farther away the closer one got to the Rockies, and by the time his train left Denver, Wilson was thinking more about high-mountain adventure than, say, what a mortar fragment might do to a man's arm. This is not to say that Wilson lacked circumspection. The last thing he had done after interviewing with Minnie Dole back in Manhattan and before boarding the train at Fort Upton was to take out the standard army life insurance policy. If he fell off a cliff, froze to death during a maneuver at 13,000 feet, or got shot in the head overseas, his father would get $10,000. But with the bus grinding its way up into the hills, with the mountain air cooling and the roadside snowbanks deepening with every mile, dark thoughts were the last thing on Wilson's mind. The next morning, as he hopped off the bus at a little whistle-stop called Pando, Wilson was astonished by the countryside. He had never seen such beautiful mountains. Built at 9,224 feet, Camp Hale occupied the bulk of a narrow, crescent-shaped valley running roughly north-south and nestled between high ridges on all sides. One southeastern arm of the valley extended toward 12,300-foot Sheep Mountain, broken by Kokomo Pass; the northwestern arm tumbled down into Homestead Valley and finally into Red Cliff Canyon. Draining the ridges to the east and west of the camp, the Eagle River passed straight through the center of the valley. A product of glacier sculpting, the valley's north end had the gravelly look of a terminal moraine. At the south end, where the valley swept off briefly to the east, the camp had turned a low hill into a miniature ski slope.[1]

The camp had been laid out on three straight dirt roads running the length of the valley, cut by twenty-one crossroads. More than a thousand buildings had been thrown up in the months before the troops' arrival, including hundreds of barracks, stables for the mules, a hospital, a field house, and a veterinary clinic. The eastern edge of the valley ran into a long line of low cliffs that would serve as fine faces for instruction in rock climbing. With scree fields at their base, the cliffs were fractured by countless chimneys and cracks, which to any climber meant one thing: routes up.

Resolution Creek poured down from a 12,000-foot ridge to the east, creating a spur off the northeastern shoulder of the valley that would become a primary route out of camp during wilderness training exercises. Below about 12,000 feet, most of the countless ridges and peaks around the camp were relatively rounded, and most were matted with trees. Above this, however, the local giants were violently jagged and broken. From Ptarmigan Pass, some six miles uphill from the valley floor, climbers could look out over dozens of 13,000-foot peaks, all within a day or two's walk from camp.

A trail led alongside Resolution Creek through mountain meadows and patchy stands of aspen. The slopes leading down to the creek—indeed, the slopes on most of the lower peaks around Camp Hale—were ideal ski-training territory and perfectly suited for avalanches. On virtually every face, avalanches had torn through the pine forests, leaving V-shaped trails of matchstick trees that looked like abandoned log drives. Pearl Creek ran into Resolution Creek from 12,150-foot Pearl Peak; recruits moving out on bivouac along the Pearl Creek trail could look down and see their barracks far below, and beyond that, 13,200-foot Notch Mountain and 14,000-foot Mount of the Holy Cross. The sun, especially on the ridges around camp, was eye-searing, especially in winter, when it bounced off the snow for a second assault on the eyes.

Six miles beyond the south end of the valley, the road wound its way up to the Continental Divide near Tennessee Pass to Cooper Hill, where the camp had built its primary ski-training grounds, including a two-mile-long rope tow. Looming like a fortress wall high to the east of Cooper Hill was Chicago Ridge, an immense, rounded 12,200-foot formation extending for some five miles.

Except for the little train depot at the north end of the valley, there was virtually nothing in the way of human habitation near the camp. The closest town of any size was Leadville, some 20 miles to the south. Denver was 120 miles away, along treacherous mountain roads that made any trip there an adventure in itself. The valley in which the camp was situated had not been the army's first choice, but a spot in Wyoming's western Yellowstone Park, in the shadow of the magnificent Tetons, had been abandoned because it was located too near a breeding ground for endangered trumpeter swans. The swans had an important ally in the person of Frederic Delano, a strong conservationist who also happened to be the uncle of President Roosevelt.[2]

A spot near Aspen, Colorado, had proved too small; one near Wheeler, some eighteen miles from the nearest railroad, too remote. Pando, an abandoned mining town situated on both the main line of the Denver and Rio Grande Railroad and the slim U.S. Highway 24, seemed perfect. The fact that the camp would be far higher than any region in which the mountain troops were likely to be called to fight did not seem to occur to those planning its construction. The highest mountain passes in the Alps, at 6,000 feet, were fully two thirds of a mile lower than the men's barracks, let alone their training grounds, which would stretch up to 13,000 feet and above. With twelve feet of snow falling on the valley in an average winter and temperatures up on the peaks routinely dropping to −30 degrees Fahrenheit, the region would have been far too harsh for most training centers. For mountain troops, it was perfect.

Once construction began on April 10, 1942, the building teams had to hurry—winter, and with it the arrival of what were expected to be 15,000 troops, 5,000 mules, and 200 dogs, was just seven months away. Complicating the process was the fact that the Eagle River, fed by rain and spring runoff from the surrounding mountains, left the valley floor a subarctic swamp for much of the year. Just to form a firm base on which to build, earthmovers gouged some two million cubic yards of earth from the nearby hills and spread it over the slush of the valley floor. Just building the road between the camp and Tennessee Pass cost close to $400,000—the most expensive road project in the state, according to a proud man named Charles D. Vail, an engineer for the state highway department whose name would later grace a ski resort built just the other side of the mountains.[3]

By May 1, the ground had been sufficiently solidified for the first heavy building to begin; by August—in a kind of proto-Levittown building mania—the work crews had become so efficient, they made bets over which team could build a barracks the fastest. One day, a crew of sixty-one carpenters and four shinglers built a two-story, sixty-three-man, insulated bunkhouse—complete with everything but doors, plumbing, and screens—in seven hours, forty-five minutes, shaving three hours off the previous national military record. The barracks were designed with fourteen windows to a floor and a small room downstairs used primarily for drying ski gear. Dedicated—though still not nearly completed—on Flag Day, June 14, 1942, Camp Hale was named for Brigadier General Irving Hale, a brilliant and broadly talented man who had driven a stagecoach during the state's pioneer days, won a Silver Star during the Battle of Manila, and later organized the Veterans of Foreign Wars.[4]

A month after Camp Hale's dedication, a provisional command known as the Mountain Training Center was established at Camp Carson, Colorado, to prepare for the final move to Hale, develop training manuals, and begin testing mountain warfare tactics. Among the first men to arrive at Camp Carson were members of the 126th Engineer Mountain Battalion, set up to experiment with the construction of aerial tramways and suspension bridges in mountainous terrain. One consultant to both groups was Major Frederick Roebling, grandson of the famous engineer who had designed the Brooklyn Bridge. By the time the mountain troops got into the war, these engineers would be asked to perform heroics matching anything done on the battlefield.[5]

ASSIGNED TO A COMPANY in the 86th Regiment, Dick Wilson was giddy after throwing his bags into his barracks with the gear he had been handed on arrival: skis, boots, a wool sweater, a parka, the whole bit, all of it top quality and more than he could ever have afforded back home. After stowing his gear, Wilson made a beeline for the barracks presided over by the "famous guys" in the 87th newly arrived from Fort Lewis—Walter Prager, Peter Gabriel, and Alf Engen among them. The Europeans had made the most of their bunkhouses. Skis, poles, and boots were lined up against the walls, and the thick odor of ski wax swirled in the cold air whenever someone opened the door. At night, the barracks jumped, with men laying down songs on guitars, mouth organs, violin, even a concertina—a small, handheld accordion on which one of the Swiss would play a rollicking polka. One tune, "Ninety Pounds of Rucksack," sung to "Bell-bottom Trousers," became the division's signature song:

> *I was a barmaid in a mountain inn*
> *There I learned this tale of misery and sin*
> *Along came a skier, fresh off the slopes*
> *He's the one that ruined me and shattered all my hopes.*

> *Chorus:*
> *Singing ninety pound of rucksack, a pound of grub or two*
> *And he'll schuss the mountains like his daddy used to do.*

> *He asked me for a candle to light his way to bed,*
> *He asked me for a kerchief to cover up his head,*
> *And I being a foolish maid and thinking it no harm,*
> *Jumped into the skier's bed to keep the skier warm.*

Chorus

Now early in the morning before the break of day
He handed me a five-note and with it he did say,
"Take this my darling for the damage I have done;
You may have a daughter, you may have a son.
Now if you have a daughter bounce her on your knee;
But if you have a son send the bastard out to ski."

Chorus

The moral of this story as you can plainly see,
Is never trust a skier an inch above your knee;
I trusted one and now look at me:
I've got a bastard in the mountain infantry.

Chorus[6]

Within a couple of days of his arrival, Wilson's ski training had begun. Hiking six miles up to Tennessee Pass and riding the rope tow to the top of Cooper Hill, Wilson could see Mount Elbert and Mount Massive, the second and third highest peaks in the continental United States. The run down the mountain was very fast; daredevils in a tuck could hit 65 miles per hour on seven-foot-long hickory boards. Some let their enthusiasm get away from them: the Sunday after pulling into camp, Wilson saw two men fall and break their legs. Wilson was an excellent skier, but he could not always protect himself from the beginners around him. One day, tearing down a brand-new run that had just been cut through the woods, he saw, too late, a first lieutenant just ahead. "Track!" Wilson yelled, to no avail; the "dumb looie" was standing in the middle of the trail. Wilson tried to swerve but ran right over the lieutenant's skis and flew off between two trees that straddled a large hole. Wilson's skis went into the hole and didn't come out. He flipped a somersault, tore ligaments in his right knee and left ankle, and instantly lost respect for superior officers who didn't know enough to stay out of the way of expert enlisted men.

Given the cartwheeling experiences of "dumb looies" and inexperienced recruits like Denis Nunan alike, one of the first things instructors taught their charges was how to fall. Early lessons in "snow tumbling" included lining up a couple of men on their hands and knees and having a third man—without skis—sprint at and dive over them onto the snow. Doing it right, the diver would relax his body, tuck his head in toward his chest, and roll without injury. It being somewhat counterintuitive to relax the neck when flying face first onto a frozen slope, quite a few of the men decided that the best thing would be to learn how not to fall in the first place.

There was certainly no shortage of expert instructors from whom to seek advice. The influx of European downhill racers in camp had grown considerably. Among the best known was the Austrian Herbert Schneider, a world-class skier whose father, Hannes, had essentially invented downhill skiing techniques back in Saint Anton. Hannes Schneider had taught thousands of Europeans to ski—including many of the best now serving in the American mountain troops—but he had been arrested in the early months of the war for anti-Nazi activities such as admitting Jews to his ski school. Only some intensive diplomatic arm-twisting by a New York banker named Harvey Gibson, an investor in New Hampshire's Mount Cranmore ski resort, had gotten the elder Schneider safe passage to the United States.[7]

Another expert-in-residence was Toni Matt, who had been the Austrian junior ski champion before emigrating to the United States; once here, he became the national downhill champion in 1939 and 1941. Matt's reputation as a daredevil had been cemented during a single run, during the infamous American Inferno Race down one of the steepest ski slopes in the country—Mount Washington's Tuckerman's Ravine. The Inferno began at the top of Mount Washington, dropped over the headwall of Tuckerman's, and ran through the trees to Pinkham Notch, a vertical drop of 4,223 feet in about four miles. Matt had been on the mountain only once before—and that had been during a dense fog—but he had gotten plenty of advice from other skiers, all of it the same: don't schuss the headwall. The only man who had ever tried to shoot down the ravine without making a single turn had broken both legs and rolled down the wall like a barrel. Matt nodded and schussed the headwall. During his descent, he reached speeds of 80 miles per hour and finished the run in a record six and a half minutes. It was hailed as the most stunning piece of skiing ever done in North America and instantly made Matt a folk hero.[8]

If the downhillers brought the troops considerable media attention, some instructors were skeptical of the emphasis camp officers put on downhill skiing techniques. Scandinavians (not least a remarkable group of eight hundred first- and second-generation Norwegians known as the Viking Battalion) felt that cross-country training would be of far more practical military use. Soldiers were more likely to travel across snowbound territory than fly down mountains. German ski troops, after all, had been trained in Finland and Norway, not in Austria. The Germans "have *not* had Norwegian instructors—thank God—but they will have had Finnish instructors and you know they are excellent cross-country skiers," a visiting colonel in the Norwegian army named Carl Stenersen wrote Minnie Dole after a lengthy stay at Camp Hale. "The German authorities are in for efficiency and they do understand that 99 percent of military skiing is cross-country skiing—and they will not allow their skiers to fumble around for months on a hill with play skiing. They know how to *travel* on their skis."

A military operation on skis meant two things, Stenersen wrote: stealth and speed. Ski troops could move through forests, hit their enemy "with the utmost ferocity," and then disappear. "Speed, speed and speed cross-country in hidden trails," Stenersen wrote. "I see the great fun of downhill running, of slalom, of course I do. And its value as recreation, fun, play and sport—in *peacetime*. But now we have to take our sport, the skiing, in the service of winning this war. Skiing is a means and way of waging war. Therefore, we must sacrifice the fun, the play, and go in for strictly military skiing as part of our work, our military duty."[9]

Stenersen's points were well taken. A formation of downhill skiers might look good to visiting generals and film crews, but what were the chances of the men needing to roar off on downhill skis in the middle of a war? The Finns had held off the Soviet army in wooded flatlands, not in the mountains. And in the places the troops were most likely to be sent, such as Italy, the Germans either did or soon would occupy virtually all the high ground anyway. There would be no swooping down on enemy troops. At best there would be long, difficult slogs through the flatlands and into the foothills, regions where Nordic skiing techniques would be exclusively useful. Once in the mountains themselves, winter rock-climbing techniques would become far more useful than downhill ski turns.

If arguments over philosophies of ski training occupied Camp Hale's ranking officers, far more pressing to the men on the ground was the valley's horrible air. Indeed, if Dick Wilson's earliest days were ebullient, the feeling did not last long; those first few moments, for those first few soldiers, would turn out to be the only moments when anyone considered Camp Hale to be an unblemished paradise. In the early days, the snow on the ground only just covered the debris left over from the frenzied construction job; discarded nails beneath the snow made even a quarter-mile jeep trip an uncertain affair. Worse, even this late in the season, the creek running through the heart of the camp had turned the valley into a quagmire of muck that would torment the men virtually until the day they left.[10]

Far worse than the mud was the combination of altitude and soot that came to plague Wilson and virtually everyone else in camp. Situated in a valley with steep mountain walls on all sides, Camp Hale required a significant expenditure of energy just to get trains in and out and for the men to stay warm. To climb roadbeds with 4 percent grades—among the steepest in the country—trains on their way to and from the town of Leadville required three snorting locomotives, each of them belching coal smoke into a valley that rarely enjoyed a purging breeze. Heating the buildings required burning some five thousand tons of coal per year, and—given the army's reliance on sooty soft coal—the valley quickly began to resemble a high-altitude industrial city, complete with foul air and so much ambient soot the valley became known as "The Land of Black Snow." After just a couple of weeks, Dick Wilson wrote home asking for cough drops to soothe a throat made chronically raw by the soot in the air—a condition that became so ubiquitous it earned its own name: "The Pando Hack." As their health worsened, Wilson and five others from his barracks were admitted to the hospital, two of them on stretchers; fully one hundred others arrived with the same affliction the same day. By the time the troops left the camp just two years later, some seventeen hundred men would have transferred out just because of breathing the air.[11]

SHORTLY BEFORE DICK WILSON landed in the hospital, the army, eager to bump the ski troops up to fuller military strength, gave Minnie Dole a new assignment: find 2,500 skiers and mountaineers to fill the new camp's vacant barracks with two new regiments, and do it in sixty days. Once again Dole kicked into high gear. He buttonholed his friends at the National Ski Patrol, writing hundreds of letters asking for volunteers from the country's premier skiers. He toured New England colleges, tempting students with the chance to ski the Rockies and serve their country at the same time. After sixty days, he had a thousand more recruits than the army had asked for. By the time Wilson got out of the hospital, his regiment had added 180 men from New England alone.[12]

Many of the recruits came into New York to meet Dole in person and were given signed papers to present at their home induction offices to ensure their assignment to the mountain troops. With enthusiasm running so high and so many patriotic young men pounding on his door, Dole sometimes found himself face-to-face with angry mothers, wondering why, if their sons had been promised a spot in the ski troops, they were slogging through basic training at some base in Louisiana. In addition to being a recruiter and cheerleader, Dole also became a fixer; with a few phone calls, he could usually find a missing boy and get him a train ticket to Pando.

Like many other recent high school graduates, Art Delaney learned about the ski troops from *Life* magazine; unlike most others, Delaney discovered the magazine on a train home from Alaska. A baseball star from Valley Stream, Long Island, Delaney had fled his suburban neighborhood in 1939 to seek one last adventure before heading off to college and arrived in Seward, Alaska, with four dollars to his name. He quickly landed a construction job with the Army Corps of Engineers, which was building a base at Fort Raymond. The men under whom he toiled were typical of the early years of frontier Alaska, itinerant roughnecks with fabulous stories to tell about wine, women, and building the Grand Coulee Dam. Delaney was in Alaska when the Japanese bombed Pearl Harbor; for the year following, he watched as an intense paranoia swept over the men around him. Alaska had long been a magnet for roustabouts from the Lower Forty-eight, and the fever of war took hold of them in a manner Delaney found frightening. Paranoid vigilantes roamed the streets sticking guns in people's backs; others threw up a barbed-wire compound and forced in a dozen Japanese Americans—including the wealthiest man in town. Delaney decided to go home and join the air corps.

On the train home, however, he saw the article in *Life*. Flipping through the pages, he saw a photograph of a sergeant dressed in a white-hooded suit with a rifle on his back and skis on his feet. It was Walter Prager, the debonair Swiss ski coach from Dartmouth and world champion racer. Delaney also saw a photograph of a soldier dangling from a rope as he demonstrated "how a rock belay and a stout rope can save a soldier's life." It was the world-famous Swiss mountain guide Peter Gabriel. He also saw a team of soldiers, crampons on their feet and axes in their hands, traversing a vertical wall of ice, their lives relying on a single length of rope pinned to a wall of snow overhanging a crevasse. "Mountain troops say they would rather be on a ridge a thousand feet above the enemy rolling rocks down on him than below him in a valley shooting up with a battery of 155s," *Life* reported.

The article also included an address for the National Ski Patrol, 415 Lexington Avenue, where volunteers could sign up. As soon as his train stopped at New York's Grand Central Station, Delaney walked straight over. Two weeks later, after convincing three friends to write letters testifying to his prowess on the baseball diamond, Delaney, who had never been on skis, was back on a train west, this time bound for the mountains of Colorado.

He showed up at Camp Hale the week of Thanksgiving, even before the men from Fort Lewis had arrived, and was assigned to L Company of the 87th. At twenty-one he was older than many of the new boys showing up for training, and his work with the rough lot of men in Alaska convinced him that he could handle whatever the army threw at him, perhaps better than some of the prima donna skiers from New England. A group of NCOs "made it known to the recruits that they were gonna damn well learn to be soldiers before they learned to ski," he said. "A lot of these recruits looked at these mountains and thought they were joining a great military ski club."[13]

More like Denis Nunan than the unit's younger skiers, Delaney remained clear about what the men were in fact training to do: kill Germans. As in any infantry division, the endless repetition of standard army training—gutting dummies with bayonets, cutting silhouettes in half with machine guns—was meant to make murderous violence a matter of instinctive routine, something soldiers didn't have to contemplate. The countless hours of ski training simply made it easier for men—most of whom would have been repulsed by such acts in their civilian lives—to detach their minds from more grim assignments.

Since the mountain troops were learning to be frontline soldiers, they would not have the luxury of depersonalized, long-distance bombing runs or remote missile launches. They could count on fighting highly trained—and far more experienced—German soldiers virtually hand to hand with rifles, pistols, and knives. They would fire, and receive, countless mortar shells and machine-gun rounds and would see, at very close quarters, their skiing partners, as well as their enemies, torn to shreds. No matter the romance of their public image, the mountain troops were, in the end, training like any other unit to inflict as much suffering on their enemy as efficiently as they could. One insight Nunan had picked up during his rifle training stuck with him. The army, he learned, had decided not to use hollow-point "dumdum" bullets because they were too effective at killing people. More effective were regular bullets, which merely wounded their victims; tumbling through tissue and splintering bone, standard ammunition left terrible infections in its wake, and it takes more enemy soldiers to care for the wounded than it does for them to bury—or not bury—the dead.[14]

If the commanders leading the troops were still trying to figure out what mountain training might mean, they had little trouble understanding the parallels between surviving in the wilderness and surviving on the battlefield. Training in the mountains, at its best, trains climbers and soldiers alike to prepare fastidiously and respond instinctively to disaster. A soldier, like a climber, can never know when danger will appear. He can only prepare for it as rigorously as possible so that when it does come he will react spontaneously, like a martial artist who blocks a punch without having to give it a moment's thought. The chaos and fear implicit in moments of precipitous personal danger are far too overwhelming for an untrained body and mind, no matter how gifted or strong. Practice, exposure to simulated crisis, is the only way. And in the frozen mountains of Colorado, simulated crises were everywhere.

In January 1943, a nineteen-year-old soldier from New Jersey named Bob Frauson was part of a team ordered to live for two weeks at 13,000 feet and eat nothing but dried cocoa powder and pemmican. Vilhjalmur Stefansson, the Arctic explorer, had convinced camp officials that if Eskimos could survive on pemmican, so could mountain troops. The purpose of the test was to see how the men would respond to the high-calorie food under conditions that had their metabolisms running at full tilt. Just staying warm up on Homestake Peak would be a challenge; the men were also given exhausting ski maneuvers to do and spent their nights in snow caves.

The men were divided into three groups, eating pemmican with 40 percent, 60 percent, or 80 percent fat. Predictably, given his natural dislike of lard, Frauson was put in the 80 percent group and soon found himself "sweating fat." Frauson solved his problem by boiling his pemmican and pouring the fat into the snow. By the time he and his companions returned to Camp Hale, their stomachs had shrunk so dramatically that they were unable to eat the steak dinners camp administrators had prepared for them.[15]

A month later, Art Delaney took part in what became known as the Homestake Maneuvers, an exercise in which a reinforced detachment of 1,000 men and a battalion of pack artillery hiked out into the field near 13,209-foot Homestake Mountain, a few miles southwest of Camp Hale. What the men were doing in the woods was not clear to them; the whole thing seemed like an excuse for camp officials to see how much terrible weather the men could take living at nearly 12,000 feet. The weather was horrific, with blizzards blowing horizontal snow and temperatures the coldest of the season. Loaded down with ninety-pound packs, the men moved out on snowshoes and skis at a brutal pace of 106 steps per minute, which even the most acclimatized men found hard to maintain. Some of the newer recruits, fresh from lives lived at sea level, had not yet become acclimatized and had no idea how to protect themselves from the elements or even how to operate their portable stoves. Men fell out all over the place, disappearing into the woods and doing their best to wander back to camp. Art Delaney was fine going up, but once at altitude he wandered off course and got lost for two days. The warmest it got was 10 degrees Fahrenheit; at night, the soldiers had to rub their feet for an hour to thaw them out enough for the pain not to keep them awake. The only useful thing the men learned, it seemed, was to respect the laws of the mountains more than the laws of the military bureaucracy. At one stage, Lieutenant Colonel Rolfe, the camp's commanding officer, ordered a platoon to pick up some supplies that had been parachuted in and landed on a steep slope overlooking

Homestake Lake. Major Walter Wood, one of Bob Bates's old companions from the Alpine Club, in Colorado as an adviser along with Bill House and Minnie Dole, advised against the move, since the slope was loaded with snow and could slide at any moment. While the two men argued, an artillery commander decided to practice a little snow safety and fired a few shells into the slope to test the stability of the snow, a precursor of an avalanche control technique that would become standard after the war. The shells did the trick: the entire slope came down in a rush, virtually filling a lake below.

After two weeks in the woods, the men came down out of the mountains in a march they dubbed "the retreat from Moscow"; more than a quarter of them were suffering from frostbite and extreme exhaustion. Some of the things Wood and House observed—officers sleeping in tents while soldiers froze outside, men carrying absurdly heavy loads—resulted in a ferocious report to General Leslie James McNair, chief of the army ground forces. Dole wrote separately that the standard military management was inadequate, even dangerous, when applied in such extreme circumstances. The staff at Camp Hale was "rank-happy, with 'rank' at the top and brains at the bottom," he wrote. "I saw boys—good, husky boys—so exhausted and scared they deliberately stood around and froze their feet so they could get out."

McNair turned around and fired off a letter to Rolfe, complaining that the men on the Homestake Maneuvers had been given inadequate equipment and training for such a rigorous exercise. "A high percentage of the personnel fell out due to sickness, fatigue, frostbite and fear," the letter said. While acknowledging that Camp Hale had significant organizational problems given the influx of new recruits, McNair blasted camp officers for neglecting the considerable pool of expertise it had among its enlisted men. "The large proportion of experienced woodsmen, mountaineers, guides and trappers in the enlisted and lower commissioned grades provides an excellent source of technical knowledge. This source should be used to the utmost in the development of instructional training technique which is founded on time-tested mountain and winter procedures."[16]

Not long after this, Rolfe was relieved of his command. He was replaced by Brigadier General Lloyd Jones, a veteran of skirmishes against the Japanese in the Aleutians. If the men were glad to see Rolfe go, they didn't exactly welcome their new commander with open arms. Minnie Dole's lasting image of Jones was of a man so frail he had to sit on a radiator just to stay warm.[17]

AS CAMP HALE BEGAN to fill up with new recruits and word spread about the hardships they survived as part of their weekly routines, media interest in the mountain troops began to grow at a bewildering rate. If the men had trained in relative obscurity at Fort Lewis, they became media darlings from the moment they stepped off the train in Colorado. *The Denver Post* announced their arrival under the headline "Jeeps, Mules and Toboggans Tote Camp Hale Guns in Snow: Demountable Artillery Carried over Trailless Mountains by Tough Men, Animals and Machines—And Men are Toughest of All."[18]

World-famous Arctic explorers such as Vilhjalmur Stefansson—the proselytizer of pemmican—could be photographed teaching recruits how to survive wintry blasts by digging themselves snow caves or building igloos. Inside the barracks, reporters noted the men's preference for pinning up pictures of mountains, rather than starlets, above their bunks. Francis Sargent, later a governor of Massachusetts, remembered his peers, while on leave, climbing up the sides of Denver hotels. "My God, half of the sonuvaguns in the outfit would rather go climb some rock than go down to town and look for booze and broads."[19]

By the middle of the troops' first winter in Colorado, the goings-on at Camp Hale had become so intriguing to magazine writers and film crews that the men were constantly being asked to ski for the cameras. Some of the films were for recruiting purposes, so camp officials had no trouble asking the men to alter their schedules. It didn't take long, however, for the media attention to wear thin. Denis Nunan, among others, began to complain that the presence of film crews was beginning to compromise daily training. During a day with Columbia Pictures up on Cooper Hill, soldiers were asked to tow a toboggan full of movie gear up a slope in waist-deep snow at 11,700 feet—a chore that left all the men crumpled with exhaustion. Their collapse did not make the final cut.

When Warner Bros. showed up to make a training film, *Mountain Fighters,* on Cooper Hill, they picked Dick Wilson, finally released from the hospital, and sixty others to do the skiing. The *Mountain Fighters* film (in Technicolor!) became perhaps the apotheosis of the romance the country had developed with the ski troops. The film opens with a burst of triumphant trumpets as cameras pan across a group of men rappelling down cliffs, skiing in perfect synchronization, and marching, weapons shouldered, through a wintry mountain camp. Suddenly a bombastic voice booms out a message intended for ears far beyond the men the film was intended to recruit.

"Near the top of the Continental Divide, American soldiers are learning the highly specialized art of mountain warfare as no other soldiers have learned it before," the voice intones. "Camp Hale—high in the Colorado Rockies. Here the United States Army has its great mountain training center. Here, surrounded by the awe-inspiring grandeur of towering snow-clad peaks, our mountain divisions are being trained for the vital role they will play in the destruction of the Axis. And what men they are! Every one a volunteer! Many are world-famous skiers and mountain climbers! Many are amateurs, and many are greenhorns. Men from the ski slopes of New England, men from the High Sierras of California, men from Norway, men from Denmark, men from Sweden, and men from Switzerland. Yes, even men from Germany and Italy. These are the United States mountain troops!"

The film then cuts from footage of men in training to a series of scenes obviously staged, with rock-jawed actors playing the roles of sergeant and recruits. During a sequence in which dozens of fully outfitted soldiers sweep down a slope in a "military ski test," the narrator again almost gasps with excitement.

"And here they come! Shooting down the long white slope like a string of comets! Watch them do that first fast turn, still keeping formation as they change direction! Then into another turn and moving faster still! From this they start a stem christiania, and now they're really getting hot!"

The scene then shifts to the men, now fully trained and wearing green wool overcoats, boarding a smoke-belching troop train, en route to fight in "the mountains of Europe."

"That long-awaited day has arrived. The strenuous weeks of training are over. They're all real mountain fighters—hardened, deadly efficient! More than a match for anything the Axis can throw against them! Yes, it's been tough skiing for these boys and they've certainly had their ups and downs. But at last it's good-bye to Camp Hale, good-bye to the Rockies they've climbed and conquered. Maneuvers are over—now the real fighting starts! Today, for the first time, American mountain troops, well equipped, well trained, and determined, are fighting side by side with the united nations in the inevitable destruction of the German war machine!"

The film's final segment has the mountain troops patrolling the slopes of an unnamed mountain range, where, in a melodramatic battle sequence, they take a ridgeline from a group of "Germans" who outnumber them "ten to one." Again the narrator's voice cuts in, now rising with almost hysterical pride. As he speaks, the musical accompaniment melts into "The Star-Spangled Banner."

"There they go! The hard-hitting mountain troopers! The fighting daredevils of the heights! America's proud contribution to the battles of the high country! Marching steadily forward beside their comrades of the united nations! They conquer mountains and men, that liberty might live forever as they fight on to victory!"[20]

Denis Nunan's opinion of the film—and all the media hype—was less than charitable. "We get more publicity than FDR it seems, and $\frac{9}{10}$ of it is bunk," he wrote home. All the acting for the cameras "makes us wonder if we are in the Army to fight the war or to be stooges for Hollywood. It also causes us to wonder about there being a war on, with us parading up and down in front of a camera while the boys in Africa are being pushed all over the map!"[21]

CHAPTER FIVE

CLIMBING AND FALLING

N MAY 1943, TEN MONTHS after halting the German advance across Egypt at El Alamein, Allied forces completed the recapture of North African territory with a breakthrough in Tunisia that yielded nearly 250,000 German and Italian prisoners. But it was the north, on the Russian front, to which the world had once again turned its full attention to the perils of winter warfare. After a heady advance that carried them seven hundred kilometers and cost the Soviet army two million lives, the Germans in the autumn of 1942 still faced an incomprehensibly vast expanse of Russian territory and an equally deep reservoir of Soviet replacement troops. Hoping to protect the drive to the Caspian Sea's critical oil reserves and dreading another humiliating Russian winter, Adolf Hitler ordered his troops to attack Stalingrad. Fighting a *Rattenkrieg*—a "rat's war"—amid the rubble left by German bombers, German general Friedrich Paulus's 250,000 soldiers captured large chunks of the city by the end of September. Rather than launch an all-out counteroffensive, Soviet strategists decided to surround the city with a force amounting to 60 percent of the entire armored strength of the Red Army. Hitler refused to withdraw the troops; Hermann Göring assured him that the encircled soldiers could be resupplied by airdrops from the Luftwaffe. What followed became a debacle widely considered to have been the turning point of the war.

As autumn turned to winter, temperatures plummeted as low as −30 degrees Centigrade. German supply planes were either frozen on the ground or shot from the sky. Soldiers within the city were left to eat their horses and their leather belts; those who didn't die of malnutrition became infested with lice and infected with typhus. By the end of January 1943, when Paulus finally surrendered his 90,000 remaining German soldiers, more than a million people, fully half of them civilians, had lost their lives. As devastating as the battle was for the Russian people and the Red Army, however, its impact on German military confidence was crippling.[1]

The German general Frido von Senger, moved from a post as a liaison officer in Italy, had been given command of a brigade within the 17th Panzer Division and ordered to try to relieve the trapped German Sixth Army. The relief effort failed, as the attack had, in part because of an endlessly replenished swarm of Soviet soldiers and in part simply because of the difficulty of surviving in relentlessly freezing weather. "Only those who have seen the facial expressions of men grown apathetic through exhaustion can form any idea of the loss of fighting power and strength involved," Senger would write. "The continuous suffering of the troops affected me physically. The cold was visibly sapping their strength."

For Senger, this would just be the first of a series of winter battles that would test not only his leadership skills but his perseverance in a military establishment whose political leaders he abhorred. After growing up in Baden-Baden in Bavaria and studying for two years as a Rhodes Scholar at Oxford, Senger had served eleven years in the German military, where he eventually took command of a cavalry regiment. A devout lay Benedictine and a man of quiet scholarship, Senger had nonetheless proven himself an exceptional career military commander. Despite a professed loathing for the Nazi regime, Senger rose through the ranks and was already in the army high command by the time of Hitler's rise to power in the summer of 1934. Within a year of his stymied efforts at Stalingrad, he would help oversee yet another terrible cold-weather war, this time in the mountains near Cassino in southern Italy. Then, following Field Marshal Albert Kesselring's plan of a slow and punishing withdrawal up the peninsula, Senger would make highly effective use of the rugged Italian landscape, a geographic feature that would cripple American and British forces for nearly two years. By the time Senger's crack troops withdrew for their final stand in the northern Apennines, they would turn their field-tested wills against men who during most of the Italian campaign were still learning to ski in Colorado.[2]

WITH THE STEADY DRUMBEAT of magazine coverage continuing to trumpet the mountain troops' exploits, a second wave of recruits began pouring into Camp Hale. Articles in newspapers around the West urged "rock climbers, trappers, packers, guides, prospectors, and timber cruisers" to contact local recruiters or, in a pinch, ski patrollers.[3]

Gene Hames was the perfect candidate. After graduating penniless from western Montana's Missoula County High School, he figured he had two choices for work: he could join the Northern Pacific Railroad as a brakeman, or he could go to work in the woods. The Anaconda Copper Mining Company needed men with strong backs to open a logging operation fifty miles east of Missoula in the Blackfoot Valley, so in 1937, Hames signed on as the company's youngest timber faller for $1.10 a day. Growing up on a ranch in the shadow of the Bitterroot Mountains of western Montana, Hames was used to a certain amount of hardship. He slopped barns from an early age and, as there was no plumbing or electricity in his house, fetched pails of water from Burnt Fork Creek. His father, who had once worked the manganese mines down near Philipsburg, had moved up to managing the cattle and alfalfa operations on a ranch near Stevensville. Montana winters could be particularly trying on both the animals and the people who tended them. For heat, the family relied on potbellied stoves in the living room and kitchen; to get to school, Gene and his five siblings would saddle up horses and ride, two to a horse, in all weather, four and a half miles each way.

Arriving at the mining camp, Hames joined two hundred other men living sixteen to a bunkhouse, stacked up in bunks and warmed by good stories and a log on the fire. The camp cook, a huge man who had served in the First World War, ran the place like a drill sergeant—there was no talking allowed during meals, other than to ask for more salt. Though the food was bland, there was plenty of it. Hames put on forty pounds of muscle his first year on the job, and he needed every ounce.

He started work as a top loader on a tie car, helping lay tracks into a new stretch of forest Anaconda planned to log. Later he became a sawyer, working first a two-man, six- or eight-foot crosscut saw, and then a timber faller. The men cut down the trees, limbed and measured them, and lopped off the tops. The logs were then skidded out of the woods with horses and loaded onto railroad cars using a steam-operated machine called a sliding-ass jammer. Men were paid a fixed rate per thousand board feet, so the harder and faster they worked, the more money they took home. Hames quickly discovered why lumberjacks have one of the world's most dangerous jobs: a moment's inattention with an ax could mean a splintered shin; a tree that fell a few angles off could hammer a man into the ground like a peg. Men known as "choker setters," who drove the big cats that dragged trees from behind steel cables, got their arms caught and ripped off. Hames managed to avoid these common accidents, but once, while he was smashing a steel wedge into a tree trunk, his hammer shot a sliver of shrapnel straight into his chest, an eerily battlelike injury that required surgery to remove.

Hames had a couple of older brothers who were in the military—one had joined the Marine Corps the day after Pearl Harbor, the other had been drafted into Officer Candidate School at Fort Sill, Oklahoma—and he decided that once he came of age he had better figure out where he would best serve his country. One day, while getting his red 1936 Pontiac convertible fixed at a garage in Missoula, a man told him about a magazine article he had read, raving about a new unit of elite soldiers known as the "mountain troops." He suggested that a boy with Hames's skills in the woods might try it out. Although Hames had never heard of the troops, the chance to combine military service and wilderness training seemed good to him. He sent in an application, was sworn in at a recruiting office in Butte, and two weeks later joined E Company of the 86th Regiment.[4]

If Gene Hames stumbled onto the mountain troops almost by accident, Hugh Evans seemed destined for them. After growing up in Marin County, California, Evans decided to follow his older brother to New Hampshire's Phillips Exeter Academy. In 1938, he took a train to Michigan, then made his way to Exeter, a gorgeous hamlet about an hour north of Boston. Exeter offered many things Evans expected—proximity to the White Mountains not the least of them—and at least one thing he didn't: a young man named Bob Bates, not ten years older than Evans, who had just arrived there as an English teacher fresh from his attempt on K2. To Evans, what

Bates knew about literature mattered far less than what he knew about mountains, a field in which he was already something of a legend. As a boy, Evans had hiked and skied through the wilderness of northern California's Sequoia and Yosemite National Parks, rock climbed along the Pacific coast, and completed a six-week pack trip through the High Sierra. But for the fourteen-year-old Exeter freshman, Bates, whose exploits in the last six months alone had put him at the forefront of international mountaineering, gave Evans his vision of what it meant to be a hero.[5]

By the time Evans was nearing graduation four years later, Bates had taken leave from Exeter and was playing his central role in the formation of the mountain troops and the testing of its equipment as a major in the army's Quartermaster Corps. In mid-January 1943, Evans wrote Bates that he had spent the summer as a camp counselor in the Sierras, where he had done quite a bit of rock climbing and backpacking. "The main reason for my writing is to ask you how I can get into the mountaineering troops," Evans wrote Bates. "After Exeter I would like very much to be able to get into these troops because the chance of getting drafted is getting pretty big."[6]

Bates wrote back two weeks later, advising Evans to send his application to a colleague in a recruitment office in Cambridge, Massachusetts, and to ask him to put it through channels. "Don't shoot me if the mountain troops don't make any first ascents," Bates wrote. "I think you'll find them a good bunch though they haven't done much real mountain work yet." Bates added a note that could only have added to the heroic appeal he held for Evans: "Slept outdoors in an Arctic suit at 20 below with a 10-mile wind the other day. Some day head up to the Hudson's Bay Country. It isn't pretty but the people who live there are grand."[7]

Privately, Bates was worried about Evans. He was at the age when boys think they are invulnerable, an illusion that would certainly be tested by serving in the mountain troops, who, if they ever saw battle, would surely be sent straight into the teeth of the fighting. "I was afraid Hugh would be all gung ho and get killed," Bates would say. "I was very scared the mountain troops were going to know more than most people, and would be sent to lead people and get knocked off right away." After completing basic training at California's Fort Ord, Evans was on his way to the Rockies, where he would initially join A Company of the 85th Regiment.[8]

Gene Hames and Hugh Evans arrived in Colorado after most of the first winter's training had been completed. Evans found himself—without having gone to noncom school and with virtually no experience as an army leader—made a sergeant and leader of a squad. He spent his early weeks working with pitons and helping train recruits in the art of rock climbing, arriving at the climbing sites early and setting up fixed ropes for the men to climb. Like every other new arrival, he discovered new depths of hunger and fatigue. One weekend in Denver, he chronicled his time in a list that could serve as a template for all soldiers on weekend pass: "10% dancing, 15% buying clothes and finding out about plane reservations, 25% sleeping and 50% eating. I have never eaten so much in such a short time in my whole life."[9]

On July 15, with some thirteen thousand men now in camp, the official name of the mountain troops was changed once again, to the 10th Light Division (Pack, Alpine), with three full regiments: the original 87th, the 86th, and the new 85th. One temporary regiment, the 90th, was also formed but would later be broken up, its men divided among the other units. In addition to the three main regiments were three artillery battalions, a medical battalion, three quartermaster pack companies, antitank and antiaircraft batteries, a signal platoon, and the mountain tram– and bridge-building 126th Engineer Mountain Battalion. "Light" divisions were best suited for fighting that required little equipment—in mountains or jungles, or for airborne or amphibious landings in which invading forces could rely on pack mules or local bearers to help move gear. The 10th's heavy-weapons companies that had been formed previously were now disbanded, their mortar sections attached to other companies.

For many of the European recruits, one of the first things to do in Colorado was attain U.S. citizenship. In early May, Walter Prager, Torger Tokle, and five dozen others, most of them Norwegians, had presented a petition from the Immigration and Naturalization Service to District Judge William A. Luby. Luby granted the petition, calling the group "some of the finest mountain soldiers in the world" and "examples of marvelous physique and endurance." The division eventually had fully five hundred foreign-born soldiers. What these men had to teach their American comrades went far beyond the lessons learned on the ski slopes; they also conveyed their anxieties about the sweep of terror that had consumed their home countries.

A favorite camp pastime was trying to divine where the division's services might finally be needed. Though rumors continued to swirl about a possible insertion somewhere in the Pacific, the chances of its being deployed in Europe jumped dramatically in the middle of July 1943, when the Allies launched Operation Husky, an amphibious assault on Sicily that would become one of the largest combined missions of the entire war. Even while the Africa campaign was still under way, Churchill had been talking up plans to invade Italy with Roosevelt at the Casablanca Conference in January 1943. With the Russian front draining so much blood and so many resources from the German army, the prime minister argued, the time was ripe for an advance from the south. Roosevelt and Marshall argued that committing to an invasion of Italy would pull critical resources from the cross-Channel operation scheduled for the following year. The flatlands of northern France would be far easier to navigate than the endless mountains of the Italian peninsula. History argued their case as well: Italy had never been successfully invaded from the south.[10]

In the end, Churchill got his way. When a dead Royal Marine officer, Major William Martin, floated up on a remote Spanish beach with a briefcase chained to his wrist—its contents indicating a major attack on the Balkans—the Germans thought they had scored an intelligence coup. They were wrong. Martin—the legendary Man Who Never Was—was a decoy. An Allied invasion was indeed just eight weeks away, but it would come farther south, on the island of Sicily. Over the course of the next thirty-eight days, half a million Allied soldiers, sailors, and airmen fought German and Italian forces for control of what Allied commanders hoped would be a major point of control for Mediterranean shipping and supply.

The Allies had a lot going for them. An island of deeply independent people, Sicily had suffered under one form of occupation or another for centuries and had no particular fondness for the German army or its 300,000 Italian stand-in troops. The Italian soldiers on the island were disconsolate over the course of the war, and many were poorly trained; some of the officers did not even know how to fire their own weapons. When he arrived to become the German liaison officer with the island's senior Italian commander, General von Senger was shocked at the paucity of the island's defense networks—indisputable evidence of the sorry coordination between the Axis armies.[11]

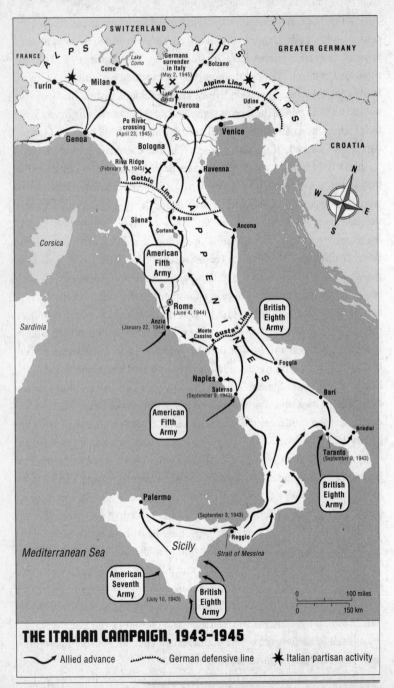

THE ITALIAN CAMPAIGN, 1943–1945

Allied advance ⁓⁓⁓ German defensive line ✴ Italian partisan activity

Yet as would be the case for the remainder of the Italian campaign, nothing went as smoothly as the Allies hoped. A formation of British gliders were forced by flak and bad weather to ditch into the sea, drowning 252 men. Only 12 of 147 gliders landed on target. More than 3,000 paratroopers from the U.S. 82nd Airborne were scattered by heavy winds over a thousand square miles; they missed their target by such a wide margin that Italian observers figured there were as many as 30,000 men floating down from the skies.

Despite these early gaffes, the Allied amphibious forces landed with great success. Under the command of British general Harold R. L. G. Alexander, the Allies bombed airfields, rail lines, and coastal enemy positions. The American troops were led by Lieutenant General George Patton's Seventh Army, the British Eighth Army by Lieutenant General Bernard L. Montgomery. Two days after the initial landing, the Allies had placed more than 80,000 men, 7,000 vehicles, and 300 tanks on the island and captured six airfields. Six weeks later, despite ferocious counterattacks by the armored Hermann Göring Division, the island fell. Patton's men raced to be the first to arrive at Messina. German and Italian armies suffered five times the losses of the Allies, yet a German force of just 60,000 men had managed to tie up a 467,000-man Allied invasion force for more than a month and succeeded in evacuating far more troops than expected. Though the Allied victory was complete, it would come to be seen as the first in a long series of battles that took far longer and cost far more in terms of both personnel and matériel than the strategists ever expected.

Beyond the immediate military fallout, the defeat in Sicily convinced Italian king Victor Emmanuel III to force Benito Mussolini from office on July 25; under cover of darkness, the king and his *capo*, Pietro Badoglio, gathered their families in Rome and fled for the port town of Ortona, and thence to Brindisi, by then under the control of Montgomery's Eighth Army.

Though some Allied strategists argued that the Italian campaign should end in Sicily, Churchill once again pushed for a full invasion of the mainland peninsula. Pushing north all the way to the Po River valley, he maintained, would not only wrest a critical agricultural and manufacturing base from the Germans but could open up new avenues into southern France or through Yugoslavia's Ljubljana Gap into Austria. Churchill said the Allies should at least capture Rome and then secure a defensive front stretching east from Livorno to Ancona. More modest plans called for an endpoint north of Naples and the capture of the Foggia airfield sixty miles to the east. One of the most valuable bases in Italy, the Foggia field would allow Allied planes to reach as far north as southern Germany, Austria, even Poland, all of which were beyond the reach of planes based in England. Once again Churchill prevailed. The war in Italy continued, albeit with chronic shortages of men and equipment, which continued to flow north to France.

If the Allied high command was determined to make Italy a third front, its severe limits on troop strength would seriously hinder any progress northward. Adding to the challenge was the remarkably complex makeup of the American and British armies themselves. Alexander counted twenty-six different nationalities fighting for him, notably substantial units from Canada, India, New Zealand, and Poland. The American army would oversee, among others, the all-African-American 92nd Infantry Division; the all-Japanese-American 442nd Infantry Regiment (which included among its soldiers future U.S. senator Daniel Inouye); a small Brazilian Expeditionary Force; and the 6th South African Division. If this astonishing diversity made for a rich contrast with the German army, it hardly made military coordination any easier. Having to cope with everything from vast differences in languages to food requirements (Muslims wouldn't eat pork; Sikhs wouldn't eat beef) to divergent political desires for the war itself, the American Fifth and the British Eighth Armies would just have to make do.[12]

Meanwhile, in August, behind the scenes and without warning the Germans, top Italian military officials arranged an unconditional Italian surrender with General Eisenhower. As soon as the Germans learned of the Italian capitulation, everything on the peninsula changed. Almost immediately, German soldiers, tanks, and airplanes were everywhere, aiming an opposition force not just at the southern coastline but, in moves that angered their former allies, occupying much of northern Italy as well. Following the 26th Panzer Division moving to reinforce the battle in Sicily, the 44th Panzer-Grenadier Division spread out below Bolzano. Arguing that the Alpine passes were inadequately protected from Allied air raids and fearing the Italians might cut the passes off behind the forces already in country, Field Marshal Erwin Rommel set up Army Group B headquarters in Verona. Soldiers poured into Trieste to prevent Yugoslav forces from inching west. To many Italian civilians, it began to seem as though the Italian army had surrendered not to the Allies but to the Germans.

After Sicily, the German command had wrestled with what to do if the Italians dropped out of the war. How deeply should the German army commit to defending the Italian peninsula, and at what cost? Rommel argued that there weren't enough resources available to occupy the entire country. Better, he said, to concede everything to the south and concentrate resources on building up defenses along the Brenner and Ljubljana Passes in the Alps.

Field Marshal Kesselring, head of German Command–South, took the opposite position, arguing that twelve German divisions—the same number Rommel wanted in the Alps—could tie up as many as twenty Allied divisions for two years or more. The preservation of German power in northern Italy would also mean continued access to the highly productive agricultural and manufacturing centers in the Po River valley; why simply concede Turin, Milan, Bologna, Verona, and Venice? Besides, the peninsula's waves of mountain chains gave the Germans a remarkable geological advantage. If the Allies broke through one mountain defense, there would always be another one waiting. It would take two years for the Allies to win what Rommel was willing to give up in a day. Moreover, Allied air bases could be kept farther away; Mussolini could be restored to a form of leadership; and Hitler could fulfill a long-held desire by reclaiming sections of northern Italy lost by his native Austria in World War I. Besides, Kesselring argued, the Allies would never make it as far as the Alps. Even if they somehow managed to push north of Rome, the German strongholds in the Apennines—the last line before the Po River valley—would never break. Kesselring had nicknamed the Apennines position the *Gotenstellung*, or "Gothic Line," for the Gothic kingdoms ruled by Germanic tribes in Italy in the sixth century, but Hitler declined to use the name, fearing a collapse in morale if the line were ever to break.[13]

As the former chief of air staff under Göring and a leading commander in the battles for Britain and Malta, Kesselring was widely known for his military optimism and had long had Hitler's ear. But beyond Kesselring's remarkable ebullience was Hitler's fear of losing the oil, bauxite, and copper deposits in the Balkans to the Allies—and worse, of allowing a direct line of communication between the Allies and the Russians.

Back and forth the arguments raged, until Hitler decided in favor of Rommel. German troops would concede southern Italy and make their stand in the northern Apennines. But even as he was transmitting the order, Hitler abruptly changed his mind and canceled the telegram. Instead, he made Kesselring the commander in chief, Southwest—in charge of the Tenth and Fourteenth Armies—and transferred Rommel to the western front, thus effectively changing the course of the war in Italy. Over the next eighteen months, 200,000 men would die fighting for the strip of land that Rommel had urged be given up.[14]

The Allied push up the Italian mainland began on September 3, 1943, with Canadian and British forces of Montgomery's Eighth Army crossing the Strait of Messina and landing, under four hundred tons of heavy artillery and air cover, near Reggio di Calabria. Over the next five days, Operation Baytown advanced a hundred miles, to the instep of the peninsula's boot. On September 8, Italy officially surrendered, and the next day—even as German forces took control of most major Italian cities—four divisions of the new American Fifth Army, under the leadership of Lieutenant General Mark Clark, landed on the beaches of Salerno to begin Operation Avalanche. The port of Naples lay just fifty miles to the north.

When the 36th Infantry Division, a National Guard unit from Texas, first landed at Salerno, it had reason to hope it would meet little resistance. Italy had surrendered; perhaps the war was over. But coordination problems began even before the landing: the Allies in Italy were a hodgepodge gathered from a dozen different nations; they spoke different languages, used different equipment, and even had different goals for their participation in the war. Their German enemy, suffice it to say, faced no such difficulties.[15]

Worse, a shortage of adequate landing craft made it difficult for the Allies to put armored vehicles on the ground, and troop strength was never brought to full capacity because of the buildup for Operation Overlord in France. Entire divisions that had fought in Sicily were already on their way to Britain. The commander of the naval operation would later criticize the timing of the Italian government's surrender announcement, since the assumption of an easy victory had led to a lack of discipline and alertness among his men. The reality on the beach was far less promising. Barking German loudspeakers on shore invited the invading forces to "come on in and give up."

Some British units, coming ashore, landed in the wrong place after following an errant rocket barrage that left an entire division fully exposed. American troops seemed unsure whether to advance on the rough inland country or simply hold the beach. General Clark's command ship was pushed so far out to sea by German planes that it lost its ability to communicate with the ground forces during much of D-Day. When Clark finally asked his ground commander his thoughts on the battle, the general responded, "All I've got is a prayer."

Perhaps most critically, General Clark had called off a prelanding bombing in the hope that it would allow the invasion to advance unnoticed. This proved to be a major miscalculation. The commander of the lone German division guarding the beachhead hoped only to spar with the four landing divisions before retreating to guard the road to Naples, where, along with reinforcements arriving from the north, it would stage a savage counterattack.

In the first four days, Allied planes flew 3,000 sorties and dropped more than 2,100 tons of bombs in support of the 189,000 ground forces and 30,000 vehicles that had landed near Salerno. Yet despite heavy damage inflicted on advancing German tanks from offshore, smaller German attack units were able to keep the Allies bottled up on the beach until the notorious Hermann Göring Division, which had caused so much trouble in Sicily, could arrive from Naples, followed by the 26th Panzer Division and 29th Panzer-Grenadier Division. The Luftwaffe carried out the heaviest German air attack of the Mediterranean campaign, mercilessly bombing and strafing the landing craft. What Clark had hoped would be a quick, surprise victory turned into a bloody stalemate that only increased the Germans' confidence in their ability to hold the peninsula. The German counterattack lasted five days, and the Allies would not have survived without substantial British reserves from North Africa and help from exhausted veterans of the Sicily campaign. In the end, Kesselring ordered a disengagement on September 16, his forces having suffered only 3,500 casualties, one third those of the Allies.

But the Germans, it turned out, also misplayed Salerno. Hitler, who never thought the Allies could be defeated in southern Italy, refused to commit more than four divisions and thus missed a chance to throw the Allies back into the sea. As a result of the strong German showing, Hitler decided to defend Italy fully. On September 17, with Rommel reassigned to France, Kesselring announced the military occupation of all of the peninsula. Had the Allies won more convincingly at Salerno, Rommel's plan might have won out and saved Italy and both sides a long and terrible war. Two weeks after taking control of Salerno, Allied troops took Naples as well. Kesselring ordered his troops to withdraw first to the Volturno River and later to the "winter line," a heavily fortified position about seventy-five miles south of Rome. As they retreated, the Germans destroyed or mined every bridge and roadway they could, as well as fuel depots and electrical and water stations. With winter coming, the Allies' chase required monumental engineering efforts just to keep the troops moving north. When the cold weather arrived, their burdens would increase by an order of magnitude.[16]

WITH OTHER AMERICAN SOLDIERS seeing so much action in Italy and elsewhere, the training at Camp Hale grew to seem increasingly onerous, a Sisyphean experiment that felt less like military preparation and more like a curse. With the arrival of the spring of 1943, daily snowfall made life in the valley a muddy misery. As Denis Nunan started rock-climbing school for the third time since joining the mountain troops, his mood darkened once again, especially after he nearly broke his neck during a fall on a miniature glacier that sent him sliding fifty yards into a creek. Blizzards continued right into May. The men grew desperate for warm weather. During maneuvers above 12,700 feet on Elk Mountain, Nunan's unit couldn't see more than thirty yards ahead, which meant crossing a cornice just ten yards wide whose adjacent abyss was invisible. Men dropped out left and right from the combination of eighty-five-pound packs, thin air, and snowshoes.[17]

But when it finally arrived, spring weather also meant an explosion of color in the mountains, where wildflowers bloomed in the alpine meadows. Waterfalls poured over cliffs lining the eastern edge of camp, along the trail leading to Kokomo Pass. The air suddenly took on a hint of sage and buzzed with the dry rattle of grasshoppers. Mountain jays flitted from lightning-blackened tree snags to scraggly dead sage bushes sitting like elk antlers against the rocky peaks. In warm weather, the men could fish and play football in the meadows. But even in spring, daylight in the valley was in short supply. With so many high peaks around, the horizon was 4,000 feet higher than the men's barracks.

As the aspens leafed out, their bark a waxy skin of white suede, they reminded the New Englanders of the paper birches back home. The mountains themselves, their slopes scarred by rock slides, seemed a cross between the jagged White Mountains of New Hampshire and the rounded Green Mountains of Vermont; swelling up to the east of Cooper Hill, the smooth sides of Chicago Ridge looked like a chunk of Vermont dropped from the moon.

As the last of the snow finally left the ridges and cliffs around Camp Hale, ropes and pitons replaced skis and snowshoes. Companies set off from camp on mountain maneuvers lasting a few hours to a few weeks, practicing attack or defensive strategies with everything from advance scouts to full artillery support. The ramblings of the mountain troops led to a number of stories within the ranks that, though probably apocryphal, tell a kind of truth about the rigors of their work. One popular story had it that a soldier marching on patrol near the top of Sugarloaf Mountain picked up the voice of an air corps pilot talking to a controller at the Pueblo Air Base. "Am at 11,000 feet," the pilot reported, noting that, as per air corps regulations, he would be turning on his oxygen. "Coming in for a landing. Gliding. Gliding." The soldier, unimpressed, promptly broke onto the channel: "Sugarloaf mountain patrol to 10th Division headquarters. Coming in at 12,000 feet. Walking. Walking. Roger."[18]

The troops had become famous for their ski training, but they quickly learned the seriousness with which the army had decided to approach its mountaineering training as well. "The untrained mountain soldier has two foes—the enemy and the mountain," a military climbing manual stated. "But he can make a friend and ally of the mountain by learning to know it. The mountain can give him cover and concealment, points of vantage and control, even, at times, food, water, and shelter."[19]

The climbing instruction the men received was taught by men of no less celebrity than their ski instructors. One day, a Canadian officer came upon a young man scrubbing floors and recognized him instantly. There, on his hands and knees, was "The Highest Man in the World," Paul Petzoldt. Petzoldt's journey to Colorado had been as indirect and bizarre as that of anyone else in camp. In 1938, after the rest of the original K2 team had left for the United States, Petzoldt—soon joined by his wife, Bernice—had remained for several months to explore India and indulge a curiosity about Eastern religion. One day, in the city of Srinigar, the couple had run into a retired California physician and missionary named Dr. Johnson, who was in town with his wife to escape the heat in their adopted home city of Punjab. The pair had become ardent followers of a sect led by a local spiritual guru and had established a tuberculosis sanitarium at the sect's compound. When the doctor learned of Petzoldt's interest in Indian religion, he quickly offered him a job as a bookkeeper at the clinic.

The doctor's wife was a passionate mystic but also moody and withdrawn, and she was particularly cool toward Petzoldt and Bernice, who was openly skeptical of the woman's unblinking confidence in the Hindu path to enlightenment. Somberly declaiming one evening on the best way to raise one's feminine *kundalini* up the *sushumna* until it unites with the male *shasrara*, Mrs. Johnson was unamused by Mrs. Petzoldt's rejoinder that "perhaps a swift kick in the rear end would do the trick as well."

When Bernice Petzoldt fell ill a couple of days later, she became convinced that Mrs. Johnson had tried to poison her; a comment from Petzoldt to that effect sent an enraged Mrs. Johnson grabbing for a shotgun she kept to fend off mad dogs. She and Petzoldt began to wrestle for the gun. He pulled it from her, threw it out an open window, and bolted out into the night—where, in a dark outdoor courtyard, he crashed into the old doctor, knocking him to the ground. Petzoldt kept running, not realizing whom he had run into. When he came back a few hours later, he learned that the elderly doctor had smashed his head on the pavement and died. Petzoldt wound up in jail and facing the wrath of the Indian cult for whom the doctor worked.

Attorneys for the cult told Petzoldt that if he would plead guilty, they would get all witnesses to testify on his behalf and the charge would be reduced. If he didn't cooperate, the cult could make things very difficult. Petzoldt agreed to the request and was released on bail. After a series of negotiations and the hiring of a local lawyer, Petzoldt brazenly changed his guilty plea to not guilty. A tense three-day trial concluded with Petzoldt's acquittal. The world's most famous mountain climber decided the time might be right to go back to Wyoming.[20]

Petzoldt had been busy since his return, christening mountains in South America, putting up new climbing routes in the Tetons, and, in October 1941, climbing Wyoming's Devil's Tower for the first time ever, to rescue a world-record-holding (and embarrassed) parachuter who had landed on the peak without considering how to get down. During his years in the Tetons, Petzoldt, who after the war became the founder of the National Outdoor Leadership School, had developed equipment and techniques for getting injured climbers off mountains, often with makeshift litters made by lashing a backpack to poles cut from saplings. When he was finally discovered scrubbing floors at Camp Hale, Petzoldt was offered a position as a sergeant, with three squads working under him, training the medical corps in mountain evacuation. Though his work was pioneering within the ranks of the military, Petzoldt was merely perfecting techniques he had developed in the Tetons: teaching climbers to avoid dangers by learning the subtleties of mountain geology and weather. Falls, he taught, were just barely behind enemy fire on the list of dangers to mountain soldiers. Petzoldt taught teams of medics inventive ways to pull men off snowy slopes, using chicken-wire sleds in which injured soldiers could be tucked inside sleeping bags and either guided down the mountain by men on skis or strung up on "zip line" wires and lowered down a cliff face with a series of slings and carabiners. Petzoldt's rescue training would prove to be one of the mountain troops' most effective and enduring legacies.[21]

JUST AS THE MEN were becoming experts in scaling steep cliff faces, the 87th Regiment was ordered to pack up for, of all things, a crash course in amphibious training at California's Fort Ord. Why, the men wondered, would the army possibly want mountain troops for a sea operation? They would not find out until they were steaming their way north to fight in one of the most desolate, weather-beaten places on the earth: the Aleutian Islands.

CHAPTER SIX

OPTICAL ALEUTIAN

NIGHT WAS THE WORST. As the troopship bellied through an ocean the color of gunmetal, anxious soldiers were tossed around in their bunks with each passing swell. Terrified of rumors about Japanese submarines—"tin fish," Denis Nunan called them—the ship's officers kept red-eyed enlisted men careening out of their bunks, reaching groggily for their life jackets, and stumbling out into belowdeck passageways, utterly black save for the eerie glow from wall-mounted boxes of fire hoses. There they would wait for one of two sounds: the dull burst of a depth charge from their own ship or the terrible explosion of a torpedo tearing into the side of the ship's hull.

Night after night the alarms sounded, and night after night they proved false. Eventually, lying in bed deep below the surface with only a sheet of metal between him and the hungry ocean, Nunan got so jaded that when the warnings went off he would say a little prayer, listen for the depth charge, and go back to sleep. This, he thought, was a hell of a place for the world's most famous mountain troops.[1]

Flailing around the hold of a ship bound for the Pacific was about the last thing any of the men of the 87th Mountain Infantry Regiment had expected. For two years, they had trained in some of the highest mountains of the United States and Canada; though they had yet to see battle, their exploits at Camp Hale had made them among the most famous soldiers in the American army. Through much of their training, the men in the mountain troops had cast their eyes not on the Japanese but east: either they would defend the United States against a German invasion in the mountains of New England, or they would take the battle to the mountains of Europe. Most of the members of the 87th—skiers and mountaineers even before they joined up—had arrived from New England and had a far clearer idea of what a battle with Germany might require of them.

The Japanese, by comparison, were a shadowy lot. On June 7, 1942, six months to the day after Pearl Harbor, the Japanese had occupied two islands, Attu and Kiska, barren, windblown chunks of rock dangling at the end of the Aleutian chain southwest of the coast of Alaska. The Japanese strategy—eventually placing some ten thousand soldiers on two tiny islands—perplexed the American public and army brass alike; perhaps they were simply hoping to contain the Americans at their base at Dutch Harbor, perched on another island five hundred miles to the east. Or perhaps they were up to something bigger. "There is little doubt now that their grandiose scheme envisioned an actual assault, by way of Alaska, on our Pacific northwest," one writer put it at the time. "The Japs wanted—and, make no mistake about it, they still want—to set foot on United States soil some day. It is more than a matter of military strategy; it is an emotional desire, a deep-seated and fanatic ambition that colors all their national thinking. And our apparently undefended Aleutians, which had served in prehistoric times as a land-bridge for invading hordes from Asia, offered once again a logical avenue of invasion for these modern barbarians striking at our shores."[2]

To a nervous War Department, still shaken by the debacle at Pearl Harbor, the Aleutian Islands indeed seemed like perfect stepping-stones for a Japanese invasion of Alaska and points south: Attu lay just 720 miles from Paramushir; Kiska was 200 miles closer to the Alaska mainland. In May 1943, in Operation Landcrab, the army sent the entire 10,000-man, fully reinforced 7th Infantry Division to capture Attu. Operation Landcrab was a disaster, not least because the troops had been poorly prepared to fight on such inhospitable ground.

As the 7th Division landed on Attu on May 11, 1943, they found the freezing, wind-battered island covered with wet snow—a major problem, since the relatively inexperienced troops had not only been trained in the desert, they had been issued standard dryland gear. With their feet soaked from the moment they disembarked and nowhere to dry them out, a full third of the men began to develop crippling cases of trench foot.

Worse, the 2,400 Japanese troops occupied every inch of high ground. The men of the 7th Division landed with no opposition, but the Japanese retreated into the interior mountains and waited. For the next eighteen days, American troops crisscrossed an island only fifteen miles wide, slogging through snow and mud so deep even bulldozers got immovably stuck. At one point, Major General A. E. Brown became so apprehensive about the terrain and the invisible Japanese troops, he managed to move his men only 4,800 yards in forty-eight hours. Even as the invasion stagnated, rumor had it that one lieutenant, whose supplies somehow never found him, survived for twelve days eating nothing but fish he managed to catch and rice he captured from the Japanese.

Finally, on May 29, with an American victory at last in sight, one thousand Japanese soldiers staged a banzai raid, screaming to high heaven as they poured out of the fog with fixed bayonets. Initially, the Americans fled in terror. The desperate Japanese attack took a heavy toll, including the killing of the American battalion commander, Major J. E. Siddons; his executive officer, Lieutenant Colonel James Fish; and scores of infantrymen. When the Americans regrouped, they managed to kill half the raiders, mostly with mortars and a 37-mm gun fired from atop a hill. As the attack ran its course and the Japanese realized the inevitable, five hundred soldiers clasped hand grenades to their chests and died a modern variation of a traditional military death.

By the time Attu was taken, 2,351 Japanese were dead, with several hundred more presumed to have been buried during the three weeks of fighting. Five hundred forty-nine Americans were also killed—only Iwo Jima would be bloodier—but that did not begin to tally the misery. All told, there had been 3,829 casualties, including 1,148 wounded. Tellingly, given the poor preparation for the arctic weather, fully 1,200 men suffered injuries caused by the severe cold, plus more than six hundred illnesses, many of them caused by exposure. After the battle, General George Marshall confessed to Minnie Dole that he "should have sent Alpine troops to Attu." For the next campaign, for the island of Kiska, he would.[3]

———

A TREELESS, BARREN ROCK, Kiska wasn't exactly Alpine terrain, but the Kiska Volcano, which rose 4,000 feet from the sea, and the unchangingly terrible weather, called for surefooted men trained to withstand extreme conditions. "All around were cliff-walled shores and, when visible, a bright green matting of waist-high tundra scrub and deep lush mosses—a great green sponge of slopes rising to a rocky knife-edge crest nearly eight hundred feet above the shore up in the fog," a lieutenant named George Earle recalled, noting that the island enjoyed just eight clear days a year and nearly incessant "knock-down deafening wind."[4]

The suicidal intensity of the Japanese resistance on Attu only served to ratchet up the War Department's anxiety. Early reports from the army general staff indicated that 6,000 to 10,000 Japanese troops had constructed an intricate series of tunnels and underground battlements high on Kiska's promontories that would be next to impossible to root out without a swarm of soldiers willing to fight hand to hand. And in fact, the Japanese enclave was far more complex than the army imagined. During the fourteen months the Japanese occupied the five-by-twenty-mile island, they had scattered along its perimeter several minisubmarines; an airfield, seaplanes, and Zero fighters; trucks, tanks, and enormous ammunition dumps. Machine guns and artillery pieces, from antiaircraft pieces to 125-mm naval guns, had been set up to oversee the island's harbor and coves. Inside the caves, according to Brian Garfield's account, *The Thousand Mile War,* the Japanese had constructed miles of tunnels, massive ammunition dumps, barracks, three hospitals, dental clinics, mess halls, machine shops, photo labs, telephone switchboard centers, and recreation rooms. The entire operation had been excavated with shovels and pickaxes, reinforced with wood struts and beams, and thoroughly ventilated by a system of pipes leading to the surface.[5]

To prevent the bloodbath on Attu from recurring on Kiska, the War Department decided on a far more massive attack, this time with more than 34,000 troops, supported by 450 aircraft, plus battleships and cruisers from the Pacific Fleet, attached to the Amphibious Training Force 9. The spearhead of the assault would be the 87th Mountain Infantry Regiment. In June 1943, two weeks after the fighting ceased on Attu, the men of the 87th left the mountains of Colorado for amphibious training at Fort Ord, California. From there they boarded ships and steamed toward Kiska.

At Ford Ord, the men of the 87th found themselves learning, among other things, the mechanics of Japanese weapons. Denis Nunan considered Japanese workmanship and ingenuity "something to marvel at." The men also got a lot of practice scrambling down cargo nets strung from the sides of landing craft and wading through roiling surf to secure beachheads. The landing craft rocked so violently that by the time the men reached the jumping-off point they were already soaked to the skin. Camp Hale, it seemed, had done little to help the men get their sea legs, and many of the men got seasick even on the shortest excursions. Although the navy proved impressive in landing some of the men right on the beaches—and thus completely dry—the soldiers still found themselves spending much of their free time cleaning salt and sand from their weapons.[6]

As they trained for an amphibious assault, the men of the 87th still had no idea where they were going to be sent; they had been told that they would be dropped on a beach and would have to fight their way through surf, sand, brush, and maybe even snow. Many of them didn't care what the circumstances would be; after so many months of training, they were aching to see some action, to put their training to the test. The prospect of battle also had some of the men writing home telling their families not to worry about them. "You must expect me to go someplace someday, so although it won't be for some time yet, when I do leave please don't let it get you, nor must you worry," Nunan wrote his mother. "Just trust in God and St. Chris to take care of me. I'll keep well and have no fear of the future. [I'll] be careful and wear my rubbers when it rains!" Nunan reassured his family that he was not in the army to become a hero. "Booby traps and medals are all the same to me," he wrote. "You're healthier without either!"[7]

As the country's only mountain troops, the 3,000 men of the 87th Regiment, organized in three battalions, were ordered to lead the charge, take the beach, and then move on to control the island's high ridges. Once the hard work had been done, 15,000 troops from the 7th Division—half of whom had survived Attu—would move in, along with 5,000 men from the Alaskan 4th Regiment, 5,300 from the Royal Canadian Army, and 2,500 commando rangers, the First Special Service Force. All told, just under 35,000 troops would be attacking the island. With the exception of those who had fought on Attu, the invasion force, including the force commander, Brigadier General Joseph L. Ready, was green. The army expected a 20 percent overall casualty rate. Among the 87th, soon to be out on the front edge, the rumor was that the brass expected 80 percent to die on the island. "They told us on Adak that the going would be tough, that some of us were going to drown in surf, and if we didn't get it we'd see our friends and comrades drop," Nunan later wrote. In anticipation of such heavy losses, the army had already begun filling the vacated barracks back at Camp Hale with new men.[8]

UNBEKNOWN TO NUNAN and the rest of the invasion force, the Japanese had decided on a plan that would become one of the war's most remarkable and least remembered: they would withdraw their troops surreptitiously from right under the nose of the American blockade. Initially, the plan was to use 5,000-ton submarines, for months the only means the Japanese had had of supplying troops on Kiska. Admiral Shiro Kawase was ambivalent about this plan, since it would take as many as fifty trips to evacuate all his men this way, and with the Allies building their forces on Attu, a full-scale invasion seemed imminent. The U.S. Air Force was already bombing Kiska heavily; it launched some fifteen sorties a day in June and more in July. The soldiers on the island were suffering from severe deprivation during the bombing; they were so short of food at one stretch that when an American bomb blew dead fish to the surface of the harbor, camp cooks added them to the menu: "Roosevelt's rations," they called them. Clearly, for the Japanese leadership, there was no time to lose.

Admiral Kawase came up with a plan that even his own officers thought crazy: he would mount an attack on the Allied navy near Kiska. While the skirmish was on, a rescue ship under the cover of a heavy fog would steam right into Kiska harbor to evacuate every Japanese soldier on the island. On Wednesday, July 21, the Japanese rescue fleet left the Kuril island of Paramushir with three cruisers, an oiler, and eleven destroyers. It steered far south of the range of American patrol planes, to a point five hundred miles south of Kiska, where the destroyers refueled and waited for a fog to settle in.

The Allied invasion was set for the second week of August 1943. On July 19, just two days before the Japanese fleet would sail from Paramushir, Rear Admirals Ike Giffen and Robert Griffin launched a two-pronged assault on Kiska that included the battleships *Idaho, Mississippi,* and *New Mexico,* as well as five cruisers and nine destroyers. Their six-inch guns lobbed 424,000 pounds of shells onto the island and, combined with further attacks by American and Canadian planes, seemed to have locked the island up tight.

An hour after the bombing stopped, Giffen and Griffin received radio reports that seven enemy ships had been seen on a radar screen moving west of Kiska. They were to be intercepted immediately. Vice Admiral Thomas Kinkaid, overseeing the operation, was certain of what the blips represented. Tokyo Rose had been predicting an American invasion of Kiska; a Japanese periscope had been sighted near Attu; for weeks, American intelligence had been picking up increased human and radio activity on the island. Plainly, the Japanese were preparing to reinforce and defend their last remaining Aleutian island—possibly as early as July 25, according to intelligence reports. Kinkaid acted with conviction: he sent the entire fleet surrounding Kiska in search of the seven ships and sent the two destroyers already blocking Kiska's harbor in support as well. On July 23, Kinkaid ordered four PT boats to keep an eye on the vacated harbor, but heavy weather blew in from the west, and the PTs, in danger of foundering, returned to Amchitka, one hundred miles to the east. Kiska harbor was wide open.

By July 24, after several days spent scanning the seas for the seven mysterious Japanese blips, Giffen and Griffin figured they had missed their chance; Kinkaid ordered them to return to Kiska. By nightfall on the twenty-fifth, the fleet was ninety miles southwest of the island. The Japanese evacuation force lay four hundred miles to the south, still waiting for fog.

An hour after midnight on July 26, the *Mississippi* picked up seven blips on its radar, 58 degrees off her bow: enemy ships, fifteen miles to the northeast. Seconds later, radar screens on four other ships picked up the same images. In an instant, men were at their battle stations, the entire fleet made a turn to the left, and guns began blazing at the target 22,000 yards away. Twenty minutes later the blips abruptly changed course. The Japanese ships were zigzagging, the *Mississippi* reported. But the images were weak and getting weaker. Gradually, by twos and threes, the images disappeared altogether. Thirty minutes after the shooting had begun, Admiral Giffen called for a cease-fire. The enemy had vanished without ever having been seen.[9]

Now, in addition to a phantom enemy, Giffen and Griffin had an additional problem. Since battleships at cruising speed swallow 200,000 pounds of fuel oil in a day, and far more at combat speed, their fleet was in serious need of refueling. The oil ship *Pecos* was in the vicinity, but it would take the fleet twenty-four hours to fill its tanks and get back to guarding Kiska. In those twenty-four hours, Admiral Kawase made his move.

On cue, a thick fog descended on the Aleutians, covering Kawase's approach as well as masking a furious effort by Japanese soldiers on Kiska to blow up every ammo dump and machine shop on the island. Twenty miles from the island, Kawase ordered his own cruiser to stand guard while Rear Admiral Shiro Kimura led the final approach. As the evacuation fleet of eight ships moved into Kiska harbor, 5,183 soldiers boarded scores of tenders and made their way off the beach. In less than an hour, they were gone.

For the next three weeks, using everything it had, the Eleventh Air Force bombed Kiska, now inhabited largely by Arctic foxes and a few stray Japanese dogs. Three hundred fifty-nine planes kept up a withering assault; on August 4 alone, 135 sorties dropped 304,000 pounds of explosives. Other planes dumped tens of thousands of surrender leaflets. The pilots reported that, strangely, they were receiving no antiaircraft fire. "The whole thing looks suspicious and baffling," one wrote. "We are told that five thousand or more may die in taking the sinister island, but we wonder . . . did the Japanese evacuate by submarine?"[10]

Despite these misgivings, Admiral Kinkaid decided to launch a full-scale assault on the island. If Kiska proved to be nothing more than a massive training exercise, so be it.

ON THEIR SEVENTH DAY at sea, a thick yellowish fog descended on the Allied invasion force and never disappeared. The troops arrived on Adak, 150 miles from Kiska, three days later, unloaded their gear, and spent a week getting used to the remarkably unpleasant conditions. The Aleutians were known for some of the worst weather in the world, and the men in the mountain troops were beginning to see why. The force left Adak on August 13. D-Day had been set for August 15.

The island of Kiska is shaped like a broad whale's tail, its flanks jutting northeast and southwest. A large volcano looms over the northeastern-most tip; Kiska harbor lies on the eastern side of the island, opposite the point where the two flanks spread apart. Given the terrible damage the Japanese had inflicted from their mountain perches on Attu, the plan for the assault on Kiska called for three separate landing forces to attack the precipitous western edges of the island before moving inland and knock-ing the Japanese off the interior high ground. Attacking from the west, it was hoped, would surprise the Japanese, since their guns had presumably been placed to cover the only decent harbor on the island's eastern shore.

Leading the assault, the 87th's 2nd and 3rd Battalions would attack the southwestern leg of the island; the regiment's 1st Battalion would attack the Kiska volcano on the northwestern leg. Once the mountain troops had captured the high ground, thousands of regular infantry would swarm the island in support. On D-Day plus one, a second wave would attack a beach a few miles from the volcano.

The day the battle began, Denis Nunan's mother sent her son a prayer, written in a firm-handed calligraphy. "God, Father of Freedom, look after that boy of mine wherever he may be," it read. "Walk in upon him, talk with him during the silent watches of the night and spur him to bravery when he faces the cruel foe. He is my choicest treasure. Fail him not—and may he not fail you, his country and the mother that made him."[11]

WITH JUST HOURS to go before they landed, the men of the 87th Moun-tain Infantry Regiment began, some for the first time, to confront the pos-sibility that they might not return home. Nunan kept a letter tucked into his shirt just in case it turned out to be his final words to his family. In it, he reported that he had just taken communion from Father Bracken, whom he had known since his early training days. He had also, he hated to say, been ordered to shave his fine red-and-gray beard—to prevent infec-tion in case of a wound to the face, he was told. He did manage to keep a terrific soup-strainer mustache and goatee.

"I'm carrying this letter into combat and if anything happens to the writer I hope someone will mail it—but on the other hand I hope that it will never have to be mailed," he wrote. "Am just writing you to let you know that I am fine, and to give you an idea of how the Irish feels a few hours before going into combat. I want you to know that although it will be a dirty job, I am going in with a determination to win and return home soon and safely. From now on it's up to God and my special friend St. Chris. Don't worry about receiving this—remember that I went without fear, even though I wanted terribly much to get another chance to enjoy life."[12]

Once the sun had gone down on Sunday, August 15, the men of the 87th boarded assault boats and began circling. At 3:30 A.M., a detachment of American and Canadian commandos landed in rubber boats, hoping to strike the ridgeline in advance of the larger assault. Three hours later, as the sun rose, five PT boats and a group of transports made a move on Gertrude Cove—a feint intended to draw Japanese attention away from the main assault on the island's western shoreline. When the 87th finally hit the shore, soldiers found the landing areas rockier and nastier than they had expected. They had to jump into the surf and begin their assault soaked to the waist.

As soon as they hit the beach, the men of the 2nd Battalion began running with their rifles and rucksacks up a talus slope that lifted 3,000 feet into the clouds. Within an hour the heavy fog had draped itself over the whole island; the winds kicked up to 50 miles an hour. Almost as soon as they hit land, the men could tell this was going to be a strange day; as he waded ashore, an ensign named William Jones ran not into a Japanese machine gunner but a dog named Explosion that he had given to some men at the Kiska weather station fifteen months before; the dog had somehow survived the brutal Allied bombing runs.[13]

Making his way up the ridge, Denis Nunan stumbled on a grave. The marker read, "Here lies a gallant American aviator who sacrificed youth and courage for his Motherland." The marker was signed, "Nipponese Army, 1943." Who were these Japanese soldiers, he wondered, who would go to such trouble to bury an enemy, and where the hell were they?[14]

The troubles on Kiska started compounding from the moment the 87th landed. The island was wrapped in such a dense fog that maps were useless. In the few moments when the maps could be checked against the hills, they were worse than useless: a ridgeline that looked straight on the map turned out to be curved on the ground. Soldiers moving along the top of the ridge thought the forms they could dimly make out were the enemy and found themselves firing on their own men.

"They had us terrified before we landed," Private First Class Murray de Camp Spear, a New York insurance man and veteran amateur skier, told the writer and fellow member of the 87th Hal Burton. "The whole theme was the Mysterious Orient and the Inscrutable Jap: They were going to wait until we all were ashore and then pounce on us. When we got ashore and didn't find any Japs, the scuttlebutt was that they were hiding in the crater of Kiska volcano, ready to dash down and bayonet us. And then with all that, there was rain, mist, and a penetrating, nasty, 35–40 mile an hour wind that actually drove a couple of the men out of their minds. We finally dug in atop a hill. We were certain we had to stay awake or the Japs would kill us all. Every time a figure was dimly visible, somebody would let off a few rounds or throw a concussion grenade. My carbine jammed, and all I had was a GI hunting knife. I figured I'd be bayoneted any minute. Just a little distance away was my sergeant, Clyde Limoge, with his messenger, John Lonnaissen. 'Sarge,' I yelled over. 'I'm unarmed and I'm scared. I want to come over to be with you.' 'Come ahead,' yelled Limoges. I came bounding over, leaped into the foxhole, and Lonnaissen shot me in the groin. He'd been asleep, and he thought I was a Jap."[15]

Major Robert Works, operations officer for the 87th, moved up to the ridge to look for the E Company commander, Captain Ev Bailey. Hiking through the fog, he was as terrified of being shot by his own men as of dying at the hands of the Japanese. Works could barely see his hand in front of his face, he would tell the writer Flint Whitlock, let alone the faces of the ghostly soldiers he encountered on his way up. Every ten yards during the climb, Works was stopped by an Allied soldier in a foxhole or behind a rock and asked for the password, "Long limb," which Japanese soldiers were said to be unable to pronounce. The wind was howling so loudly he could barely hear their commands.

A command post was set up to maintain radio contact with the men on the front edge of the assault; commanders back on the lowlands wanted news of Japanese dead and wounded. Finally, Works found Captain Bailey.

There had been no Japanese killed or taken on the ridge, Bailey reported, though his men had received a great deal of enemy fire. Works told Bailey to order his men to cease their fire. Taking prisoners alive was critical to learning more about the Japanese strategy on these islands, so from now on Allied troops would be allowed to use only bayonets to continue the fight.

Continuing along the ridge, Works came upon a machine-gun team that had yet to hear the word about the cease-fire. Suddenly, just ahead in the fog, he and the gunner saw a shadowy group of soldiers approaching just fifteen feet away. The soldiers had not yet noticed the machine gun. Just as the gunner was about to let it rip, Works heard one of the approaching men utter the password: "Long limb. Long limb." Then: "Jesus Christ! Don't shoot!" The men were members of the so-called Devil's Brigade, which had preceded the 87th up the ridgeline.

The commandos had covered much of the island southwest of the volcano. To their astonishment, they had discovered only empty gun emplacements. There were no Japanese soldiers on the island. But every time they moved forward to relay the news, they were taking fire from their own men, shooting through the fog. Radioing the news back to the command ship, Works was rebuffed. The Japanese could not possibly have escaped, the navy reported. The blockade of the harbor was utterly secure.[16]

Art Delaney's platoon was down low, beneath the ridge. Delaney was terrified. "With all that fog coming in, you could almost *see* the Japs coming at you," Delaney said. "We shot at anything that moved." With patrols out looking desperately for the enemy, the sporadic gunshots that rang through the mist seemed proof of the density of Japanese bunkers. Delaney's platoon guide, Harvey Nokleby, kept insisting that his men keep digging themselves in through the frozen tundra, in case the going got tough. Despite his own precautions, Nokleby took a bullet to the head and died right at Delaney's feet.[17]

Over on Ranger Hill, a promontory south of the volcano in the middle of the island's northeastern flank, members of the 3rd Battalion had discovered a fine position to set up a radio crew near an abandoned Japanese gun position built around a 75-mm gun on wheels. The communications chief ordered his men to vacate the position and sent in a team from the

Alaska Command to move the gun. As they approached, the ground around the gun exploded, sending bodies flying into the air. The Japanese had planted pressure mines underneath the gun. Walter Galson, who saw the explosion, watched a good friend die. Galson rose to help him but felt a firm hand on his shoulder. An old forest ranger lying next to him told him to stay put. "You stay here," the man said. "There's not a damn thing you can do."[18]

Roger Eddy, a second lieutenant in K Company, reported a lot of rifle fire near his position above Gertrude Cove. "Every time a helmet poked up through the fog everyone would let go, and a lot of people simply fired because they thought they saw Japs in the murk," he recalled. "We were all scared stiff; we were green; and everybody expected to die." One terrified machine gunner opened up on what he thought was an attacking Japanese unit, only to learn that it was his own battalion headquarters. Responding to the fire, the headquarters called for help from the nearby I Company commander, who sent out platoons to beat back the perceived attack. One of the platoons was led by Wilfred J. Funk, the grandson of the lexicographer and son of the president of the Funk & Wagnalls publishing house. Before enlisting, Funk had worked on Mount Rushmore; he was known for having swung by a rope from Teddy Roosevelt's mustache to Abe Lincoln's lower lip. Both Funk and Second Lieutenant William Hamill, the leader of the other platoon, were killed in the ensuing melee. One of Eddy's sergeants was shot between the eyes.[19]

In all, 24 men were shot dead by friendly fire on Kiska; four more were killed by land mines. Fifty men were wounded, and 130 more came down with trench foot. Seventy-one men were killed and 34 wounded when the patrolling destroyer *Abner Read* hit a mine in Kiska cove. Of the casualties on Kiska, a large majority—20 of the dead and 55 of the wounded—were from the 87th. Art Delaney, for one, never stopped thanking the Japanese for evacuating their troops. "God knows how many lives they saved," he said. For once, the army and the media decided to keep the exploits of the mountain soldiers quiet.[20]

AFTER THE DEBACLE, the 87th remained on the island for more than four months. They set up Quonset huts and built a makeshift base with a hospital, supply dump, the whole bit. "The one thing the military hates is an idle private," Delaney said. "If he's idle long enough, he'll start thinking about his situation. You gotta keep him busy."[21]

Domestic life on Kiska was grim. Constantly wet from a fine mist that never blew off the island, teams of soldiers built shelters from salvaged lumber, tin, and canvas. Despite the short days and perpetual cloud cover, the men were issued only a candle and a half per month and learned to live in almost unbroken darkness. They learned to bathe with their helmets, to eat cans of beef they found among the provisions the Japanese had abandoned, and to boil water for their endless stream of laundry. The rations the men consumed were as gray as the weather, and when Nunan opened a package from home to find a can of Vienna sausages, he had to laugh. Thanks for the "Cocktail a la Viennese," he wrote home, but since he was forced to eat so many of "their big brothers," he had begun to think of his mess kit as little more than a "pooch dish."[22]

Predictably, the Kiska blues were put to song:

I'll tell you a story as well as I can
Of the biggest dry run of the Ski Trooper clan
They trained in the winter, they trained in the fall
Then came to an island with no Japs at all!

What? No Japs at all? Yes, no Japs at all!
We learned how to ski and we learned how to climb,
We learned how to stay out in any ol' clime
We jumped on our skis when they gave us the call—
Then came to an island with no Japs at all!

One soldier shared a letter from his grandmother reminding him not to drink too much beer and to be careful with the girls. To fend off boredom, some climbed the volcano; others adopted Aleutian blue foxes. "All I could think to tell my tent mates at night was: 'Set the alarm and put the fox out,'" Bob Livermore, an original member of the 87th's Glee Club, wrote home. Other men discovered new uses for weapons. Spawning salmon could be killed with hand grenades. Stovepipes were cleaned by dropping in a sack of gunpowder, with the downside risk of blowing up a tent. Tent pegs could be fashioned from artillery shells.[23]

Life got so dull that even the usually cheerful Denis Nunan began to lose heart. This was hardly the war that he, or the magazines, had come to envision for the mighty mountain troops. Civilians "must remember that some campaigns never end in a blaze of glory midst a romantic setting," he wrote home. "Many end in loneliness midst sand, mud, fog or rain. Let the civilians see more of those pictures—see pictures of our own dead— the horrible wastes of war—maybe such pictures will make people think twice before they beef or strike at home."[24]

Eventually, the remaining members of the 87th moved down to the Kiska harbor area, where they began unloading ships, building roads, and constructing camps with both tents and huts. Denis Nunan's admiration for Japanese ingenuity grew the closer he inspected their handiwork. The winter gear the evacuated soldiers had left behind was excellent. Inside their cave network, they not only had electricity—mocking the 87th's candles—and plenty of stored food, they had well-equipped hospitals, with satellite field dressing stations dug into hills all over the island. All the health care, apparently, was needed even in quiet times; there were rats and mice everywhere. Not only were the underground facilities vast and complex, but the Japanese techniques for moving huge coastal gun emplacements up to the top of the ridges baffled him. Had they still been inside their ingenious cave system when the invasion troops arrived, he wrote, "they could have raised the devil with us," Nunan wrote. One thing the 87th managed to do that the Japanese apparently never did was get an airstrip working; with the help of a team of Canadian soldiers, engineers also helped build a massive dock.[25]

Later it dawned on the men that their real task on Kiska, once the mission against the Japanese had proven a tragic farce, was—once again—to test extreme-weather equipment, this time tropical mountain gear that might be used in the islands of the Pacific. What they also learned was that they had almost been shipped to the Solomon Islands, where the marines had been having a great deal of trouble. Only a reversal of fortune in the marines' favor allowed the 87th to return to Camp Hale, where their future would continue to be agonizingly uncertain.[26]

The 87th left Kiska in dribs and drabs, the last departing by the end of December. Denis Nunan boarded a merchant ship in the middle of a blizzard on December 1; after brief stops at Adak and Dutch Harbor, the ship steamed on to Seattle. The depth of the losses the army had expected the 87th to suffer became apparent only after the men returned to Camp Hale. An entire regiment, the 90th, had been brought in from Camp Carson to replace them.

Just before arriving at Camp Hale, Denis Nunan sent home two pieces of scrap he had picked up on Kiska: a red piece of metal from the Rising Sun emblem off a downed Japanese Zero and a shard from the wrecked American P-40 flown by the pilot the Japanese had buried with such dignity.[27]

CHAPTER SEVEN

THE MARCH UP THE BOOT

A S THE MOUNTAIN TROOPS were landing on Kiska, half a world away Generals Mark Clark and Dwight Eisenhower had begun studying the beaches of Anzio, twenty-five miles north of Naples, and the nearby mountains of Cassino as possible breakthrough points on the Italian front. If the Allies could take the hills overlooking the Liri Valley and complete a pinch with a major landing at Anzio, they could complete the capture of the lower third of the peninsula and open a gateway to the great prize of Rome. The ambitious Clark was determined to make history by taking the Italian capital as soon as possible, preferably before his mentor Dwight Eisenhower invaded France the following summer. Ever since West Point, where Clark had been two classes behind Eisenhower, the two close friends had enjoyed similarly meteoric careers. In the late 1930s, they had crossed paths at Fort Lewis, where Eisenhower was a lieutenant colonel, Clark was a major in charge of plans and training, and George Marshall was a brigadier general. In May 1942, Eisenhower, then chief of the War Plans Division, had asked Clark to accompany him to England to discuss sending American troops into the war in Europe. Eisenhower later picked Clark to be his immediate subordinate in charge of II Corps, then as his deputy commander in charge of the invasion of North Africa, which Churchill had decided should precede any invasion of northern France. (The British prime minister repeated to Clark a comment he had made to Stalin: "Why stick your head in the alligator's mouth at Brest when you can go to the Mediterranean and rip his soft underbelly?")[1]

In December 1942, Eisenhower had named Clark to head the new Fifth Army, in advance of the invasion of southern Europe; President Roosevelt had personally awarded Clark the Distinguished Service Cross for his work at Salerno. For Clark, Rome would mark the high point of his impressive career. "It was perfectly clear that the capture of Rome prior to that invasion would be of tremendous psychological importance to the Allied cause," he would write. "Thus we were, in a rather definite way, engaged in a race against time to break the enemy's Gustav Line and reach Rome before the invasion of France."[2]

Anticipating a series of quick victories on the mainland, George Marshall sent a Hollywood film unit, with John Huston serving as director, to shoot what he assumed would become a true-to-life training film of the anticipated liberation of the town of San Pietro. Things didn't go quite as smoothly as Marshall hoped. On December 12, 1943, American tanks rolled into town and were immediately ravaged by antitank fire from within the town and from the heights above it. Soldiers trying to escape were wiped out by machine-gun fire. Over the next week, as two more assaults were made, one third of the nine hundred civilians who had refused to flee were killed, along with hundreds of casualties to the 36th (Texas) Division and the 82nd Airborne. Huston's documentary captured some of the most vivid combat footage ever recorded—so vivid, in fact, that Marshall had the film shelved for the duration of the war.

San Pietro was only one of the early skirmishes that proved how difficult the taking of Italy would become. On the way north to Cassino, on January 20, Clark—as usual bickering with his British commanders, who urged him to delay the move—ordered his Fifth Army across the Rapido River. The German 15th Panzer-Grenadier Division, waiting on the north shore of the river, had a field day. General Fred Walker's 36th Division took nearly seventeen hundred casualties; to those who fought there, the Rapido became known as the "Bloody River." Scandalized by his unit's losses, General Walker, who had taught Clark, then two ranks below him, at the Army War College, considered the attempted crossing a gross violation of basic principles of infantry warfare. After the war, the division's veteran's association convinced Texas state legislators to call for a congressional investigation of the "fiasco" at the Rapido that had seen "an inefficient and inexperienced officer . . . destroy the young manhood of this country."[3]

Two days later, on January 22, nearly 350 ships deposited 36,000 Allies on the beaches at Anzio. Major John P. Lucas, in command of VI Corps, wrote in his diary that Anzio would likely turn out no better than the Rapido; he felt "like a lamb being led to the slaughter." The invading forces met no German response for twenty-four hours (Hitler thought the move was a feint before an invasion closer to Rome), but the Allies failed to seize the opportunity to move twenty miles closer to Rome. Remembering the missed chance at Salerno, Hitler agreed to a request from Kesselring for a massive counterattack, and soon the Fourteenth German Army moved into the hills above the Anzio beachhead. They began pummeling the landing force with heavy artillery—as infantry and panzer units sped south from Rome, just thirty miles away, and six divisions began moving in from southern France, Germany, and Yugoslavia. Within days virtually all available German reserves had arrived to support the counterattack. Instead of a force of 20,000, the Allied forces found themselves battling a force of 120,000 Germans, of whom 70,000 were combat soldiers. Hitler was determined to "lance the abscess south of Rome"; his commanders used the largest weapons in their arsenal, including 150 cannons larger than 105 millimeters and a pair of guns each weighing 218 tons and capable of firing 280-mm shells up to thirty-six miles. In one of the campaign's most humiliating encounters, Colonel Darby's Rangers lost almost all of 767 men from the 1st and 3rd Battalions in an ambush during the battle for Cisterna di Latina; Darby was so devastated by the trap that he broke down and wept. By mid-February, Churchill would confide to a friend that the month had represented his most anxious moment of the war.

With Anzio going so badly, Clark had little choice but to increase the pressure at Cassino, which Anzio had been intended to support. But things at Cassino were not going well either, in part because of mountainous terrain and heavy snows. "Thousands of men have not been dry for weeks," the journalist Ernie Pyle reported. "They dig into the stones and sleep in little chasms and behind rocks and in half caves. They live like men of prehistoric times, and a club would become them more than a machine gun."[4]

The Germans relied in part on their crack 1st Parachute Division, considered one of the finest units anywhere in the German army, and on the XIV Panzer Corps, an army-sized unit commanded since October by General von Senger. Fresh from his assignments near Stalingrad and, more recently, as a liaison officer to the Italian army in Sicily and Sardinia, Senger was startled to see how overwhelmed his soldiers were by the frigid mountain climate. Even seasoned soldiers expected the battlefields in southern Italy to be "a land of sunshine, sea and oranges." Instead, they found battlefields at 2,000 meters, where "the raging snowstorms seem to exterminate all life." The magnified shock of the bombing within the region's valleys stunned even the sturdiest veterans. Splintering rocks multiplied the horror inflicted by shrapnel. "In the mountains the soldier felt lonely, and the proximity of death was more real under heavy fire," Senger would write. "The demoralizing effect of the intense bombardment was increased tenfold by the echoes from the valleys."[5]

In the mountains, the evacuation of the wounded was far more trying than on conventional battlefields. Soldiers had trouble adjusting to mountain rations. Food prepared in the lowlands was always cold by the time it reached the men on the upper ridges. Senger tried to improve things, with little success, by covering the rations in straw.

To Mark Clark, taking the mountains surrounding Cassino with standard infantry troops would turn out to be "the most grueling, the most harrowing, and in one respect perhaps the most tragic of any phase of the war in Italy." The Germans had constructed a massive defensive position in the mountains behind the town, complete with heavily reinforced stone-and-earthen walls and underground chambers. Some of the German hideouts were so deep that during one of the Allies' most intensive bombing runs, a group of cloistered German officers never interrupted their hand of cards. There was never any question of German surrender; an order had been given to the German soldiers that they were to die before they relinquished the hills. "When I think back on the weeks and finally months of searing struggle, the biting cold, the torrents of rain and snow, the lakes of mud that sucked down machines and men, and, most of all, the deeply dug fortifications in which the Germans waited for us in the hills, it seems to me that no soldiers in history were ever given a more difficult assignment than the Fifth Army in that winter of 1944," Clark would write.[6]

Complicating the attack on the mountains of Cassino was the presence of the Benedictine Montecassino Abbey, which had sat atop a hill southwest of the city since A.D. 529. Although some strategists, notably the New Zealand Corps's General Bernard Freyberg, wanted the monastery taken out as a potential German stronghold, Clark worried that it housed only monks and an irreplaceable collection of art. Moreover, Freyberg argued, a pile of rubble is often more useful as a defensive position than an ancient building. Although the Germans had promised the Italians that they would not use the monastery as a fortress, the Allies had trouble trusting them; just a couple of days before the planned attack, the Luftwaffe had bombed a hospital tent on the Anzio beach that had been marked with a runway-sized Red Cross. "If they could ignore the laws of humanity about living men," an Italian-American soldier named Daniel Petruzzi would write, "why would they coddle the wood and canvas artifacts of a long-ago civilization, parts of it preserved in a 'dead language?' "[7]

After threatening to pull his troops out of Cassino unless the abbey was bombed, Freyberg finally won out, and on February 15, 225 Allied bombers dropped 576 tons of explosives on Cassino. The monastery, among other buildings, was utterly destroyed; officials later estimated that it had taken tons of bombs for every German paratrooper killed. *The New York Times* called it "the worst aerial and artillery onslaught ever directed against a single building." With the bombing complete and the enemy "softened up" for an infantry invasion, the time seemed perfect to take Cassino once and for all. The trouble, again, was that the foot soldiers, in this case the 4th Indian Division, had had no training in mountain warfare. The supply lines, which depended on eight hundred mules because of the steep terrain, were completely inadequate. The assault was slow getting started, and the Germans crushed its first waves. The following night, a British battalion lost 130 men and 13 officers in an unsuccessful move on another hill; later, three more Indian battalions and a New Zealand battalion were also rebuffed.

The slopes beneath the abbey were left charred and stripped. "From the desolate cathedral on the southern outskirts of Cassino we looked across stagnant pools of water to where the ruined shops and houses rose tier on tier against the steep bare slopes of Abbey Hill," Homer Bigart wrote in the *New York Herald Tribune* on May 20. "The terraced olive orchards rising almost to the monastery were reduced to successive levels of blackened stumps. Not one flower, not one blade of grass, lived in the gardens of the town. Twisted trees, defoliated by the fragments and concussion of thousands of bombs and shells, reached dead limbs out of pools covered with greenish slime."[8]

Holding aloft a large crucifix, the abbot managed to lead a number of survivors to a Red Cross station at the bottom of the hill, but several hundred refugees were buried in the rubble. The artwork inside was more fortunate: in October 1943, as the Allies neared the Volturno River, a German lieutenant colonel named Dr. Maximilian Becker, who had an English mother and a German father who had lived in Saint Louis, had asked the local bishop to crate everything up and ship the artwork north. Despite their promise not to use the monastery as a defensive position, the Germans did build gun emplacements and ammunition dumps in the building's shadow. After the bombing, the German officer who had removed the artwork asked the abbot to sign a note certifying that "inside the enclosure of the sacred Monastery of Cassino there never were any German soldiers."[9]

From January 16, when the offensive started at Anzio, to March 31, when the German defense of Cassino was abandoned, the Allies suffered more than 52,000 casualties, compared to less than 38,000 for the Germans, and were no closer to Rome. Criticism of the Italian campaign began to grow louder. "There is not the slightest doubt that the original decision to invade Italy proper was based on a belief that the Germans would not give battle in southern Italy, and that if they did they could not possibly maintain more than three or four divisions there because of their very long supply lines and our own mastery of the sky," the journalist Eric Sevareid wrote. "But some day people will want to know whether the returns balance the enormous investment of Allied lives, ships, transport, and planes. They will ask if we could not have achieved almost as much by stopping in southern Italy at the Volturno line, securing our ports and our bases and using the bulk of our forces in more fruitful encounters elsewhere. They will ask 'Did not the Italian ground fighting really become a war of attrition and nothing more?' " To Clark, there was only one real lesson to be learned from Cassino: "Aerial bombardment alone never has and never will drive a determined enemy from his position."[10]

George Marshall would later confess that one thing might have turned the tide at Cassino and advanced the war in Italy considerably: mountain troops. The only specially trained mountain troops the Allies had, General Alphonse Juin's Corps Expéditionnaire Français, had performed so well breaking out of the Liri Valley after Cassino that Marshall made Juin the first French recipient of the Distinguished Service Medal.

If there was one man who took this lesson to heart, it was a replacement artillery commander at Cassino named George P. Hays. "It was simple: the Fifth Army was trying to bull its way up the main roads through the valleys and the Germans held the heights and broke up the attacks," Hays wrote. "I thought the army would have to mount an attack through the mountains if it were going to be successful in joining up with its troops in Anzio."

Four months later, Hays found himself far from the mountains of Italy, commanding the 2nd Infantry Division's artillery as it landed on Normandy's Omaha Beach on D-Day plus one. The next time Hays saw Italy, in January 1945, he would indeed have his chance to see mountain soldiers in action, this time under his own command.[11]

NEWS OF THE FIGHTING in the mountains of Italy soon reached the soldiers in Camp Hale, and their frustration grew more intense than ever. As bad as it was training before Hollywood cameras when the Allies were fighting in the sands of North Africa, hearing of the grim events in the Italian mountains was much worse. What on earth were the mountain troops preparing for if not this? Adding insult to injury, some six hundred members of the original 87th Regiment were pulled out of the mountain troops and reassigned for flatland duty, even as six hundred new recruits arrived from the Deep South and bases in Hawaii. Many of these men had never seen snow before. By transferring so many men from the 87th out and watering the troops down with warm weather, flatland soldiers, the army seemed to have lost faith in its decision to maintain the troops as an elite alpine unit. "The morale in the infantry regiments of the 10th Division is very low," a chaplain named Anders Lunde wrote to Minnie Dole. "The chaps from Hawaii have hated the camp from the moment they set foot in it. They have no interest in the mountains, the snow, climbing, skiing, or any of the facilities needed for existence in this climate. Their intense dislike has acted as a pall on the spirits of those under them who have pride in being in the outfit. Many of the officers and non-coms of this group would give their right arms to be out of camp."

The chaplain also repeated a complaint that experienced mountaineers and skiers had been expressing since the troops were founded: the incompetency of the ranking officers. Although the typical officer had never been in mountain country before arriving at Camp Hale, he "has all sorts of ideas as to what the regiment should do, how it should be clothed, what equipment it should have—namely regular infantry tactics and equipment, without skis, snowshoes, etc. He has no use for what we have at hand, thinks there are too many sportsmen here. He is positive that in taking the advice of Norwegian, Finnish, Russian, German etc mountaineers and ski troopers, we are making a grave mistake. One wonders if there are no officers in the United States Army (West Pointers or regulars) who have imagination or at least open minds."

Given the unending battles over the best way to train the mountain troops, the chaplain offered a simple suggestion for improving morale, one that he felt sure would mean a great deal to the enlisted men: a shoulder patch insignia designating them as a special unit unlike any other in the army. For two years, the men had gone without any distinguishing adornments and had even been prohibited from wearing ski clothes off base; they had, in other words, no way to mark themselves as anything more than recruits fresh out of a reception center. In a pathetic effort to identify themselves as ski troopers, soldiers had been dressing up their uniforms with ski pins from Denver jewelry stores, a move that so infuriated camp administrators that offenders were given a week of hard labor and six weeks of pass restrictions. "They say that one reason the men are not provided with a distinctive insignia is that this Division is supposed to be a deep dark secret," the chaplain wrote. "As a matter of fact, in the light of certain articles in the press, this is ridiculous. I feel strongly, and I know that all of us do, that an insignia should be made available at once before the morale of the men sinks any lower."[12]

The army took the point, in its fashion. A number of designs for insignias had been proposed, including a red wolf's head on a field of white in a blue circle and a pair of crossed white skis, resembling the Roman numeral for 10, on a field of blue. As it turned out, the army would indeed soon issue the men a distinctive patch that quite closely resembled the crossed skis. But once again, perhaps to assert the primacy of traditional military training over ski training, those in charge selected a patch with crossed red bayonets, not white skis, on a field of blue that resembled a powder keg—or, some said, a pickle barrel. So disgusted were some of the men in the 87th that they wore their patch upside down.

While the camp veterans seethed waiting to see action, a rail-thin, wide-eyed boy named Stuart Abbott, newly arrived from Chicago, was spending his spare time in the hills with nothing more than a sketch pad and some pencils. Within two weeks of his arrival at Camp Hale in December 1943, Abbott had received his mountain training gear and begun the standard two-week "acclimatization school." Even on extended marches in his platoon, Abbott always carried the essentials for field observations of a different kind: *Colorado Evergreens*, by Robert E. Moore, and a small blank notebook he used for his field observations. Inside Moore's tree book, Abbott had drawn a box chart with tree names in the left column and altitude across the top, to help him recognize not only trees but their context: narrowleafed cottonwood in foothills; yellow pine up to 9,000 feet; aspen from 6,500 to 12,000 feet; Engelman spruce from 11,000 up to 12,000 feet.

In the back of his notebook, he copied short descriptions of a mountain's "Life Zones" (Alpine, Hudsonian or sub-Alpine, Canadian or Montane Zone, Transition or Foothill Zone) with elevations and tree populations at each, and a Wind Gauge chart, with velocities and their "Effect on Objects": at 0 miles per hour, "smoke rises vertically"; at 32 to 38 miles per hour, moderate gale-force wind "puts trees in motion and makes walking difficult;" at 64 to 75 miles per hour, storm-force wind "causes widespread damage."

Inside the front of his notebook, Abbott copied three guidelines from the naturalist Ernest Thompson Seton: "Keep a full and accurate journal; and remember always Science is measurement. Collect specimens of all things that interest you, make drawings of those that are not easily collected, and label everything with at least the time and place. Write of each event on the day that it happened. Do not trust your memory."

Seton would have been proud of this student. Whatever energy Abbott put into his military training, he was also determined to continue sharpening his skills as a field naturalist. During a spring outing at Silver Creek, he took note of the birds he could identify: his first Oregon junco and what he thought might be a red-tailed hawk. He measured an aspen tree felled by a beaver; the trunk, he noted, was 8¼ inches in diameter and 27 inches in circumference. Later he noted "two black chinned sparrows in aspens on S Slope and another on way home. According to RT Peterson's guide they are *way* north of their range. A Record?"

Abbott, who on his arrival was assigned to L Company in the 86th, did not really feel cut out for this military business. At six feet four and 170 pounds, he was absurdly skinny. He had flat feet, a handicap that even during basic training at Camp Roberts had nearly gotten him medically discharged. His interest in joining the mountain troops had more to do with his love of natural history. While his companions were drinking beer in Leadville or chasing skirts in Denver, Abbott, who was all of eighteen, was fantasizing about rare birds.[13]

When Abbott wrote letters home from Camp Hale, he asked for things like his little blue notebook and a Roger Tory Peterson field guide, which he had covered with brown wrapping paper. When he wrote his grandmother, he included a pencil sketch of a flying squirrel he copied out of *Audubon's America*. He was a deeply sensitive young man and, in his way, a fine candidate for a military unit that prided itself on training soldiers to become experts in the nuances of the natural world. If many in the camp griped about the unbroken wilderness surrounding the barracks, Abbott considered it heaven. Whereas they bellyached about the cold, Abbott pored over a copy of *The Friendly Arctic*, written by the explorer Vilhjalmur Stefansson, who had been hired by the mountain troops to teach winter skills, such as the construction of snow caves. His letters to his sister and mother began to express a thickening of the blood.

"While I think of it I want to ask you and Molly to quit writing me a page of goo about how cold it must of been and how lucky I was not to freeze my feet whenever I happen to describe something we do," Abbott wrote home. "Really it nauseates me. After all that's what everyone in the whole dam division does every day so when I tell you I did so and so yesterday why in hell do you have to write back like I had done something never done before and congratulate me that I was lucky to come out all right etc etc."[14]

Thankfully, Abbott had recently met a friend—a quiet natural history student from Cornell—who was equally passionate about birding, and the two planned to join in the Audubon Society's Christmas bird count. So high were Abbott's spirits that he ended a letter to a friend in Chicago by wondering how he could send a snowball home in the mail.[15]

As another Christmas season approached, the men did their best to make the camp cheerful. Each evening at dusk, carillon bells sent Christmas carols echoing down the long, narrow valley. Two large stars and a blue-lighted Christmas tree shone out from a slope behind the camp hospital. In the servicemen's club, four huge red candles, topped with flame-shaped electric bulbs, stood beside the fireplace. Ceilings and walls throughout the camp were festooned with greens. Sixty children from the nearby mining town of Redcliff performed a Christmas program. Between Christmas and New Year's, a team of five dozen men from the division's reconnaissance troops decided to celebrate the holidays by climbing Mount Elbert and Mount Massive, the second and third highest peaks in the continental United States. Breaking trail through deep snow and deadfall forests, the skiers switched the lead every ten or fifteen minutes and finished the thirty-two-mile trip in three days.[16]

Nonetheless, for many in camp, the holidays were a melancholy time. Soldiers ruminated about their families back home sitting around a fire, opening gifts, and drinking eggnog. New Year's Day 1944 dawned gloomy for Denis Nunan, and not all his melancholy came from his hangover. True, he and a friend had shared a bottle of Vat 69 the night before as they watched the fireworks. But the idea of a celebration, when so many soldiers were overseas, left Nunan feeling hollow. Ever since his legs had gotten used to the wet ground on Kiska, long hikes in the Rockies that had once seemed standard now made his feet and shins ache. Now thirty-three years old—the younger men in his unit called him "Pops"—he didn't seem to recover from illness, or from taxing maneuvers, as easily as he once had. The camp itself, more than ever, began to seem like a prison, the endless—and apparently pointless—training even more onerous. Here they were, back in Colorado, blowing snow off their gun sights and eating hamburgers that tasted like they were "made from horses that died during races back in the Gay 90s!" The celebrated mountain troops, media darlings that they were, nonetheless seemed doomed to a legacy that included little more than a lot of tough training and one embarrassing mission to a godfor-saken chunk of Aleutian rock.

Although he no longer felt "like an Aleutian rat," Nunan could see the effect of the botched Kiska campaign on his fellow soldiers. Some, he wrote, "have been drunk since they hit the States." One of Nunan's ex–squad leaders "lies dead on Kiska, the top of his head blown off by American bullets. We brought back boys without arms, legs, eyesight, even minds." This horror deepened the bitterness Nunan felt for the American media's fascination with the exploits of the mountain troops. "Did any of those pictures in *Life* show how we lived on Kiska? Did they show the food we ate? Did they show the boys being blown sky high by booby traps and land mines? Did the stories tell that the fog was so dense that we shot and killed our own men as they loomed out of the fog? There were no Japs there so they don't show the graves of our boys—but I have a friend buried on Kiska. I know a boy on the bottom of the Gulf of Alaska—a booby trap threw his mind out of kilter and he jumped overboard en route home. The pictures didn't show us working night and day—in rain, fog, snow, sleet and hail, with mud all about—unloading barges and getting the island built into another American defense post. No, you can't rely on the papers, movies, radio, etc. One has to see first hand the horrible waste of war, the bungling, red tape, ineffective management—one has to live the life of a ground force soldier to realize how rotten war is. And to think that I learned all this without a Jap on the island."[17]

Like any soldier who returns home when others do not, Nunan also began to grow philosophical. Nunan began to wonder why, when so many men were dying in this war, "I go along thru life always safe and well and with-out a care. I even went out to face the enemy, only to find that for the first time in the history of the enemy he had fled battle! I wonder what I am being saved for?" It would not be long before Nunan would find out. For the moment, he made himself feel better by mailing his mother a pair of earrings—metal insignias he had cut off the uniform of a Japanese marine jacket.[18]

DESPITE A CAMP full of bitter and exhausted soldiers, there would never be a shortage of men anxious to join the mountain troops, even from the unlikeliest places. Dan Kennerly arrived at Camp Hale at 7 P.M. on New

Year's Eve. Stepping off the train, he saw a snowbank seven feet high in front of the station and wondered what in God's name he had gotten himself into. Born to a family of Georgia cotton farmers, Kennerly had never been north of Gatlinburg, Tennessee. During his career at the University of Georgia, where he had been a standout football player, Kennerly had been given his choice of outfits to join after basic training. A burly man, thicker in the chest and thigh than most his age, Kennerly had thought at first about signing on with the paratroopers, who happened to be based at Fort Benning, just ninety miles from Atlanta, but they were full. His second choice had been the ski troops. What, he was asked by the recruiting officer, did a boy from Georgia know about skiing? What, for example, would a southerner use to wax his skis? Kennerly had to think fast.

"Beeswax," he said. The interrogating captain looked at Kennerly and grinned. This guy might make it after all.[19]

Kennerly had grown up reading about Kit Carson, Davy Crockett, and Daniel Boone and had thrilled to tales of the Civil War spun by neighbors who had served in the Confederate army, including an old codger who let the young Kennerly inspect his cork leg. As he got older, he and his friends started exploring the considerable woods around north Georgia. Smoking around a campfire, eating potatoes they had snitched from their mothers' kitchens, the boys practiced the great southern traditions of cussing and spitting and telling lies. Kennerly quickly became a master of the form, specializing in tales involving flatulence, city slickers, and gullible Yankees duped into buying "mule eggs" that were in fact painted watermelons.[20]

As Kennerly grew, he got touched by that old-time southern religion, football, and it was during a game of touch that he got his first whiff of war. He and his friends had spent the morning in Sunday school, where, as usual, the class had spent ten minutes talking about scripture and fifty minutes discussing football. Afterward, devoted to practicing what they had learned in church, they all tromped over to a field at Emory for a pickup game. In the middle of the game a friend drove up, honked his horn, and yelled for everyone to run over and listen to his car radio. The Japanese had bombed Pearl Harbor. The boys were stunned. Silently, each turned away and drove home. Of the twelve boys playing that day, four would later be killed in action.

Soon after his arrival at Camp Hale, Kennerly was assigned to A Company of the 85th Regiment and placed in a light machine-gun squad, along with other men kidded for having "strong backs and weak minds." Right from the start, he was an oddity, the first southerner many of these men had ever seen. The boys from New England had a hard time understanding his Georgia accent or how a guy who had never seen more than six inches of snow could have ended up in the ski troops.

Kennerly's inexperience with winter weather was hard to hide. The first time he tried the T-bar on Cooper Hill, he fell off, to much laughter. Soon after arriving in camp, Kennerly and his squad were sent out on a two-day combat problem; he and another southern recruit were told to put on "bear-paw" snowshoes—Kennerly thought they looked like oversized tennis rackets with no handles—and strap themselves into a harness attached to a toboggan loaded with a machine gun and ammunition. Kennerly felt like "a damn sled dog." The Yanks got a big kick out of watching him stumble along, a coon dog trying to do the job of a malamute.[21]

But Kennerly adapted well. As the men were being taught how to build snow caves, Kennerly quickly figured out that constructing a shelter underneath a rotten log would always prove easier than digging out in the open, since the ground underneath rarely froze. He learned to make a mattress for his sleeping bag out of the boughs cut from evergreen trees, which provided comfort as well as a layer of warm air between his body and the snowpack. Like all winter soldiers, Kennerly learned that nighttime was the right time to warm up and dry out his gear, and he soon developed a system: he always put his boots between the inner and outer linings of his sleeping bag; the boots' inner soles were placed underneath his knees; he put his socks inside his undershirt. When he woke up, all would be warm and dry. If the gear smelled bad, Kennerly didn't particularly mind; he figured he wasn't associating with civilized people anyway.

Another thing Kennerly learned quickly was never to drink anything after about 4 P.M. Chronic dehydration seemed a far sight better than getting up at three in the morning to urinate in temperatures running south of −30 degrees Fahrenheit.

BACK IN CAMP, the troops were confronted with another source of tension that had nothing to do with the weather. In September, a group of some three hundred German prisoners of war, most of them taken from the Afrika Corps, where they had served under Rommel, had been placed under the supervision of the camp. Though housed in separate barracks, they were placed right in among the rest of the men. The presence of the enemy right under their noses was hard for some of the men to bear. "When I see the German prisoners of war I boil inside and feel like killing them," Denis Nunan wrote. "If I ever see them and have a gun in my hand I'm afraid I will. They look so healthy, well fed, and do such light work while because of them our boys are dying in Italy!"[22]

To make matters worse, Camp Hale was now also the home of an odd collection of both native and foreign-born American soldiers that the military, for a variety of reasons, considered to be security risks, many inducted into the army by draft boards trying to fill quotas. Some were believed to be Nazi sympathizers. Without enough evidence to take legal action, the army decided to sequester some two hundred of them into what it called the 620th Engineer General Service Company, first at a camp near the Black Hills of South Dakota and then, in December 1943, at Camp Hale. The men were given duties such as making camouflage nets, digging ditches, and sawing wood. Camp officials unwisely decided to dress the men of the 620th in blue fatigues, making them indistinguishable from the POWs except for the white letters "PW" stenciled on the uniforms of the prisoners. Even more unwisely, the decision was made to house the 620th just a couple hundred yards from the German POWs. The two groups quickly found common ground, and a brisk trade in cigarettes, wine, and whiskey grew up between the two housing sections. On Christmas Eve, the 620th put on a holiday celebration in which the toasts were made in German and sprinkled among the carols were "The Horst Wessel Song" and "Deutschland über Alles." Rumors began to spread that some of the men might be planning an escape.

They were. In the middle of February, a young, English-speaking private in the 620th who called himself Eduard Müller threw on two sets of clothes—fatigues underneath and olive drabs on top—took a bus down the road to Redcliff, and paid $250 at a local garage for a 1934 Reo sedan. He drove back to camp, where, as he pretended to fix a flat tire, two German prisoners slipped away from work detail and hopped in. After thirty-six hours of driving, two flat tires, and two narrow escapes from law enforcement, Müller ran out of gas just seventeen miles from the Mexican border. The three men started walking and were arrested almost as soon as they crossed the border by a Mexican customs official, who figured they were escaped German POWs from nearby Amarillo. The three men did not look to be suitably outfitted for a long journey. All they carried with them was several boxes of candy bars, a couple of pocket knives, canteens, and a compass. Müller was perhaps the best prepared. In his pack he had a change of underwear, an electric razor, and a whole cured ham.

After being turned over to U.S. officials, Müller's two companions identified themselves as German nationals Erhard Schwichtenberg and Heinrich Kikillus, both veterans of the Afrika Corps. In Schwichtenberg's wallet was a note that read, in German, "Believe me, when the hour comes, I shall without doubt gladly give my life for Germany." Müller also carried a military pay record saying he was twenty-four years old; had been born in Schwarzenholz, Saar; held the German-Italian Memorial Medal; and had been captured at Casablanca. His plan had been to lead his companions to Argentina, then to Spain, and finally to Germany. Only the last bit was true. In fact, his real name was Dale Maple, and he was an American. Maple was taken to Bernalillo County Jail in Albuquerque and charged with treason.

Maple's story turned out to be far stranger than anyone in law enforcement could have imagined. He was, for one thing, "one of the most intelligent men I have ever had the opportunity to interview," an FBI officer said. A native of San Diego, Maple was the son of an ironworks executive and had graduated at the top of his high school class before enrolling at Harvard. In 1941, he had earned a bachelor's degree, magna cum laude, in comparative philology—the study of linguistics—and been a member of Phi Beta Kappa. He was also an accomplished classical pianist. In college he had joined the campus ROTC but planned after graduation to make a career as a philologist. He had studied Old Danish and Assyrian and had been the first student ever at Harvard to study Maltese, a blend of Italian and Arabic. He had done graduate work in Russian, Polish, and Hungarian and was conversant with most contemporary European languages. But his greatest love was Germany—the language, culture, and, most troublingly for those around him at Harvard, the politics.

Maple had quit the Harvard German Club over political differences with the other undergraduate members. He was quoted in the student newspaper, *The Crimson,* as saying that "even a bad dictatorship is better than a good democracy. . . . The present government of Germany is as much a part of German culture as the works of Beethoven, Wagner, Dürer, or Kant." The comment led to his dismissal from the ROTC, and thence to the beginning of an odyssey that led eventually to his being charged with a crime punishable by death.

In the days after his disappearance, Maple's father, back in San Diego, felt sure his son had been kidnapped and said he was keeping two loaded pistols at close hand. If the escapees showed up in San Diego, he would shoot the Germans, one with each pistol. Officials at Camp Hale were so embarrassed by the escape—it wasn't even reported for twenty-four hours—that the army kept a lid on the story's publicity. Since Maple was a soldier, military authorities took the case from the FBI and changed the charge to "relieving, corresponding with or aiding the enemy," which, under the 81st Article of War, was the closest equivalent to the civilian charge of treason. Following the advice of a civilian attorney from the town of Leavenworth, Maple pleaded not guilty.

During testimony, a stream of doctors, some with psychiatric training, testified that Maple was apparently completely sane. One said that a childhood accident had left Maple's "brain jelly" somewhat "scattered" but that doctors could find no evidence of lasting brain damage. Another said that despite having an IQ of 152—denoting "very superior intelligence"—Maple's overall emotional demeanor seemed at odds with the severity of his predicament. "He considers himself a 'professional soldier' but he does not appreciate the inconsistency in violating his oath by escaping in the company of German prisoners of war," the physician testified. The panel of judges found Maple guilty, noting that aiding an enemy "may well be in the circumstances sufficient evidence that he adhered to that enemy and intended and purposed [sic] to strike at his own country." Maple was sentenced to hang by the neck until dead.

At the time, no U.S. citizen had ever been sentenced to death for treason. (It would be seven years before Ethel and Julius Rosenberg received the death sentence for giving secrets to the Russians and two more before they were executed.) In Maple's case, President Roosevelt elected to follow the recommendation of his army judge advocate general: "While he is undoubtedly legally sane and responsible for his despicable acts, under all the circumstances I am unable to escape the impression that justice does not require this young man's life. I feel that the ends of justice will better be served by sparing his life so that he may live to see the destruction of tyranny, the triumph of the ideals against which he sought to align himself, and the final victory of the freedom he so grossly abused."

Maple was sentenced to life in prison and sent to the federal penitentiary at Leavenworth, where he worked in the prison bakery, played the church organ, and did philological research in Old Bulgarian. The year after the war ended, the army reduced Maple's sentence to ten years; after his release, he went to work in the insurance business.[23]

As for the tumultuous 620th, the army quickly redesignated the unit Company A of the 1800th Engineer General Service Battalion and shipped it to Bell Buckle, Tennessee, where its personnel were equally problematic. The 1800th included, among others, members of the Ku Klux Klan, the Christian Front, and civilian German propagandists such as Lorence Asman, who had once sent a letter to Roosevelt that read, in part, "If you continue to destroy our wealth and our treasury, and if you continue to promote Jewish Communism, and if you continue to shed the innocent blood of our sons on foreign battlefields, then we, the 100,000,000 Christians of America, will rise up in righteous anger and tear down your tower of Babel and get you."

CHAPTER EIGHT

THE D SERIES

ALE MAPLE'S CASE caused barely a ripple at Camp Hale because the division was occupied by winter training so harsh that even the most hardened veterans found it astonishing. It got worse. At the end of March, the men set out for what became known in official army documents as the most grueling exercise in the history of the American military: the D Series.[1]

It was a remarkable sight: 12,000 soldiers set out from their barracks on skis and snowshoes. Temperatures the first day reached −30 degrees Fahrenheit. For the next month, men were ordered to carry ninety-pound packs to altitudes of 13,000 feet through storms that kept temperatures well below zero and dumped as much as eight feet of snow. By the time the exercises were over, the Army would report the "proud record" of no fatalities and only 195 cases of frostbite, 340 injuries, and nearly 1,400 cases of sickness. One history of elite military training noted that the 10th Mountain Division, "the most elite U.S. Division in the twentieth century in terms of intelligence scores, fitness and training," had suffered five times as many illnesses and injuries preparing for combat as any other American division in the Second World War.[2]

From the outset it seemed that officers wanted to see how far they could push their men. Fueling the men's resentment was the widespread knowledge that even the smallest peaks in the ranges around

Camp Hale were twice as high as any pass they were ever likely to see in Europe. Officers would drive by a group of men marching up a mountain and shout from the comfort of their vehicles for them to pick up the pace. This sort of idiocy infuriated the men on foot, who were consistently exhausted from hauling their packs uphill in the thin air above 10,000 feet. "The real story is that the brass hats just didn't realize the hardships and difficulties of winter warfare in the mountains," Stuart Abbott noted. "I guess they never will as long as they ride around with the top up on their Weasels."[3]

Given a year's training since the disastrous Homestake Maneuvers—and perhaps to avoid the tongue-lashings that had resulted—camp officials had laid out a formal checklist for small-unit leaders outlining ways to prepare for the worst. All soldiers were to be adequately outfitted for extreme conditions. Out in the field at night, men must change their socks and innersoles to avoid trench foot, hypothermia, and frostbite. Other requirements provided the enlisted men with further evidence that their COs remained oblivious to the realities of mountain training:

"No vulgarity or yoo-hooing."

"Men not to sit in snow."

"No drinking out of streams or ponds."

"Keep rifle muzzles out of snow."

"All men to eat at each meal."[4]

INCREASINGLY DISGUSTED with the increasingly dangerous training—and perhaps a little delirious from the cold—Denis Nunan began hearing rumors that the 10th was about to be sent to the South Pacific. "The hell with fighting in the Alps or Norway or the Jap Kurile Islands—we all want to head south or have the war over," he wrote home. "How the Russians do it beats us, as when you get as cold as we do you don't give a damn about anything, and you not only hate the war but hate the whole world. One gets little sleep, and due to the combination of that and the lousy food we all border on the point of exhaustion. We are taking this beating so the brass hats can get a bit of practice at handling a division in the field!"[5]

After a couple of days out, Hugh Evans had already gotten frostbitten on his fingers, toes, and ears. On Saturday, April 7, he and his men arose at 3 A.M., gulped down a cup of coffee for breakfast, and packed up for an attack exercise up Resolution Road toward Ptarmigan Pass. A glitch in communications had the men standing around in the bleak, frigid air for an hour, but they finally began a march that took them up several thousand vertical feet in less than two miles of walking. Given the steep grade, Evans's captain set a relentless pace. With the stronger hikers constantly having to stop and wait for the men behind them to catch up and the weaker hikers falling further and further behind, the line stretched and finally snapped. Typically, to keep the pace sustainable and to allow the line to regroup, company leaders allowed their men to hike for fifty minutes and rest for ten. On this day, however, the pace never let up. As soon as the men in front had caught their breath, the line would move forward, meaning the men in back never got the chance to unshoulder their packs. With more and more men denied the chance to rest, the troops began to grumble, particularly when one soldier, so sick he could hardly walk, was forbidden to return to camp. The company medic who refused to offer relief, Evans wrote, came "awfully close to being mobbed and bayoneted."

After five unbroken hours of hiking and with the sun just now beginning to appear above the mountaintops, many of the men still had not had the chance to rest. Finally, the men in Evans's platoon refused to move until they caught their breath. Evans was sympathetic but commanded his men to follow their orders. They stood their ground. Exasperated, Evans jogged up to the front of the line to speak with his captain and lobby for his men's case. He told him that his men were whipped, that the pace was too fast, and that they absolutely had to be given a chance to rest. The captain was unconvinced. He shouted at Evans to give him the names of any man who wouldn't march.

Evans refused. He had brought up the complaints of his men to prove a point, he said, not to build a case for their court-martial. He also happened to agree with them. The officer was outraged. He told Evans to give up the names or he would bust him back to private. Evans said he would rather take the bust. The captain threatened Evans with a court-martial. Evans decided to stand by his men. If this were combat, the captain said, he could have Evans shot. If this were combat, Evans shot back, he would be armed as well. In the end, Evans took the bust in rank with pride. Besides, he figured, "a non-com here is between the devil and the deep blue sea."[6]

The blizzard continued unabated. By the third week of D Series, the men, dug into snow caves at night, were so tired they would forgo searching for pine boughs for their beds, and would sleep on their overturned skis instead. During sleep, in fact, was the only time the men ever took off their skis. The snow had gotten so deep that walking around without skis, even to line up for a meal, meant sinking up to your hips. In one letter home, Evans included a line drawing of a soldier with pack and rifle walking through snow deeper than his head, looking out through a periscope.[7]

High up on the ridges, where the glare was unbearable, even the most experienced mountain soldiers felt vulnerable. Earl Clark, who had climbed with Paul Petzoldt in the Tetons before the war, at one point loaned a spare set of goggles to a fellow soldier who had lost his own. Staggering through an exercise sometime after this, Clark reached into his pack for his second set of goggles and slipped, smashing the goggles into a tree. He now faced one of the great dangers of high-mountain trekking: snow blindness. A couple of days later, the intense light reflecting off the snow had begun to take its toll. Clark noticed that his vision kept blurring, but as a lieutenant seeking to set an example for his men, he decided to try to gut it out. About four in the afternoon on the third day after he smashed his glasses, the pain had become unbearable and he was evacuated to a hospital back at Hale. Clark said he felt as if he had hot pokers in his sockets, but the pain radiated out through his whole scalp and head. The only treatment for his burned corneas was to hang blankets over the windows and wait.[8]

Men continued to fall out in droves, most from frostbite and altitude sickness, others from hallucinatory exhaustion. Some men took their rifles and smashed their own feet to get out. One morning, Hugh Evans drove down to Camp Hale in a Weasel to pick up some boots and noticed some fifteen hundred men in a line stretching from Fifth Street to Fifteenth Street, hoping to be placed on sick leave. With so many men streaming down to the camp hospital, General Lloyd Jones had issued a draconian order: men could no longer retire to their quarters. They would be either in the field or in the hospital. No exceptions. Medics would eye each man, take his recent medical history, and decide on the spot whether he could come in from the field.[9]

For virtually every soldier who survived the first three weeks without breaking a bone or losing a finger to frostbite, Easter Sunday proved to be the worst day in the field. Caught in a snowstorm out near Ptarmigan Pass,

Dan Kennerly heard thunder—something he didn't think possible in winter. Thunder at 11,500 feet is not like thunder in the lowlands. It is cataclysmic. Kennerly felt as though he were right inside the thunderhead, which, in fact, he was. That same day, Denis Nunan went twenty-one hours, in the snow, at altitude, carrying his ninety pounds, on a piece of bread, some peanut butter, and a mouthful of pineapple juice.[10]

Stuart Abbott and his crew were posted way out on an open ridge, about 12,000 feet up, well above the timberline, overlooking Vail Pass. Around daylight, the clouds closed in and it began to blow and snow hard. With new snow piling up over their boots, Abbott and his men stood around until 10 A.M. in what was beginning to look like the worst gale of the season. To protect themselves from the elements, the men dug down about four feet into the snow, built a fire, and waited it out.[11]

When the umpires finally called the D Series to a close, soldiers fired off every bit of ammo they had left. "We used more ammo in those few minutes than in the rest of maneuvers," Dick Wilson wrote home. "I saw one machine gunner run through five belts—1000 rounds—as fast as he could, in two minutes."[12]

When it was all over, the judges overseeing the maneuvers—the same "brass hats" Stuart Abbott had seen driving around in their snow vehicles—tabulated all the trials the men had withstood, all the peaks they had climbed, all the storms they had survived, and concluded that the mountain troops deserved a rating of "satisfactory." Needless to say, this did not sit well with the men who had lived through it. General Jones instantly became the object of a general wrath that would not dissipate for the rest of his tenure; he was held personally responsible for everything from "chickenshit" camp duties to poor camp morale. Not surprisingly, Jones underplayed the severity of the maneuvers. "During late March and until mid-April we had some large scale division maneuvers here in the higher altitudes and much bitter cold," he wrote Minnie Dole. "We learned many lessons on clothing and equipment. Altogether the training was the most valuable we have had."[13]

AROUND THE SAME TIME as the men were coming back to camp from the D Series, an ambulance driver named Conrad Brown was returning to

America from service in southern Italy. Near the front, he had once shuttled a group of nuns to safety from the war zone near the Sangro River to a nunnery atop a nearby hill. Driving up and down the hill all night, Brown heard the same story over and over: as a reprisal for partisan guerrilla attacks against the German army, German soldiers had killed every man in the nuns' town.

Brown, a Quaker, had never had an interest in the sharp end of the military, but the German atrocities changed his mind. He returned to New York and sought out Minnie Dole. During their interview, Dole asked him how life in southern Italy had been. Had there been any snow down there? Lots, Brown said, even near Naples, where palm trees were the norm. There was snow on Vesuvius. In fact, Brown said, his skis had fit quite nicely in the back of the ambulance, in the brackets where the stretcher was hung. Dole was ecstatic with the weather report and told Brown he would be meeting with General Marshall later that week. Brown could have a place in the mountain troops, Dole said. And the mountain troops, Brown couldn't help thinking, might soon find a place in Italy.[14]

Dole and John Morgan of the National Ski Patrol met Marshall on April 19. Dole began by blaming the terrible results of the D Series not just on incompetent leadership but on the recent willingness of the army to allow nonmountaineers into the troops in the first place—50 percent of whom, he said, had immediately applied for medical transfers because of altitude sickness. "The daily sick rate is out of all proportion to the number of personnel involved and seriously interferes with coordinated training," Dole said. "A spot check of three companies exposes the fact that only 40 percent of the personnel were qualified for training in mountainous terrain."[15]

Dole pressed Marshall to find a commanding officer for the troops whom they could believe in. "It is my feeling that the trouble has been that no officer of high enough rank has existed who understood the great difficulties of mountain warfare to champion the cause in the War Department without fear of severe censure. A lack of knowledge and a lack of sympathy in the higher echelon leads only to wasted effort and poor results."[16]

Marshall reiterated his enthusiasm for the mountain troops and explained that the reason the 10th Mountain Division had not yet been pressed into service was directly connected to its specialty training. To the military establishment, the 10th's reliance on skis and mules had marked it as anachronistic and unfit to face the Germans in France. When the mountain troops had been offered to Eisenhower's chief of staff, General Walter Bedell Smith had seen the division's table of organization and had just one thing to say: "All those mules? Hell no!"

Marshall emphasized that he did not share Smith's opinion. "You must remember that I have only one mountain division, and if I commit it at point X and shortly thereafter I need it much worse at point Y, my problems of transportation are so great I can't get them there," he told Dole. "I am forced to hold it in reserve. Of course I realize that the Attu campaign was a winter, Alpine operation. This task force was made up under the direction of the 4th Army and did not come to my personal attention. The 87th Mountain Infantry Regiment should have gone. When the Kiska task force was made up I personally gave orders that they were to go."

Given the progress of the war in Italy, a peninsula studded south to north with mountains, Marshall admitted that he had made a mistake by not sending the division to help take Cassino. "If I had had a winter trained mountain division in Italy during the winter of 1943, the entire Italian campaign might have gone differently," he said. "The largest center of communications that the Germans had was just the other side of Cassino. With a mountain division I could have wiped it out, but as it was we were held up for 17 days by heavy snows and couldn't move."[17]

When it came to the war in Europe, it appeared clear to Dole that Marshall would not make the same mistake again. Indeed, in Italy, the breakout from the pincer points near Cassino continued to be hampered by the buildup for the invasion of northern France. In April 1944 alone, forty tank-carrying ships were withdrawn from Italy for England, along with a series of cruisers and destroyers. Once the invasion of Normandy began, the diversion of troops and matériel from the Italian front would dramatically pick up speed.

Anxious to keep his campaign relevant, Mark Clark ignored orders from Allied Commander Harold Alexander to move on the strategically critical town of Valmontone, where German forces retreating from Cassino might be cut off and captured, and decided to devote his Fifth Army to the great prize of Rome. In many minds, his decision had more to do with a desire for personal glory—especially given his old friend Dwight Eisenhower's pending move on Normandy—than sound strategic military planning. On June 4, after a nine-month, 130-mile slog that had begun on the beaches of Salerno, Clark's troops took the Italian capital. Not since A.D. 536, when Belisarius had marched in from Naples, had the city been taken from the south. For exactly two days, Italy was once again front-page news, and Clark was the hero. Away from the city, however, the German Tenth Army was escaping, and once again the Allies perhaps missed a chance to end the war in Italy once and for all.

On June 6, the Allies landed at Normandy, and the world's attention turned north. Italy was once again the forgotten front.[18]

AFTER THE DESPERATION of the D Series the morale of the 10th Mountain Division would not improve until General Jones was replaced. Rumors about the division's future swirled: England, Norway, Italy, Russia, Alaska, Burma, the Philippines. The one thing everyone counted on was a mission that would use their training. They were in for a surprise: they were headed for Texas.

On June 20, two weeks after Rome and Normandy and two months after the end of D Series, the entire division was ordered to pack up and load onto a train headed south. The army, in its wisdom, had decided the mountain troops needed to prepare for swamp maneuvers in Louisiana, and Camp Swift, Texas, was where they would train. For a time, the name "Alpine" would even be removed from the division's nomenclature. Veterans of the mountain troops were bewildered and infuriated by the move. What possible strategic advantage could there be—especially given the misery the Allies were experiencing in the mountains of Italy—in turning the mountain troops into just another standard infantry division? "To win this war, why in the h—— shall we fight it *where* and *as* the Germans want to?" the Norwegian colonel Carl Stenersen wrote Minnie Dole. "They are prepared for a summer blitz and summer warfare, but they are not prepared for *winter* warfare on a large scale. Why not surprise them with a large scale winter offensive next winter?"[19]

Located thirty-eight miles southeast of Austin, 52,000-acre Camp Swift was seven or eight times as big as Camp Hale and in some ways much more pleasant. The landscape was greener, the barracks were cleaner, and there were swimming pools. For many of the men, however, nothing the camp, the state of Texas, or the South could offer offset two inescapable facts: heat and bugs. Temperatures were so high that men broke out with boils, heat rash, and impetigo; Hugh Evans's company drank 480 Cokes a day from vending machines alone, a number that did not include frequent trips to the PX after hours. Some became so delirious that, in an ironic parallel to Colorado altitude sickness, they were given medical discharges. Between Easter and the Fourth of July, the mountain troops had learned to train through a temperature change of at least 120 degrees.

Everywhere they looked, they saw cockroaches. And scorpions. And spiders. And snakes. Arriving in the midst of one of the hottest Julys in fifty-two years, the northern boys wilted. The day they arrived—wearing full mountain uniforms designed to protect them in winter weather at 12,000 feet—the men were asked to walk seven miles, in searing heat, from the train depot to Camp Swift. Gene Hames saw more men collapse and fall out during that walk than in all his time at Camp Hale. Hames was lucky. After only three weeks, he was sent to Officer Candidate School at Fort Benning; he would not rejoin the division as a second lieutenant in K Company of the 85th until December.[20]

Others were not so fortunate. As far as Denis Nunan was concerned, "they can give this place back to Mexico." The forty-four-hour train ride from Colorado left him little patience for water that tasted "flat and oily." The swimming pools were so chlorinated they ruined his sinuses and so full of sweaty soldiers that all you could do was stand up. The cedar and oak trees around camp "were so scrubby they give no shade except to ants." He developed a terrible case of poison oak, which made the long, fast marches—in one stretch of a couple of days, they did nine miles in two hours, fifteen miles in six hours, and twenty-five miles in eight hours—all the more miserable. After such long days, the best he could look forward to was another night on the Texas ground, which he considered the hardest soil he had ever encountered.[21]

Stuart Abbott, the naturalist from Chicago, was not nearly so put off. He spent his free time in Texas fishing, paddling a canoe, and swimming in the bathwater-warm lakes near Austin. The landscape and the creatures that inhabited it seemed utterly strange to him; if the soldier in him resented the heat and the constant marching, after a few weeks the young natural historian considered the place a "paradise." Contrary to what he had imagined, the landscape was not desert but high-grass prairie and hardwood forest. Out on a two-week field maneuver, he caught an armadillo by the tail. To his adoring sister, Molly, who continued to send an endless stream of homemade cookies, Abbott wrote a note of encouragement about her interest in playing the piano. "Piano lessons are a good thing," he kidded her, "as long as there is a thousand miles between us."[22]

Soon after settling into their new digs, the division's journalists launched a new version of the Camp Hale newspaper and immediately took to reporting the weather. Initially called "The Ski Zette—Texas Edition," the first issue had a simple forecast on its front page: "No Snow." Perhaps to bring some cool air to the barracks, editors put a half-page panoramic photo of Mount McKinley—"Pin-Up Mountain of the Week"—across the top of the newspaper's back page. "Pictured in all its snow-capped glory, Mt. McKinley looks cool and inviting to the perspiring mountaineer 'deep in the heart of Texas,' " the caption read. The photo, not surprisingly, had been taken by Bob Bates's old climbing partner, Bradford Washburn.[23]

In early November, the army announced a pair of startling decisions. First, the division would be reorganized for the addition of heavy-weapons companies. Prior to the change, the 10th had been modeled after the German Jaeger, or light division, with only three battalions of 75-mm pack howitzers that could be broken down and carried on pack mules. Now the division would be adding big water-cooled machine guns and 81-mm mortars. Under the command of Brigadier General David L. Ruffner, the artillery units would also include three battalions of light (75-mm and 105-mm) artillery, but not the usual fourth battalion of medium (155-mm) guns, so the division still did not reach "regular infantry" status. Since most of the men for the new weapons companies were to come from the existing rifle companies, the 10th started asking for volunteers. Dan Kennerly, the football player from Georgia, immediately signed up to begin training with heavy machine guns.

The second announcement was, for most of the men, equally jarring: the army had decided to close down Camp Hale and sell its assets for surplus. Already, it seemed, the division's history was beginning to disappear. "Now that Camp Hale is to be closed, I believe that nearly all of us, both military and civilian, cannot help viewing the prospect with considerable regret," the camp's commanding officer, Lieutenant Colonel J. A. Chase, wrote. "While all of us have complained about various things at times, when we are actually confronted with the abandonment and probable ultimate destruction of the camp, we cannot help feeling sorry. In climate and scenery there is undoubtedly nothing like it in the United States, if in the world."[24]

But with all the excitement at Camp Swift, there was little time for sentimentality about Camp Hale. In mid-November, word came that all soldiers with families on the base should send them home. The men began turning in their training uniforms and drawing fresh gear, including new combat boots instead of shoes and leggings. As a sniper, Stuart Abbott was also issued a new 1903-A A4 rifle with a Weaver scope.[25]

In addition to new gear, the division was also being issued a new commanding officer. For most of the men, this came none too soon. Things had gotten so bad between the men and General Jones that in late October, in the middle of a boxing match, Jones had been loudly booed as he got up to award the trophy. In response, the entire division had been put on restriction. "You can imagine what the mental state of this unit is when they start booing their own commander, and hate with a fierce hatred every officer above the rank of captain," a soldier named Robert Ellis wrote home.[26]

Jones had finally succumbed, no doubt thanks to the bad air at Camp Hale, to a bronchial condition that he had first contracted in Alaska. The man Minnie Dole claimed had to sit on a radiator just to stay warm was told by medical staff that he was unfit to lead the mountain troops overseas.[27]

About this time, in Washington, Minnie Dole was waiting to speak to General Clyde Hyssong about the division's morale problems when the general swept into his office and introduced him to a wiry man wearing an old trench coat with a musette bag slung over his shoulder. A slim, short, sharp-angled man with shrewd eyes, oversized ears, and deep wrinkles running from his nostrils to the corners of his mouth, General George P. Hays could have walked right out of a Bill Mauldin cartoon. He certainly had the field experience. Born in China, the son of missionary parents, Hays had served in the First World War as a young artillery lieutenant in France. During the Second Battle of the Marne, he had had seven horses shot out from under him as he moved between command posts and two

French artillery batteries, trying to secure accurate supporting fire. On his twelfth sortie, Hays had taken a piece of shrapnel in the leg and ended up in a field hospital. He had been awarded the Congressional Medal of Honor for his efforts. After recuperating, he had fought in the Argonne, where he had been decorated with one of two Silver Stars he would earn over his career. In World War Two, Hays had spent a brief tour as an artillery commander at Cassino and had later landed at Omaha Beach; he had then served in the siege of Brest, where artillery fire had helped blast out some 40,000 entrenched Germans.[28]

During their initial meeting, Dole told Hays about the years of ill will the mountain troops held toward their commanding officers and how desperately they needed a man in charge whom they could respect. For two years, the mountain troops had "resented the fact that the staff has gone too much 'by the book,' not admitting that training and maneuvers at high altitude require elasticity of thought," Dole told Hays. "They need a good fight talk, with some appreciation of them and their long and arduous training mixed in."[29]

Two days after arriving in Texas, Hays acted on Dole's advice, to broad enthusiasm. On November 26, Hays assembled all his officers and noncoms into the camp's field house. "As I looked down on them from the platform, I thought what a fine looking body of men they were, and how lucky I was to get command of such a fine division," Hays would write. "I told them that we were going to have good times as well as bad times in our combat overseas, and that as far as possible my policy was to make everyone as comfortable and to have as good a time as possible as long as we accomplished our missions."[30]

Hays's speech marked a sea change in the division's morale. "We were greatly pleased with him, and we all expect him to be much better than 'old lady Jones,' " Dick Wilson wrote. "We are all greatly relieved to get rid of General Jones, who as far as we were concerned was incapable of handling a Cub Scout Troop."[31]

If Hays made the soldiers feel good about their training, his arrival also left little doubt that the time was nigh for their insertion into the war. On November 18, Stuart Abbott sent his mother the only document she needed to realize that this time, her worries about her son leaving for war were justified: a GI will. He also reported that a rotten tooth had finally been replaced, and while it wasn't "a perfect match in color or symmetry it is pretty good."

On November 29, the 86th Regiment boarded a train for an unknown destination. Three weeks later, the remaining regiments, the 85th and the 87th, boarded old steam-driven passenger trains and set off for Camp Patrick Henry, the army base nearest to the division's port of embarkation at Newport News, Virginia. The trip took three days. The enlisted men slept sitting up—all but one, who jumped off the train en route.[32]

On Christmas Eve, the train stopped for several hours near Decatur, Georgia—Dan Kennerly's hometown. Restless after the long ride, some of his buddies asked Kennerly to go out and find some beer and whiskey. Ever resourceful, Kennerly looked out the window and realized he knew of a liquor store exactly half a block from where they were stopped. A lieutenant, choosing national over personal security, told Kennerly he could go as long as he didn't pick up the phone and tell anyone of the troop's whereabouts. This seemed fair enough, and off Kennerly went. Once in the store, he saw a pay phone, and it was all he could do not to pick up the receiver and dial his parents. Back on board, Kennerly looked out the window as the train passed within half a block of his family's house. He could see the Christmas tree lights on in his own living room.[33]

Although they would not learn this until they were halfway across the Atlantic, the next time the mountain soldiers would set foot on solid ground, they would be in Italy. And they would arrive not as the 10th Light Division but as "The 10th Mountain Division"—complete with a new curved shoulder patch reading "Mountain" to go over the barrel and crossed bayonets. As small a gesture as the patch and the new name were, it made the men in the division swell with pride. After three years of training, they were finally being recognized as the elite unit they were.[34]

CHAPTER NINE

SEE NAPLES AND DIE

THROUGHOUT THE SUMMER OF 1944, the stripped-down Allied armies moved north from Rome with real success. After two weeks of heavy fighting in July, they took Florence, Pisa, and the western port town of Livorno, known in English as Leghorn. For the first time in months, it seemed as if the war in Italy might finally be bearing some fruit, and Churchill quietly began dreaming of the possibility of driving all the way to Vienna, a move he hoped would balance Stalin's postwar designs for Eastern Europe.

Churchill's ambitions were tempered by the four hundred miles that still lay between Venice and Vienna, and, more immediately, by the massive troop demands of the twin operations in France: Anvil (later renamed Dragoon) to the south and Overlord to the north. Just keeping the Italian campaign alive required endless battles with Washington. American enthusiasm, which had always been soft, was in no danger of firming up with things going well in France.

"My interest and hopes centre on defeating the Germans in front of Eisenhower and driving on into Germany, rather than limiting this action for the purposes of staging a full major effort in Italy," Roosevelt cabled Churchill at the end of June 1944. "For purely political considerations over here, I should never survive even a slight setback in Overlord if it were known that fairly large forces had been diverted to the Balkans."

Eisenhower, never enthusiastic about the Mediterranean campaign, assured the primacy of Overlord with a massive shift of men and matériel—including Truscott's entire VI Corps—from Italy to southern France. Between mid-June and the end of July, more than a division a week was withdrawn from the Italian front. The American Fifth Army was reduced by more than 40 percent—about 100,000 men, including a full third of its artillery battalions—and was left with just 153,000 soldiers.[1]

The most important ally of the Germans continued to be the mountainous Italian landscape. Although the construction of German defensive positions in the northern Apennine Mountains had begun as early as 1943, work on their entrenchment had picked up speed in the spring of 1944. The Todt construction agency forced thousands of Italian civilians to clear fields, lay mines, destroy bridges, and build positions along the ridges overlooking the highways throughout the region. By the time it was completed, the "Gothic Line" was 14 miles deep and stretched some 120 miles, from Livorno on the Tyrrhenian Sea to Rimini on the Adriatic, and it was pocked much of the way with howitzers, mortars, heavy machine guns, and mines.

Despite the withdrawal of American troops, Churchill and Harold Alexander, in command of all Allied troops in Italy, concocted a strategy they hoped would still manage to break through this line and cut the Germans off before they could escape through the Alps. At first Alexander hoped to feint a move toward the Adriatic and then run a full Allied assault up the middle of the peninsula—straight through the heart of the Apennines. To force the Germans into a final showdown south of the Po River, and to keep enemy soldiers from fleeing north, he ordered air attacks on all bridges across the Po in mid-July.

Oliver Leese, the general in charge of the British Eighth Army, had far less confidence in the planned mountain assault. After fighting north all the way from Italy's boot, his men were barely standing from battle fatigue. Even if they somehow managed to win the battle in the mountains, they wouldn't have the strength to chase the Germans through the plains. Just as troubling, the Allies had lost their only mountain troops when General Alphonse Juin's French mountain soldiers, who had fought so effectively at Cassino, had been stripped off to support Operation Anvil in southern

France. Rather than making a desperate run through the mountains, Leese argued, the Eighth Army should make the Adriatic feint the real thing. The landscape was far more gentle in the marshy lowlands near the water and offered British soldiers a narrow line to break through, after which they would be in a position to cut around behind the German defenses. Instead of forcing a trusted commander to fight a battle against his strategic instincts, Alexander acceded. On August 25, the British attack would go forward along the coast, with 1,200 tanks, 1,000 guns, and ten full divisions. The mountains would be left to the Americans.

Mark Clark, never trustful of his British partners, was hardly unhappy to have the central mountains to himself. Unlike his superiors in Washington, Clark had long considered the push through Italy good military strategy. Engaging the Germans in a broad Italian campaign diverted the Germans' attention from France and kept their forces spread far more thinly than they would like. On a more personal note, Clark could hardly have failed to notice how quickly—in just forty-eight hours—the world's attention had turned from his victory in Rome to the beaches of Normandy; ever since then, his army's efforts had essentially been ignored. With the British focused on controlling the Adriatic coastline as summer turned to fall, Clark hoped to smash through the last ramparts of the Apennines and seize Bologna. With this stroke would come control of the arteries leading north to the Po River valley, the Alpine lakes, and—ultimately—the Brenner Pass, which served as the main gateway to Austria and southern Germany.

In some ways, Clark's ambitions benefited from Alexander's move, since Kesselring, having fallen for the initial British feint, had shifted the elite 1st Parachute Division over to the Adriatic to support General Heinrich von Vietinghof's Tenth Army. But Kesselring was unwilling to put all his eggs into one basket; he kept two divisions in reserve near Bologna, near the mountain chain's midpoint. As had been true throughout the Italian war, Kesselring would rely on fluid troop movements to plug any gaps that opened in the Gothic Line.[2]

Kesselring was not without his own troubles. His soldiers, many of whom had been at the front since El Alamein, were as exhausted as any of the men fighting for the Allies. German units also had to deal with relentless guerrilla attacks by Italian partisans. As the war in Italy dragged on, some 200,000 Italians took up arms against the Germans; between June and August alone, partisan soldiers killed as many as 5,000 Germans and wounded or kidnapped as many as 30,000 more. To be sure, among the partisans there were factions with acutely different agendas. Some were commanded by rabidly anti-Fascist Italian civilians; others fought under escaped Allied prisoners of war. Those who took up arms against the occupying Germans were treated brutally when captured. Nine months prior to the mountain troops' arrival and just three months before Rome was liberated, Hitler became incensed when a group of partisans bombed an SS column and killed three dozen Germans. When he demanded that ten Italians be killed for every German, 335 bullets were fired into the heads of 335 men—mostly political prisoners and Jews—in the Ardeatine Caves outside Rome.[3]

By the end of August, Canadian and British infantry units broke through an eastern coastal section of the Gothic Line, opening the way for an armored assault. Among those observing the attack was Churchill himself; this was the closest he came to the enemy in the entire war. Once again, Kesselring was on the defensive, and once again he was proving exceedingly dangerous. The assault, Operation Olive, bogged down, unable to push through to the Po valley. Eighth Army forces took a heavy hit in the process, losing fully 14,000 men.

Things went no more smoothly in the central mountains. The Germans fought Clark's troops ruthlessly in defense of the two main routes running south to north, Highway 65 to the east and Highway 64 to the west. Defending these lines were seven German divisions within the Fourteenth Army, though substantial troops had been shifted east to shore up the defense against British advances up the Adriatic. The Fourteenth Army itself was reeling from losses of men still not adequately replaced since Anzio. Many of the men were fresh recruits with just three months of training; others had never fired live ammunition. By the middle of the month, both the Futa and Il Giogo Passes, and thus the central Gothic Line itself, were finally in American hands.

By September 12, at the Second Quebec Conference, some of the highest ranking American military strategists were beginning to concur with Churchill's desire to wrap up the battle in Italy and move toward Vienna. Roosevelt's chief of staff argued that if Eisenhower needed it, the Fifth

Army should be sent off to France. But if Eisenhower did not need the reinforcements, "they should then be utilized to clear the Germans from Italy and to assist British forces in operations to the north-eastward towards Vienna."[4]

The mood at the front was less cheery. As the Germans withdrew northward, they left a horrific trail of destruction behind them, laying countless booby traps and land mines and destroying as many communities as they could. Livorno's harbor lay in ruins; every inch of the city seemed booby-trapped. Bars of chocolate and cakes of soap blew off Allied fingers. When Americans removed abandoned German corpses from the street, bodies exploded. In all, during their fastidious withdrawal, Kesselring's German Army Group C would exact 34,000 casualties from the pursuing Allied troops; single American divisions would lose 5,000 men. Kesselring now had one goal in mind: to stall the enemy assault until the arrival of another frigid mountain winter.[5]

The troubles with furthering the attack in the Apennines were legion, especially for the Americans. Clark's units were chronically short of virtually every kind of ammunition; one division was alloted the same amount of ammunition for a week that it had shot in a stretch of eight hours just a month before. The Germans seemed to have a limitless supply of shells. During the last two weeks of October, just four days passed in which American soldiers were hit by fewer than a thousand shells. On top of and behind the ridges, the German 29th and 90th Panzer-Grenadier Divisions and the 1st Parachute Division, among the best units in Italy, felt utterly secure.[6]

On the front lines, the toll on the units fighting in the mountains continued to be brutal. On October 6, Clark reported that since the first of the month he had been losing 550 men per division per day; a diminished supply of replacement officers meant his divisions could be kept at authorized strength for only four more days. In the first two weeks of October alone, 5,700 Fifth Army troops were killed, wounded, or missing in action. Mortality rates, to say nothing of troop morale, were worsened considerably by the terrible difficulty in just getting wounded men off the mountains and back to aid stations. Once reached by medics clawing their way up a slope, injured soldiers had to be carefully lowered down to a place where they could be loaded onto muleback, an ordeal that could take as long as six hours. From there, it could be another eight hours before a wounded soldier found himself in an ambulance. Many did not make it that far. Plainly, for fighting in the mountains, a more effective evacuation method would have to be conceived. The trouble was, no one currently serving in the Fifth Army had the training to do this. The only men who did were still chasing rattlesnakes around the flatlands of Texas.

And in the simplest possible terms, Clark's men needed rest. Some soldiers in units such as the 34th (Red Bull) Division had been at the front for five hundred days.

"My troops have been negotiating the most difficult mountain terrain we have had to face in Italy, involving the bitterest fighting since Salerno," Clark wrote George Marshall. "I do not yet know the answer to the psychiatric problem. It appears clear . . . that susceptibility to psychiatric breakdown is directly related to the length of time in combat. I shall continue to take every practical measure to give my troops the opportunity to rest."[7]

When a group of congressmen from the House Military Affairs Committee arrived in Rome to inspect the war's progress, they declared themselves shocked at the carnage that lay before them. "They didn't know the Italian battlefield was one of the toughest in the world," Anne O'Hare McCormick wrote in *The New York Times.* "They had no idea of the tremendous natural obstacles the GI's have to contend with in addition to the stubbornness of the enemy stand on the best defensive positions he holds in Europe."

The fault for the congressmen's surprise did not lie with the journalists covering the war. "Stories have been written and have been printed," McCormick continued. "They have even been overwritten and printed so many times that readers don't see the mud or blood any more. They don't hear the scream of shells or the thunder of fallen rockets. They don't realize what happens when towns are blasted from the earth and human beings are either buried under debris or scattered like ants when somebody steps on an anthill. The trouble is with the Congressmen. Either they didn't read the accounts of the Italian battle or they couldn't take in the meaning of what they read. They had to see war for themselves before it really registered. And this lack of realization is not their fault. It is because the thing is indescribable."

Ever since his arrival in Italy, Kesselring had proven himself a master of defensive maneuvers, winning admiration even from Allied strategists who deplored the general's unwavering devotion to Nazism. "Where the attack came up against good divisions the enemy's efforts were out of all proportion to the results," Kesselring would observe. "Their belief in a quick victory ebbed, symptoms of fatigue became increasingly apparent and their blows feebled. The battle of the Apennines can really be described as a famous page of German military history."[8]

On October 23, his promise to Hitler of bottling up the Italian peninsula fulfilled and with another paralyzing winter just around the corner, Kesselring's remarkable command tenure came to an end when his staff car collided with an artillery piece on the road to Bologna, critically injuring him. Kesselring was replaced by General von Vietinghof, but if the master of defense was out of the picture, his strategies remained very much in place. Even with the Gothic Line fractured, the Apennines continued to demoralize the exhausted Allies. Just outfitting the Fifth Army got harder and harder as units progressed deeper into the mountains. Local supply officers were forced to hire hundreds of Italian workers to work on massive salvage and reclamation projects, turning worn-out clothing and gear into usable equipment. Repair shops, using hundreds more Italian mechanics, were forced to fix abandoned trucks and jeeps on makeshift assembly lines. Frontline troops relied not on trucks or trains but on fifteen companies of Italian mule skinners and 3,900 mules.[9]

To General Truscott, recently returned from France, breaking out of the Apennines into the Po River valley required pushing through along Highway 64, where German defenses, he hoped, would be less entrenched than they had been along Highway 65. Truscott had the 1st Armored Division ready to roll, with the 85th Division in reserve.

Winning control of Highway 64, Truscott felt certain, meant wresting control of Mount Belvedere, a big, grassy, sloped hill, wooded at the top, that rose to 3,876 feet at the western end of a ridge extending east and northeast for six miles. Belvedere overlooked Highway 64, the main route running northward between Pistoia (the town that had given its name to the pistol), Bologna, and the Po River valley.

On November 24, three infantry battalions—the 435th Antiaircraft Battalion, retrained as regular infantry; the 92nd Infantry Division's 370th Regiment; and a battalion of the Brazilian Expeditionary Force's 1st

Infantry Division—attacked Mount Belvedere and for three days held the summit. It wasn't long, however, before the troops were forced off by a fierce German counterattack, orchestrated from a separate ridgeline just to the west, a chain of peaks that came to be known as Riva Ridge. This ridgeline offered German artillery observers a clear line of sight on anyone approaching the treeless flanks of Belvedere, and since the face of Riva Ridge was so steep, there was nothing the Fifth Army could do to knock the observers off.

Two weeks later, three Brazilian battalions made a second fruitless attack on Belvedere, this time from the east, along the slopes of an adjoining peak known as Mount Castello. After successfully repulsing these attacks, German General von Vietinghof ordered the German defensive position on Mount Belvedere redesigned again. Mines, trip wires, and concertina wire were laid across every conceivable approach. In the lowlands, farmhouses and village clusters were taken over by German troops. Protective artillery and mortar emplacements were beefed up, particularly on the Riva Ridge overlook.[10]

By the end of 1944, the German positions in the Apennines had created a stalemate, with twenty-seven Allied divisions and thirty-three Axis divisions—twenty-seven German and six Fascist Italian—staring at each other across the Alpine valleys of northern Italy. The Allies had suffered terribly in their attempts to break through. The U.S. II Corps had lost nearly 2,500 men in six days in mid-October alone to the east; the British Eighth Army had suffered 14,000 casualties since August.[11]

The end of the year also brought a change in leadership. British general Harold Alexander was promoted from commander of all Allied troops in Italy to supreme allied commander of the entire Mediterranean Theater. Mark Clark moved up to take his place, and Lucien Truscott took control of the American Fifth Army. Truscott saw that the attitudes among foot soldiers on the Allied side of the Apennines were grim. Commanders were "gravely concerned" over morale problems. "For two months preparations for the offensive had given the men a renewed purpose," he wrote. "Now those who had suffered the rigors of a campaign in the mountains during the previous winter could only look to another winter campaign in higher and more rugged mountains under worse conditions of cold, rain, and snow."[12]

Spring, General Clark hoped, would be the right time to launch a double-pronged attack. The beleaguered British Eighth Army, covering the assault's right wing, would attempt to break through the German defenses, then turn west in the Po River valley to a point north of Bologna. The American Fifth, in the center of the peninsula, would break into Bologna and continue north, join the British, and envelop the Germans. If for whatever reason the trap could not be sprung near the mountains, the Allies would chase the Germans through the Po valley and destroy them before they crossed the river.

Within the ranks, soldiers wondered why it was necessary to have a spring offensive in Italy at all. Far to the north, American troops were about to cross the Rhine River, and the Russians were approaching Vienna. Why not just hold the Fifth and the Eighth Armies where they were and let time run out on the Germans? Lives would be saved on both sides. At some level, this had been a question at least since the Allied victory in Sicily, when the entire Italian strategy had come under skeptical scrutiny by the Americans, and it had continued to nag the European command all the way up the peninsula. By the time the invasion of Normandy had proven so effective, just two days after the taking of Rome, there were renewed calls to let the Italian campaign rest. Though Mark Clark was considered a highly professional and unrelentingly forceful strategist, his quixotic personal ambition and open distrust of his British counterparts made him a convenient vessel into which enlisted men poured their enmity.

But Clark remained single-minded and deeply resentful about the incessant dismantling of his troops. Clark felt certain that French forces alone could have taken Marseilles, and that, had Truscott's VI Corps remained in Italy, it would not only have ended the war there but allowed for a strong push into the Balkans. "The weakening of the campaign in Italy in order to invade southern France instead of pushing into the Balkans was one of the outstanding political mistakes of the war," he would write. Stalin "knew exactly what he wanted in a political as well as a military way; and the thing he wanted most was to keep us out of the Balkans. After the fall of Rome, Kesselring's army could have been destroyed—if we had been able to shoot the works in a final offensive."

Clark compared his remaining divisions to distance runners who had done the best they could but collapsed right before the finish line. An injection of thoroughly trained and fresh manpower was the only way the mission could continue. After three years of training, the 10th Mountain Division had finally found its calling.[13]

ON DECEMBER 11, the first third of the mountain troops, the 86th Regiment, shipped out of Hampton Roads, Virginia, on the USS *Argentina*. Three weeks later, the 85th and 87th Regiments filed onto the largest and fastest passenger ship in the United States, the USS *West Point*, a converted luxury liner once known as the SS *America*. The remainder of the division, notably three artillery units, left two days later on a smaller army transport boat, the *General Meigs*. As they loaded onto the ship, a band played "Over There" and the Notre Dame Victory March; a team of women from the Red Cross gave each man a canvas bag containing a toothbrush, toothpaste, razor blades, cigarettes, and playing cards.

In all, just under 14,000 soldiers boarded the ships: three infantry regiments of about 3,000 men each, plus three artillery battalions; the 126th Engineer Mountain Battalion; a battalion of medics, ambulance drivers, and veterinarians; and companies of headquarters men and assorted smaller units. Each infantry regiment consisted of three battalions of 1,000 men; in addition to headquarters men and medics, each battalion consisted of three rifle companies of 180 men each and one heavy-weapons company—a group of men trained to fire heavy .30-caliber and .50-caliber machine guns and 81-mm mortars. Rifle companies were divided further into four platoons of 40 men each: three platoons of riflemen and one of weapons men armed with .30-caliber air-cooled machine guns and 60-mm mortars.

Over the next few months, an additional five thousand men would join the troops as replacement soldiers, in part because the mountain troops would suffer among the highest casualty rates in the entire Italian campaign. By the end of the war, one in five men in the division would suffer a battlefield injury. One in twenty would be killed. None of their training, it seemed, could protect them from mortars and machine guns.

As soon as they were on board, soldiers were told that for the first time their letters home would be censored. They were ordered not to write anything that might even remotely be considered classified information; anything that was would either be blacked out in ink or cut out with a pair of scissors. At least on board the ship, this was a fairly easy directive to follow. The boys still had no idea where they were going.

To Denis Nunan, the ship's size was indicative primarily of the discomfort the boys would experience on the way over. "The larger the can, the more the sardines," he wrote home. The quarters on board both troop ships were extremely tight. Stuart Abbott felt as though he and the men had been "melted and poured in." When soldiers threw down their duffel bags between bunks stacked five to a tier, there was exactly enough room for the men to stand upright, arms at their sides.

Dick Wilson and twenty-one other men were jammed into a compartment below the waterline that had been built for thirteen; they felt like they were crossing the Atlantic in a submarine. Their bunkroom was in the ship's stern, right over the propeller, and the relentless vibration became a constant aggravation. The lights were on all the time except when the men crawled into their bunks at night; the bunks themselves were so closely stacked that the man above prevented the man below from sitting up. As the ship pitched and rolled, virtually everyone who didn't get sick developed sore back muscles just from trying to stay in bed. During the day, men were always searching for the few sunny spots to read or play cards or chess; at night, no one was allowed on deck at all, though they could go out on the promenade deck for a smoke. They were served only two meals a day, which, given the quality of the food and the length of time it stayed in their stomachs, suited many of them just fine; a good deal of the food, Stuart Abbott noticed, was being "wasted over the rail." For those with an appetite, the chow lines were so long that they practically had to line up for the next meal as soon as the first one was over.[14]

Winter weather kept most people inside most of the day. The foul air caused by severe overcrowding on board combined with heavy rolling waves caused a number of the men—and many of the WACs—to find their way to the leeward rail. On the sixth day out, heavy seas ripped life rafts from the decks and smashed them through the ship's port side; icy seawater poured into a bunkroom that had only just been evacuated.[15]

The departure of the troops from the United States struck a nerve in the men who had set it up. Minnie Dole tacked a map of Italy to his wall in the Ski Patrol headquarters and used a box of colored pins to mark the division's progress. "I hope that you can realize that I feel quite lost with the Division out of the country and I can only hope that everything goes well with you in every detail," Dole wrote to General Hays. As it turned out, Dole's duties were far from over. As the division went to war and started losing soldiers to injury and death, Dole would be put in charge of finding men to replace them.[16]

AS THE MEN EMBARKED, General Hays left for Washington, where he caught a plane for a meeting in Italy with General Truscott, recently promoted to replace Mark Clark as commander of the American Fifth Army. With his men crippled after so many months at the front, Truscott was thrilled to have some fresh bodies. An experienced commander, Truscott knew that soldiers reached peak performance, in terms of both physical effectiveness and psychological strength, after about 90 days in the field and started breaking down soon thereafter. Most soldiers are considered wrung out after 140 days. The men of the Fifth had been fighting almost continuously for eighteen months. The fact that the mountain troops were exceedingly physically fit gave him a shot of optimism he hadn't felt for weeks. Perhaps crashing one more wave of men over Mount Belvedere would finally bring this tortured sector under Allied control.

Looking over the plans for the attack on the Apennines—and a map of Mount Belvedere, which Truscott considered the division's primary objective—Hays could see just how intimidating the German positions had become.

"Who is going to share the bullets with us when we attack?" Hays asked.

"No one," Truscott replied. "Do you think you can do it?"

Hays said if his men made a direct attack on Belvedere, "I don't think I will have any division left." He asked for a month to get his men prepared and to see if there were any secrets to cracking the Apennines.[17]

THE *WEST POINT* MOVED so quickly across the Atlantic that it was not accompanied by naval escorts. As it passed through the Strait of Gibraltar on January 10, the ship was finally joined by four destroyers and plenty of

Convair PBY-5 and PBY-6 Catalinas. Stuart Abbott drew a delicately shaded pencil rendering of Gibraltar and included it in a letter home. Dick Wilson was less impressed. To him, the rock looked "much more impressive on the Prudential Life Insurance posters than it does when you actually see it."[18]

On January 13, the *West Point* passed the rugged, steeply hilled island of Capri, where the troops saw their first British plane, a Halifax bomber. That day—nine days after leaving Virginia, and three weeks behind the *Argentina*—the ship arrived in Naples at about 4 P.M., in a heavy rain. What the men saw shocked them. Although they could see the beautiful mountains, including the vapor-shrouded Vesuvius, outside the city, Naples itself—once the principal supply port for the Allied efforts in Italy—bore the grim scars of a country fighting to free itself from hostile occupation. Hoping to make the city's port unusable for troop arrivals and food shipments once it became clear the Allies were not going to give up at Salerno, the Germans had left sunken ships everywhere. Within the city, streets and buildings remained unrepaired after the battles of more than a year before, when Allied bombing runs and Neapolitan guerrilla attacks had forced the Germans from the city in late September and early October of 1943. As they fled, German soldiers had left time bombs in churches, government archives, and post offices, some of which blew up a week after they left.[19]

When the mountain troops arrived, they were greeted by Red Cross girls who handed each soldier two stale doughnuts, and by German leaflets that warned, "This is not Camp Hale, where you had 15,000 men skiing at the foot of Tennessee Pass." More sinister messages translated the Italian proverb *Vedi Napoli, e poi muori*: See Naples and die.[20]

As the men waited to board trains or boats for the move north, they were swamped by peddlers selling cheap rings and bracelets with the 10th Mountain patch on them. Clearly, the arrival of the division—now folded into the Fifth Army's IV Corps—was not quite as secret as had been planned. As the 86th had done before them, the men of the 85th and 87th began moving, by freighter or rail, through Livorno and Pisa and finally to a staging area in the Apennines between Florence and Bologna. The men were supposed to be supplied with vehicles, additional clothing, and equipment and ammunition, but for some reason, none of their special cold-weather clothing or gear had yet arrived.

Not far from Pisa, Dan Kennerly learned about the first casualties the mountain troops had suffered a couple weeks before, when a mine exploded near a rail line running along the border of the 86th Regiment's training area. Seven enlisted men were killed, four of them medics, and four others were wounded. A Catholic chaplain named Clarence Hagen was killed by a mine explosion while going to perform last rites. After three years of relentless mountain training, these first battlefield deaths were startling. With the exception of frostbite and hypothermia, the men had mastered themselves and their physical environment fairly well. They were men who, beyond their superior military training, had become as accomplished in certain nonmilitary skills—skiing, mountaineering, wilderness rescue—as anyone on Earth. For a group of men that had survived training unprecedented in both its philosophy and its rigor, the sudden losses seemed particularly senseless and wasteful.

But Kennerly and the rest of the troops had little time, once they arrived at the base of the Apennines, to mourn their first dead. The nearest Germans were directly above them.[21]

PART TWO

THE **ENEMY**

There is a nice sound to the phrase "mountain warfare." It has a ring of daring; it sounds cleaner than trench warfare and lighter than tank warfare. The only thing that can match it is war in the air, and that has become too deadly to be nice any more. It has also become too familiar, while war in the mountains is still strange enough to sound romantic. Except, of course, to the men who have to fight it.

—Walter Bernstein, Italy, January 1944

CHAPTER TEN

RIVA RIDGE

B Y MID-JANUARY, MOST OF THE fourteen thousand members of the 10th Mountain Division had made their way from the Mediterranean coast deep into the Italian countryside north and west of Florence. They moved mostly at night, to avoid German observers high in the mountains and snipers firing from the windows of abandoned farmhouses. As they moved further into the war zone, the men asked—or forced—Italian families to surrender their homes. They did so to provide housing for soldiers, to move civilian families away from the fighting, and to alleviate a serious source of anxiety for Allied patrols. "If you're out on a night patrol and you hear a noise inside a building," Gene Hames, the logger from Montana, noted, "you don't knock to ask who's inside."[1]

However arduous their training had been, nothing quite prepared the men for the atmosphere of war. "Many men will remember their first hours in combat more clearly than anything that happens for the rest of their days, especially if this moment comes at night," Edward Nickerson, a member of the 85th's G Company, would write. "Mine came at the top of a mountain, amid dark pine trees and patches of snow blackened by explosives and reeking sharply of cordite. Cordite [a smokeless powder made, in part, of nitroglycerine] is a stench I had never smelled before and have smelled rarely since, and I actually confused it, in my extraordinary ignorance, with the smell of dead bodies. There were also a few dead Germans in slit trenches, but their characteristic smell—of sweaty leather belts and other leather gear, and heavy, unwashed, woolen uniforms—must have been overwhelmed by the stink of cordite. In the cold, they did not smell of decomposition that first night. It's the cordite I remember, strange and penetrating and frightening."[2]

To combat late-winter rain and wet snow, soldiers hunkered down in two-man pup tents or twelve-man pyramid tents. Their bivouac areas were often swamped with mud; their foxholes, which so far they had not had to use, were constantly filling up with water. The landscape around them was mostly plowed under; even the hillsides, some as steep as 40 degrees, had been terraced and cultivated. Hand-tossed haystacks were sprinkled in fields between large, rectangular stone farmhouses. As the men moved forward, they were sometimes given the luxury—whether through the generosity or reluctant submission of their Italian hosts—of a night by a fire. Chickens and turkeys scratched in the barnyards, and roosters announced the arrival of dawn, a comforting sound for some of the farm boys from back home.[3]

Getting to the villages was treacherous. The roads were terrible and often bordered steep ravines. Trying to keep a lightless jeep on a mountain road while keeping an ear out for sniper fire was harrowing work. Veering off the roads was not an option; during their retreat, German soldiers had so heavily mined the surrounding fields that civilian injuries were commonplace. One day, Denis Nunan learned that an Italian child had been killed and two of his playmates seriously wounded when a strange piece of metal they had been playing with had exploded in their faces. The frequency of such horrors appalled him.

Moving through the villages, the division got a close look at the ravages the war had left on the homes of the local villagers. Many farms had been destroyed, livestock killed, churches bombed. More sickening for Nunan was the realization that he would likely be ordered to do the same. "War spares nothing," he wrote home. "The isolated hamlets, with walls of stone feet thick, make fortresses for the enemy to gather strength within and strike out to kill. The village churches make ideal observation posts so the enemy can watch your every move and direct death against you. The little home with its red tile roof, white walls and blue door is hiding an 88 that will blast your foxhole by night. Now, instead of rebelling within at the sight of seemingly wanton destruction, we beg the artillery and air corps to lay waste to even the innocent structure—even though it might be mellowed by centuries of laughter, the smoke of thousands of fiesta cook fires, the love of generation upon generation of family happiness. War knows no love, race or creed—only the desire to live. Even I have begged the air corps to lay waste to a church steeple as the 88s were crashing too near my foxhole for comfort. So you see, Mother and Daddy, in my short time in combat my heart has hardened and my soul grown bitter. I have killed and I shall continue to do such without flinching until peace comes to the world of war."[4]

As Dick Wilson's company made its way toward the base of Belvedere, he grew ever more astonished at the poverty of the Italian people and the terrible damage that had been done to the countryside. Eventually Wilson's platoon found its accommodations—and its relations with the local people—improving. On good nights, they would be invited into Italian homes with running water and blazing fireplaces. Local women would help the men with their laundry; young partisan fighters would show the men a good time. The partisans "are about the wildest and craziest bunch of young fellows that I have ever known," Wilson wrote home. "They are completely combat crazy and every night they take off on raiding parties behind the German lines. They bring back no prisoners; the only good Jerry to them is a dead Jerry."

Although virtually all the work Wilson's company carried out was done at night, the tension was made easier by the warmth and generosity of the people in the villages. One night before his company was to leave town, a group of partisans threw a spaghetti dinner and big dance in their honor—apparently the first time they had ever treated American soldiers so well. The destitute villagers took an entire week's ration of chocolate, gum, hard candy, and cigarettes and practically forced them on the humbled soldiers. They brought their own girlfriends for the GIs to dance with. A young Italian named Franco gave Wilson a pair of medals he had stolen off the chest of an SS trooper he had killed by chopping his head off with an automatic rifle; Franco claimed to have fifty-three dead Germans to his credit. In the morning, as the men moved out, grandmothers and little children cried and waved from their windows.[5]

On duty near Monti di Villa, Hugh Evans spent most of his days and nights on sentry duty, where he found he had plenty of time to admire the comings and goings of the Italian farmers, who somehow carried on with their lives. They invited the Americans to dances where children and grandmothers alike would spin to the music made by a man on an accordion who knew five songs: "Amapola," "The Beer Barrel Polka," "The Woodpecker's Serenade," and two others Evans didn't know. Evans and his men tried to teach the accordionist the Virginia reel, with little success.[6]

But the men's rest was rarely enough to offset their constant anxiety. Denis Nunan found himself in regular small-arms firefights with German patrols and was surprised how frightened he became. "At first I tried to tell myself that my terrific shaking was due to the cold, but later admitted it doesn't get that cold even at Camp Hale." To assuage his fear, Nunan prayed during the skirmishes and went to church when they were over. One day after mass he saw a nun wearing a large white headdress and a blue robe and slipped her a thousand lire—about ten dollars. Nunan's chaplain was so pleased with his devotion that he wrote Nunan's parents to reassure them that their boy was tending to his spiritual needs. "You will be delighted to know that Denis has been faithful to his religious duties," he wrote. "During the past few days he attended Holy Mass and received Our Blessed in Holy Communion. You need have no fear for him. The Lord will take care of him."[7]

THE DIVISION MOVED into the heart of the Apennines, setting up in and around the ancient town of Vidiciatico on the lower slopes of Mount Grande. Graced with a thousand-year-old stone tower in its tiny center, Vidiciatico offered a clear view of the long, grassy, southern slopes of Mount Belvedere, less than two miles away. Of course, given the panoramic view the Germans enjoyed from atop Belvedere, the opposite was also true. Just getting men into Vidiciatico was a chore: the main road up from the town of Silla was exposed to observation and artillery fire from Belvedere, and an eight-mile march on foot up a back road, impassable for transport trucks, served as the only solution. Vidiciatico's few hundred residents, many of whom had taken up arms against the Germans, opened their doors to American soldiers and tipped them off about German bunkers and machine-gun pits.[8]

Within two weeks, all three regiments had made it into the mountains and were set up between the Serchio River and the base of Mount Belvedere. Three colonels under General Hays commanded the three regiments: Colonel Raymond C. Barlow, the 85th; Colonel Clarence M. Tomlinson, the 86th; and Colonel David M. Fowler, the 87th.

If the men were ready, much of their equipment was not. Since the motorized troop transports had not been equipped with chains, entire companies had been forced to march eighteen miles over icy roads to camp, only to find that virtually all their specialized equipment—including their mountain boots and cold-weather sleeping bags, and most of their skis and crampons—had failed to make the trip to Italy. Apparently, the division's gear was languishing, ready for shipment, in a depot in Boston; someone in the military bureaucracy had decided that a few extra pairs of socks and long underwear would be enough. World-class mountaineers like Bob Bates, who would receive a Bronze Star and Legion of Merit for his work, had been testing gear for nearly five years; the mountain troopers themselves had tested it in the field for nearly three. But the equipment was not available at the moment the men actually needed it.

Once again, frustrated soldiers found an advocate in Minnie Dole, who forwarded complaints straight to General Marshall in Washington. "I don't care if we never see a ski—the boot is the best all-purpose boot the Army ever developed," one officer wrote. "The tragedy of it all is just this: We have spent three years developing this clothing and equipment. We may now be denied the use of it at a time when we really need it."[9]

The prospect of going into the mountains with only blankets was unpleasant under any circumstances; frigid air has a way of sneaking under a blanket in ways it can't get into a sleeping bag, and body heat has no trouble at all leaking out from under even the most tightly blanketed man. The men of the 10th knew these facts all too well. Already under acute psychological pressure, they now faced the additional prospect of sleeplessness and possibly hypothermia. Resigned to the inevitable snafus of military supply, men on patrol pulled woolen uniforms over woolen underwear, threw on field jackets, and made the best of the situation.[10]

Given its arrival late in the winter season, the division had only rare chances to put its ski training into practice. Yet even these first runs—the first time most of the men were actually moving through enemy territory—proved traumatic. "The first trip out into the great unknown land of the enemy can be more nerve-wracking to the individual than the mass movements of battle," George Earle, a captain in the 87th Regiment, wrote. "There is the long strain of silent movement, the breathless waits, the inexorable searching out of him who lies in waiting to kill. There is the physical punishment and even torture of alternately sweating up the rough terrain and lying motionless for hours on the snow—freezing in your own icy sweat. Finally, there is the fast withdrawal, possibly under fire, with no litter bearers for the casualty and only the desperate loyalty of a comrade to drag the wounded in."

Out on patrol one night, a platoon of men from the 87th's G Company climbed an escarpment southeast of Pianello where they had taken some machine-gun fire the previous night. At 2 A.M., the team watched through the darkness as three Germans dropped into a machine-gun pit. Inching their way to within five feet of the gunners, an American scout raised his tommy gun and fired. Only one shot fired. His gun had jammed. The Germans instantly opened fire, wounding a bazooka man in the leg, who managed to get off a shot that killed one of the gunners. When a call for the Germans to surrender went unheeded, the patrol lobbed a couple of grenades into the pit. When this was answered by German fire from another machine gunner a few yards downhill, that gun was also silenced with a grenade. A third German machine gun opened up from the north, and it too was knocked out. Finally the patrol was able to pick up the wounded bazooka man and return to Vidiciatico.[11]

Another night, out on ski patrol, an exhausted Denis Nunan pulled up for a break right on top of a buried German bunker. He didn't realize where he was until he smelled the smoke from an underground fire. Suddenly all he cared about was getting away without hitting the chimney with his skis or his poles. The next morning, he returned with his platoon. They waited until the Germans came out and put on their skis, then shot them all.[12]

A soldier in the 85th Regiment named Hans Aschaffenburg gave impromptu German lessons to the men of G Company. A solemn man with thick spectacles who spoke English with an inflection somewhere between German and Oxford ("That *bostord*!" he would say of a sergeant he didn't like), Aschaffenburg taught his companions how to say "Hands up!" in German and "Lay your weapons down!," then asked if there were any questions. "Well, yes, what do we say if the situation is reversed and *we* want to surrender?" someone asked. "Yeah," muttered someone else, to a burst of nervous laughter. "And how would we say 'I've always admired your fearless leader'?"[13]

Stuart Abbott shuttled back and forth from the rear areas to the front lines, where he earned his combat infantry badge for engaging in a small-arms skirmish. Abbott was also, as usual, taken by the beauty of the countryside. The crags of Riva Ridge and the rolling slopes of Belvedere were as beguiling to him as anything in Colorado. Looming over a countryside dotted with ancient stone farmhouses, the mountains seemed to possess a quietude that made the Rockies seem boisterous and raw by comparison. Out on scouting runs, Abbott climbed some of the higher hills in the region and was able, up top, to see the division's objective: the lovely floodplain of the Po River valley. If he squinted, he could see—in his mind's eye, at least—the snowy peaks of the Alps, far to the north.

Such thoughts distracted Abbott from the pain of his new false tooth; not long after arriving in Italy, he had broken it off while chewing on a K ration biscuit, and was now carrying the tooth in a matchbox. This, in combination with a homesickness he had never felt in Colorado, left him feeling bereft. "I must admit that I had never really been homesick until I got over here," he wrote home just a couple of days after his twentieth birthday. "There are times now when I get so blue it just hurts to think of home. I have found that I think most of home and what I used to do most when I am out on guard at an outpost. I guess the quiet is just naturally conducive to it. I am living for the day when I can curl up in an easy chair with a good book and an entire pan of hot buttered popcorn for the whole evening. I swear that when I am back we will go through every wing in the Rosenwald Museum and eat in the cafeteria in the basement just as we did two summers ago. You, Mollie and I will see every horseshow, play and everything else of interest that goes on."[14]

As the days went by and the snow began to melt, Abbott began taking field notes again, noting the dates when plant buds opened and chronicling the birds returning to the area. "I even heard a warbler yesterday," he wrote his grandmother. "I will really hate to leave here when the time comes, as I suppose it eventually will."[15]

IN MID-JANUARY, Dan Kennerly was assigned to his regiment's mail run. Every morning, he would take the outgoing mail to regimental headquarters in San Marcello. Occasionally, his route would take him to division headquarters in Campo Tizzaro or even corps headquarters in Pistoia. Leaving the safety of camp after midnight, Kennerly would drive jeep patrols, headlights turned off, into small villages, where riflemen would raid fortified houses and corral Fascist Italian snipers. Drawing fire during one raid, Kennerly's patrol quickly killed three Italians and captured eleven more. Transporting some of the prisoners back to camp in his jeep, Kennerly watched as packs of partisans shouted insults at the prisoners with such venom he feared they might grab the men and lynch them. Thankfully, a colonel happened to drive up at that moment and ran the partisans off.

The mail runs gave Kennerly a chance to see a lot of the Italian countryside and to stitch together, as far as he could, the placement and movements of the various regiments. He passed huge supplies of ammunition and other equipment alongside Highway 64, the main supply route between Pistoia and Bologna, and mile after mile of military vehicles and artillery. Clearly, the 10th was gearing up for a massive assault. The question was where and when. For two weeks, General Hays had been considering ways to crack the German defense of Riva Ridge, the strategically critical line of peaks running roughly perpendicular to Mount Belvedere. He ordered Colonel Tomlinson, the 86th's regimental commander, to send patrols up the ridge and find ways to climb it.

A week later, Tomlinson returned to Hays with bad news: his men had been all over the base of Riva Ridge and couldn't find anywhere to climb.

"This is a mountain division," Hays replied. "Surely they can find how to climb up that ridge. It will be a lot cheaper to capture the ridge in the first place than to suffer the casualties from hostile fire directed from there."[16]

Tomlinson left solving the riddle of Riva Ridge to Lieutenant Colonel Jefferson J. Irvin, the officer in charge of strategic planning, and Lieutenant Colonel Henry Hampton, the battalion's commanding officer. Beneath aerial maps and overlays, an operations man scaled out a wax sand-table model of the Riva ridgeline. Although not high compared to the mountains of Colorado, the half-dozen peaks comprising the 12,000 yards of ridgeline were rugged and steep and would have fit prominently into any mountain chain in the eastern United States. The lowest of the peaks (and the closest to Mount Belvedere) was Pizzo di Campiano, 3,175 feet; the highest, Mount Spigolino to the south, was just over 6,000 feet, about the height of New Hampshire's Mount Washington. The trouble with any assault on the ridge was not the height, however; it was the sheerness of the face, and the shorter promontories were among the steepest. The average grade on Mount Cappel Buso was 40 degrees, compared to just 30 degrees on Mount Serrasiccia, and Pizzo di Campiano was so nearly vertical it could be climbed only with ropes. Just finding reasonable trails up the peaks would require lengthy, detailed, and dangerous patrols. Climbing them—especially at night, and under enemy observation and fire—would require the finest mountaineering skills the men possessed. Sitting beneath the ridge, Hampton felt as if he and his men were moving around "the bottom of a bowl, with the enemy sitting on two-thirds of the rim."

Just how many Germans occupied this rim was hard to determine. Estimates ran from fifty to nearly two hundred. Riva Ridge and the Belvedere massif were controlled by Senger's XIV Panzer Corps and the LI Mountain Corps, a mountain unit in name only since few of its members were equipped for specialized fighting. Stationed atop Riva Ridge were members of the 4th (Edelweiss) Battalion and a battalion from the 1044th Regiment of the 232nd Infantry Division.

For typical flatland fighting, troop superiority of about three to one is considered optimal. In the mountains, what with the dramatic advantages held by enemy troops up high, assaulting troop superiority needs to run closer to ten to one. General Hays decided to use a battalion of about 850 men for the initial attack on Riva Ridge, with 180 more men in reserve to help hold the ridge once it had been taken. The rest of the division would take on the far greater number of Germans on Mount Belvedere.

At first a route up Mount Spigolino, at the ridgeline's southern end (and farthest from Belvedere), seemed to make sense; intelligence had determined that there were only five German soldiers up top, hunkered down in a small hut. But the idea was quickly discarded when commanders realized there would be no way to supply troops once they made it to the summit; the route was simply too steep for motor vehicles or even mules. And since the Germans were strung out all along the ridge, they could easily bring in reinforcements and blow approaching Americans back down the mountain.

Sending a large force up the middle of the ridge and then fanning soldiers out once they had reached the top was discarded as unwieldy; for a single, massive assault it would take days just to complete the initial climb, and the climbing soldiers would make easy pickings for the German artillery gunners up top. The only solution, it seemed, was to find multiple routes. Discreet units would climb simultaneously to ensure surprise all along the line. A hydra-headed attack would also prevent any of the German units from supporting one another; with all the German units under attack, there would be no way for them to move soldiers laterally along the ridgetop.[17]

The first thing the mountaineers had to do was scout out the slopes. Moving out from positions near the base of the mountains, early patrols noticed, at first, very little activity along the ridge; perhaps the Germans, having successfully defended their turf for so many months, had grown comfortable on their perch. Early on, American patrols were restricted to nighttime. But with the Germans on top of the ridge apparently oblivious to—or unconcerned about—the increasing activity, patrols were slowly allowed to pick up, like water slowly beginning to boil around lobsters in a pot. More aggressive and conspicuous patrols tromped around the base of Belvedere, hoping to trick the Germans into thinking that Belvedere was the only thing the Americans were interested in.[18]

In fact, the lull since the last attack on Mount Belvedere had left some German officers doubting the strength of their own defensive position. General Frido von Senger, in command of the XIV Panzer Corps, set up opposite the mountain troops, had never shared Kesselring's confidence in the Gothic Line. The obsession with panoramic observation points required that defensive positions be constructed on forward-facing slopes, which in turn required the removal of swaths of trees to clear lines of sight. To Senger, these bare spots were a dead giveaway.

Worse, the strength of their position atop the mountain range risked making his soldiers overconfident and soft. Once they settle into a comfortable position, and set up shelters and reliable sources of food, even the best-trained soldiers develop a powerful resistance to movement, Senger knew. Remaining in one place, especially high above an enemy, is far safer than advancing or retreating along a road. There is less risk of ambush, less stumbling through unknown territory, less fear. But as soldiers construct makeshift layers of security, they lose their edge, their instincts become dull, their appetite for battle begins to wane. The chaos of war ebbs, and memories of the relative comforts of civilian life creep in. "The more intensively troops build up a position that is not attacked and the more accustomed their minds become to all the details of a position and the anticipated defensive fighting to take place there, the more useless they become for actual mobile fighting," Senger would write. "They are surprised by the mission that is suddenly thrust upon them because they have lost the mental flexibility required in adapting themselves to changed conditions."

Senger knew this was dangerous. He took to inspecting his line in a small, unmarked Volkswagen, wearing no sign of his rank on his uniform. The vehicle's anonymity, he hoped, would save him from the fate suffered by another division commander, who had been ambushed and shot.[19]

One afternoon, Bob Frauson, the soldier who had survived two weeks on Homestake Mountain eating nothing but pemmican, led two others in A Company from their headquarters near La Ca' to the base of Mount Spigolino, on the ridge's southern end. With no ice axes and only rubber shoepac boots on their feet, they climbed through the snow to a point high on the peak, all the while peering through the trees for German lookouts. Suddenly one of Frauson's men fell hard and slid down the slope. He was prevented from sailing over a cliff only by a collision with a large outcropping of rock. Frauson scrambled down after him. Just as he got him anchored to the rock, his other man came sliding down the hill. Frauson leaped forward and with a flying tackle kept his second man from going over the cliff. "You know, it's getting late, and all we're gonna do up here is get ourselves captured," Frauson told his men, both of whom now had sprained ankles. "Besides, today's my twenty-first birthday."

Frauson led the limping men back down to Poggiolforato, a small town stuck in the no-man's-land between the Allied and German lines. The village was dead. Halfway through town, Frauson heard the creak of a door hinge and saw an old man and a very young boy peering out of a house. When he saw the soldiers were Americans, the old man invited them in to share the only food they had: chestnut pancakes. With one of his companions translating, Frauson learned that the man and his grandson had been away for a couple of days, and when they had returned they had found their entire village murdered. A German patrol had rounded up every living person—about two dozen people—forced them into a house perched on a slope above the town, and burned the house to the ground.[20]

On January 15, a patrol of five expert mountaineers led by Sergeant Carl Casperson of B Company set out to scout the climb up Pizzo di Campiano, the peak immediately facing Mount Belvedere, to assess the strength of the German emplacements. The patrol, moving with rifles and ammunition but without packs, skied as far as they could, but when the cliffs became too steep they cached their skis and began free-climbing up the rock face.

Nearly five hours after leaving their camp at Ca' di Julio, a tiny hamlet of stone houses and barns, the men hauled themselves up to the lip of the ridge. Suddenly a dog barked. A German soldier came through the trees to the edge of the cliff, looked around, and turned back. No one there, as far as he could see, and who could blame him? The cliff was unclimbable. Just below his line of sight, Casperson and his men crouched against the side of the wall.

Again the dog barked. This time, three Germans—one carrying a carbine, the other two unarmed—came to the edge, and saw the climbers. Carl Casperson and another soldier named Sangree Froelicher raised their tommy guns, and Casperson ordered the men, in English, to put their hands in the air. The German with the carbine—as much in danger of falling dead from surprise as from the American weapons—moved for his gun. Casperson and Froelicher let go with their tommy guns, killing all three Germans, and bolted back down the cliff. German mortars and machine guns opened up all over the ridge. Clearly, the early intelligence had underestimated the German presence on the ridge. There weren't three positions on Riva Ridge, there were at least eighteen. There wasn't just one observation post, there were at least four. How many men were up there was still anybody's guess.

Back on the ground, the reconnaissance team reported that any assault on the ridge would indeed require more than one route. Theirs, now dubbed Route Number 1, was difficult enough to rule out all but the best climbers. The last section of the climb would almost surely have to be conducted using fixed ropes. For a large-scale attack, more routes would have to be found, both for less skilled climbers and to get ammunition and supplies up for the duration of the attack and for the defense of the ridgetop. More exploration patrols were needed.

With the whole precipitous ridgeline covered by snow and ice, even assessing possible routes up the ridge was proving difficult. The fact that so few mountain supplies had made it to the front made the patrols that much harder. Soldiers cut up mattress covers to fashion makeshift tunics. In the absence of crampons, which they couldn't even get from local alpine clubs, soldiers fixed "creepers" made of knotted ropes to the soles of their leather and rubber shoepacs to help with footing on icy slopes. They borrowed skis from local Italian ski clubs and used them with regular GI shoes; there were so few complete sets of skis, snowshoes, and winter camouflage clothing that soldiers swapped them from platoon to platoon and company to company regardless of fit. For all the equipment testing, for all the months spent training at altitudes three times higher than anything they would climb in Italy, when the moment of battle finally arrived the mountain troops had to rely on the one thing they had come to have more confidence in than technology: their instincts in rough country. Even without their fancy gear, the men had deep reserves of alpine intelligence.[21]

Finally, with the help of some local partisans who knew the mountains well, a trail was picked running from tiny Ca' di Julio up to the summit of Mount Cappel Buso that even mules could navigate once the deep snow had been sufficiently packed down. The trail to the summit, they estimated, would take a soldier, unloaded, about four hours of rough hiking. The trail was wide enough to allow mules to pass in both directions and did not require technical climbing at any point. The only problem was that the route was completely exposed along its entire length—right, left, and

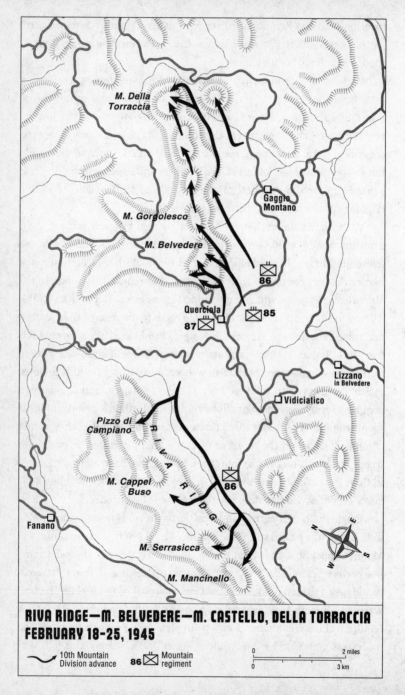

RIVA RIDGE—M. BELVEDERE—M. CASTELLO, DELLA TORRACCIA
FEBRUARY 18-25, 1945

10th Mountain Division advance

86 Mountain regiment

0 — 2 miles
0 — 3 km

front—to small-arms fire. Like much of the rest of Riva Ridge, Route Number 2 could be scouted only at night.[22]

WITH TWO ROUTES already scouted by the end of January, the 86th spent the first two weeks of February off the front in corps reserve in the town of Lucca, twenty-five miles to the southwest, to rest up and train for one of the most daring assaults of the war. Soldiers practiced moving over the roughest terrain they could find. A local marble quarry offered them the chance to buff up their technical climbing skills, to prepare them to carry weapons and supplies up a vertical face. This final training was little different from the rock climbing they had practiced for years at Camp Hale, except that now figuring out how to find a toehold on an icy rock face while making sure their grenades remained in their pockets was no longer a game.

Meanwhile, one platoon from the 86th, under the command of Lieutenant Wilson Ware, remained at La Ca' to continue patrolling the two trails leading to the ridge and to try to find others. Ware and his men quickly discovered two more: Trail Number 3, discovered by Lieutenant John McCown, led directly to the top of Mount Serrasiccia. Moving first across a deep gorge, the trail crossed the Dardagna River before ending near a set of abandoned buildings fifteen hundred feet below the top. From this point, reaching the summit would require scrambling over very rough terrain; at least six fixed ropes would be required for troops to make it over a series of rock ledges and two small cliffs. Because of its difficulty, Trail Number 3 would initially be used only for supply and evacuation until lateral routes could be established from the peak of Mount Cappel Buso.

Lieutenant Gordon Anderson of Company A discovered a fourth route that led south along the Dardagna before heading up a steep talus slope, through a tree-covered canyon, and up to the summit of Mount Mancinello by way of Mount Cingio del Bure. Although thick tree cover protected this route from small-arms fire from the flanks, anyone following this route would be extremely vulnerable from above, where the Germans could look right down upon them.[23]

Company F found a fifth route from Madonna del Acero up to Le Piagge, the high ground south of Mount Mancinello.

As the final routes were selected, Lieutenant Ware kept vigilant patrols over the trails and kept his eyes on the changing winter weather. Plans for the attack were kept strictly secret; no orders were to be given until seven days before the attack was to be launched. Some of Hays's advisers were skeptical about the plan to attack Belvedere at night. One officer showed the general a study printed by the Fifth Army describing its bad luck with the Apennines the previous fall.

"When was this published?" Hays demanded.

"Three months ago."

"Well then, don't you think by now the enemy has a copy? He wouldn't expect a night attack, and we should be successful."[24]

THE TASK OF TAKING the ridge, Hays decided, would fall to a select group of men from the 1st Battalion of the 86th Regiment, plus one additional company, F-86. They would attack the ridge under cover of darkness and as quietly as possible, to avoid arousing suspicions on Riva Ridge and on Mount Belvedere across the valley. If all went according to plan, Riva Ridge would be secured without the bulk of the German defenses on Belvedere realizing it.

The plan was that at one hour after midnight, the night after Riva Ridge was secured, the full force of the 85th and 87th Regiments would attack the Belvedere-Torraccia massif. The 87th would split into three sections on Belvedere's western edge, pushing through the hamlets of Corona, Rocca Corneta Polla, and Florio. The 85th, in two halves, would move up the center and eastern flanks until it had secured the length of the ridgeline. At daylight, after this attack, the air corps would arrive in a flurry, bombing and strafing German positions in support of the assault. Again, if everything went according to plan, the mountaintops would fall like dominoes, from the five peaks of Riva Ridge to the three large humps leading northeast from Belvedere to della Torraccia. If the attack on Riva Ridge failed, the plan to attack Mount Belvedere would have to be scrapped. Three months before, Americans had held Belvedere's summit for all of three days before being forced off by a German counterattack. There was no way General Hays was going to put that many elite soldiers in a shooting gallery. For the men of the 86th, hanging it out on the cliffs of Riva

Ridge in the division's first real wartime mountain maneuver, the assault offered the chance to finally prove their value to the American fight in Europe.

At their training ground at Lucca, men were organized into assault forces. Officers initially decided to handpick the regiment's best mountaineers to form assault platoons for the mission's spearhead but decided instead to keep small units intact. Company commanders were asked to pick existing platoons to lead the way. In addition to the assault teams, captains chose trail parties of three or four men that would lead the platoons up the mountain. On the most difficult routes, Numbers 1 and 3, the trail parties would drive pitons into the rock using hammers wrapped in cloth to muffle their sound and fix ropes up the face. As they reached their respective summits, the trail teams would yield to the assault platoons.

The men were told that after they had secured the ridge they would be relieved within twenty-four hours. This turned out to be an underestimation of vast proportions. What they were not told was that the army expected a 90 percent casualty rate. Some seven hundred of the soldiers were not expected to return in one piece. Medics in the battalion aid station far below the ridge feared that casualties would overwhelm their capacity to treat them.[25]

As the time for the assault neared, each platoon leader was given a map of the ridge. Quietly, at night, soldiers settled into tiny clusters of homes in Ca' di Julio and Farno, villages clinging to the shadows beneath the ridge named for the several generations of families that were their only inhabitants. The soldiers were ordered to remain inside old stone houses with guards posted at all windows and doors. By February 12, the snow—most of it melted, the rest packed down by frequent patrols—was no longer an issue. Soldiers could finally move about without skis, which came as a relief even to people like C Company's Howard Koch, a platoon leader who had become an expert mountaineer at Camp Hale. He found himself a platoon leader, helping to plan the assault on Serrasiccia.

During the lead-up to the attack on Riva Ridge, Koch saw the tension starting to play on the minds of the soldiers. At San Marcello, he watched a major named Graham Espey screaming at some Italian children who made the mistake of asking the wrong man for a food handout. Coming to the kids' defense, a mortar man got into it so deeply with the major that

Koch worried that the officer might end up facedown in the dirt. Intervening, Koch asked the apoplectic major to join him for a cup of coffee. Espey turned his fury on Koch, and only an intervention by Captain Worth McClure kept the major from having Koch arrested for insubordination. A short time later, the battalion commander, Lieutenant Colonel Henry Hampton himself, stopped by to inspect Koch's platoon. Koch thought his time had come. "I understand you've met Major Espey," Hampton said. "Don't you worry about a thing."[26]

ON FEBRUARY 15, three days before the assault, the battalion commander and each of the company commanders flew over the ridgeline for a final reconnaissance. Although the pilots of the small planes were forced to remain far above the summits to avoid fire from below, the flights did allow the officers to scan the ridgeline. They noted that a knife-edge they dubbed Ridge X, running west of Mount Cappel Buso and perpendicular to the rest of the ridgeline, would provide an exceptional observation point for the attack on della Torraccia and Belvedere and would make a good place to add to the posts to fend off any German counterattacks on Mount Serrasiccia.

The final plan was now in place. The men of the 86th's 1st Battalion would attack Riva Ridge in five columns, using the five different trails. Captain Kenneth Seigman's B Company, supported by machine gunners and two mortar sections from D Company, would attack Mount Cappel Buso. Captain Worth McClure's C Company, with mortar and machine gun support from D Company, would climb Trail Number 3 to take Ridge X on Mount Serrasiccia. Captain Percy Rideout, a former champion ski racer, would lead F Company, with mortar and machine-gun support from H Company, up Trail Number 5 on Cingio del Bure. Meanwhile, Captain William Neidner, a former cross-country ski racer, would lead A Company up Trail Number 4 to Mount Mancinello; leaving a platoon there to hold the summit, the company would proceed on to relieve C Company on Mount Serrasiccia. C Company, in turn, would shift over and make the assault on Ridge X.[27]

The most difficult assignment, the technical climb up Pizzo di Campiano itself, would be carried out by a single platoon, split off from

Company A and led by Lieutenant James Loose. Before the assault was over, Loose and his men would become the first real heroes of the 10th Mountain Division, and not simply because they managed to climb the unclimbable.

Since the overarching objective in taking Riva Ridge was to assist in the assault on Mount Belvedere, the plan dictated that once the ridge had been secured, men would haul four .50-caliber machine guns and one 75-mm pack howitzer to the top of the ridge. Once there, the guns could fire directly on the German line between Rocca Corneta, a strongly held natural fortress to the east of Pizzo di Campiano, and the towns of Polla and Corona. But getting such heavy equipment up the mountain would be no easy trick; the howitzers alone weighed 1,300 pounds. Supply for the whole operation would be handled by thirty small mules from an Italian pack company and a porter platoon from the 86th made up of men not assigned to the assault platoons. Officers made the supply priorities clear: ammunition up, first and always. Second, evacuation of wounded soldiers down. Third, food and water up.

Communications during the attack would be a special challenge, since the need for silence made the nighttime use of radios out of the question. Just prior to the assault, a small advance party laid phone wire, concealed in the snow, from battalion command at Farne to all areas of departure. The plan was for a wire team to follow each column during the assault and provide hourly location reports back to command.

The soldiers themselves were heavily loaded. Riflemen carried ninety-six rounds of ammunition, twice the usual amount. Those with carbines carried at least two extra boxes of fifty rounds each. Most men in the weapons platoons carried two thousand rounds per light machine gun; others carried even more, though they were told to drop the extra rounds if the going got too difficult. Each member of the mortar squads packed twenty-four rounds; optimistic about the potential targets awaiting them once they reached the top, even officers and sergeants agreed to carry three mortar shells apiece.[28]

Each assault platoon would be equipped with one of the new A-6 machine guns and at least six tommy guns. From the ground, weapons in support of the climbs would range from field artillery and .50-caliber machine guns firing directly on Pizzo di Campiano and Mount Cappel Buso to 75-mm pack howitzers firing from near La Ca' to a platoon of medium tanks in position for direct fire on Pizzo di Campiano, Mount Cappel Buso, and Mount Serrasiccia. Like the men assaulting the ridge, the troops manning the guns were given orders not to fire until ordered by the battalion commander.

Once the ridge had been safely secured, engineers would attempt an audacious project: building a 1,500-foot aerial tramway from the top of Cappel Buso down to Ca' di Julio, to help bring supplies up and the dead and wounded down. This feat of engineering, though not completed until after the fighting was largely over, proved to be one of the division's most remarkable accomplishments.[29]

By far the best thing the 86th had going for it was surprise. As the men knew from the three unsuccessful attempts the Fifth Army had already made in the area, no amount of fire from below could knock the Germans off Riva Ridge. The other advantage the men of the 86th had, given their fitness and training, was speed. All ascents were to be done between nightfall and sunrise on the morning of the nineteenth. At eleven on the night of the nineteenth, the real show, the battle for Mount Belvedere, would begin, under the full fury of the entire rest of the 10th Mountain Division.[30]

THESE FINAL DAYS had left the men on the ground extremely jumpy. Asleep one night under a tree, Dan Kennerly, the football player from Georgia, was awakened by a noise that sounded "like a Chinese New Year's celebration." He jumped to his feet, sure the war was on, only to discover that one of the kitchen mules, carrying two garbage cans full of pots and pans, had panicked and gone racing down the valley through his entire regiment. Grateful for the cause but worried that the noise might alert the enemy, Kennerly finally became convinced that every German for miles around must be "deaf, drunk or sound asleep."

On Friday, February 16, the men about to attack Mount Belvedere were treated to a rare address by General Hays, who spoke to them in a natural amphitheater. Kennerly couldn't take his eyes off the man who over the next weeks and months would determine the fate of the Italian campaign and the thousands of soldiers who fought in it. Hays reminded

Kennerly of an old, saddle-worn cowhand. The general was wiry and had dark, deep-set eyes, his thin black hair topping a tanned, deeply lined, and weather-beaten face. His head seemed too big for his body, and he had the biggest ears Kennerly "had ever seen on a human."[31]

Hays began by saying that he had never before discussed a combat plan with troops at the ground level, but that the intelligence and esprit de corps of the 10th had left him feeling these were "the finest troops I've ever been associated with."

Once Riva Ridge had been secured, Hays said, the attack on Mount Belvedere would utilize the entire force of his division, plus supporting artillery, armor, and airpower. Five battalions would make the initial assault, he told them. The 85th's 3rd Battalion would assault the summit of Mount Belvedere. The 85th's 1st Battalion would take Mount Gorgolesco, just to the right of Mount Belvedere. Simultaneously, a two-pronged attack by the 87th would attempt to secure Belvedere's left flank, the 1st Battalion capturing Valpiana Ridge to the northwest, the 2nd Battalion capturing the area between Corona and Florio. Over on the right flank, the 86th's 3rd Battalion would move along the lower reaches of the mountains, parallel to and in support of the 85th.[32]

Then Hays paused. He cast his eyes over the men. They leaned forward to hear him. The 10th would spearhead the campaign, Hays said, and each soldier, no matter how tough the fighting got, must push ahead relentlessly. "Continue to move forward," Hays said. "Never stop. Always forward. Always forward. Always forward. If your buddy is wounded, don't stop to help him. Continue to move forward. Always forward. Don't get pinned down. Never stop. When the assault comes, you must get into the enemy's position as quickly as possible. You must move fast. Don't give the enemy time to recover. Shoot him. You must take his position.

"In the days to come, those of you who survive must learn to relax and enjoy yourself," Hays continued. "You will be given time out of the line when you can rest and see the sights. You should go to all the historical places that you can in Italy, because remember you may not get back this way again. To the victors go the spoils. Take trophies, souvenirs, cameras, guns, pistols, and watches, ship them home. Someday you can show them to your grandchildren." He paused again.

"Good luck."

The general, Dan Kennerly decided, would make a hell of a football coach.[33]

On the morning of the assault on Riva Ridge, Sunday, February 18, Dan Kennerly and his first gunner marched through ankle-deep mud with backpacks and machine guns on their backs toward the departure point near Mount Belvedere. The going was slow and eerie. A thick fog covered the ground, and the foot soldiers had to peer into the soup just to see the man in line ahead. They passed houses with shadowy figures inside and braced for sniper fire. In the near distance, cannon fire echoed across the valley.

Later that night, Kennerly looked up to see powerful antiaircraft searchlights beamed on the peaks of Riva Ridge; reflecting off the low-hanging clouds, the floodlights created a kind of false moonlight. Beamed from seven miles behind the front, the lights were intended to blind the Germans on top of the ridge even as they kept the slopes—and the 10th's approach—in complete darkness.

Once the sun went down, the evening of the eighteenth turned wet and cold, with temperatures in the valley hovering just above freezing. How cold it would be on top of the mountains was hard to predict; all the men knew was that it would be colder than it was down below. Remarkably, for troops who had spent three years testing mountain equipment, the men assaulting Riva Ridge and Mount Belvedere would have to make do without their sleeping bags, which still had not arrived. If they ever found a chance to sleep, which seemed unlikely, they would have to wrap themselves in wool blankets.

A dusting of new snow had covered the mountain's upper slopes and left the valley floor a swamp of mud and ice. Sporadic shell bursts flared and died over the upper slopes, casting a glow over the top of Mount Belvedere. Poring over their maps of Riva Ridge just a few hours before the attack began, officers in A Company had decided that their objective, Trail Number 4 to Mount Mancinello, would be too difficult for their men to cover in time to be effective. Just to the south, trail Number 5, which had been assigned to F Company, seemed far easier, and since F Company was scheduled to depart nearly three hours later, Captain Neidner and an Italian-speaking messenger took off for regimental headquarters to ask permission to switch trails. The sudden change in plans was unnerving so close to the time of attack, but permission was granted. The attack on the ridge would proceed along four trails instead of five.[34]

AT 7:30 P.M., THE SUN DOWN, Bob Frauson and the rest of A Company—minus its platoon under Lieutenant Loose, over on Pizzo di Campiano—took off for the top of Riva Ridge and moved westward toward Mount Mancinello. Each man had a piece of white adhesive tape with his name on it stuck to the back of his helmet to help the line stay intact. The trail up the valley along the side of the river was good, and the company moved quickly. After a mile and a half of walking, A Company turned west and began to climb.

Almost immediately the hiking got tough. The trail on the way up the mountain was poorly marked and tangled with brush. The footing was terrible, particularly in the dark. At first the men were given a five-minute break every half hour, but as the march went on the breaks became more and more frequent until finally the entire line stopped for five minutes after every ten minutes of walking. With the slope so steep and the darkness so complete, just keeping track of the man in front became next to impossible.[35]

Every odd stone, every misshapen tree, became in the darkness the silhouette of a German soldier. Although the men in the assault platoon, with their lighter loads, were able to move along quite easily, the wire team kept falling farther and farther back. Finally, communications with battalion headquarters—scheduled for every hour during the climb—had to be abandoned.

When the bulk of A Company reached the summit of Cingio del Bure just before 1 A.M., two men from the assault platoon reported that the peak had been secured with no resistance. The Germans were either still sleeping or had abandoned their position. More heartening still, it turned out that in their overconfidence about the security of their position, the Germans had not placed lateral communications of their own along the ridge top; there was no way for any of the besieged outposts to call ahead to the others. Once the wire team caught up, A Company reported its success and set off for the main objective: Mount Mancinello.[36]

Once again, the assault platoon, under Lieutenant John Youmans, made quick work of the trail and arrived on top of the thinly wooded peak of Mount Mancinello without meeting resistance. The rest of the company arrived at 1:30 A.M. Platoons spread out to secure the snow-covered ridge; a fog that crept in at 2:00 made walking near the edge of the east rim's seventy-foot cliff treacherous. Looking northwest, toward the German side of the mountains, the men could tell, even in the dark, that the slope was far gentler than the one they had just climbed; more a sloping meadow than a precipitous drop, it fell off into a broad valley.

Once they reached the top of Mount Mancinello, A Company tried to dig in but found the open, snowy ground impenetrably frozen and rocky. Moving quickly, they gathered as many stones as they could carry and constructed defensive positions. The men paired off, not only to protect each other's backs but to share blankets and body heat. Sleeping on top of a mountain with so little protection would require a great deal of energy simply to stay warm. When the wire team finally arrived shortly before 3:00 in the morning, Captain Neidner was finally able to talk to a sergeant down at Poggiolforato, more than five miles away. About this time, down at the base of Trail Number 2, a platoon of pack mules—having already marched some twenty miles under the guidance of the Italian Alpini—began moving 50-mm machine guns to the top of Mount Cappel Buso, where the guns would support the attack on Rocca Corneta. One mule carried a howitzer tube to the top and immediately dropped dead from exhaustion.

Moving anxiously up Mount Serrasiccia, Howard Koch and the rest of C Company had done their best to feel their way in the blackness. If darkness protected the climbers against being seen by the Germans, it did nothing to prevent their hearing the attack, and to Koch the approach seemed thunderous. Heavy breathing. Boots crunching over snow. Rifle butts and rucksacks banging into rocks. To allay his fears, he kept his eyes focused on the backside of the man in front of him. The footing here, too, was awful, and the line moved haltingly, like an accordion. From time to time someone up front would quietly tap in a piton and drop a rope for the others to use as a handhold. A loud slip could have been disastrous.

Once on top, the advance party discovered a series of small wooden huts the Germans had built along the ridge. They sneaked up to one but, peering in through the windows, couldn't tell if anyone was home. They didn't knock. They dropped grenades down the chimney and blew the door off. Nobody home. As the rest of the advance team occupied the hut, one of Howard Koch's machine gunners, Jacques Parker, moved off to a wooded area to collect the rest of the company. As he walked through the darkness, whistling out a birdcall he had told his men would be his signal, Parker prayed the men in his company wouldn't mistake him for a lone German. A hand reached out and yanked Parker behind a tree. He had made it.

C Company dug trenches in the snow near where the main ridge met the slope to Ridge X and waited. They were in charge of a piece of high ground between A Company on Mancinello and B Company on Cappel Buso, but with no communication wires yet running along the ridge, they had to run foot patrols between the teams on their two wings. Since the German reinforcements were bound to come up the comparatively gentle slope from the towns of Fanano and Sestola, all the men in C Company had to do was wait. All along the ridgeline an eerie mist had begun to settle in, covering the peaks with a soup that left the assault troops straining to see even their own men. Yet the cover the fog provided was more than anyone could have hoped for. The climb had been completed in utter secrecy.[37]

Heavily armed with submachine guns and grenades, a squad from A Company's assault platoon took off in the fog and snow to search for an underground German shelter that intelligence had revealed would be waiting for them. Visibility was terrible; even in the growing daylight, men could still see only about ten yards ahead of them, so the squad had to move gingerly along the precipitous edge of the ridgeline. Twice the men set out, and twice they returned without having found the shelter. Neidner decided to wait for the fog to lift. Bob Frauson, who had saved two men from slipping over the cliff during the reconnaissance climb the month before, dug a grave for a dead German soldier, but the man did not stay buried for long. When a member of A Company straggled to the summit sometime after the rest of the unit, Frauson saw he had made the climb in regular army shoes. He told the soldier that there was a nice pair of mountain boots on the dead German's feet; all he had to do was dig him up and swap shoes. He did.[38]

At 4:15 A.M., the deep voice of Colonel Tomlinson, the regimental commander, boomed over Captain Neidner's phone, demanding news. No one had heard from the team on Pizzo di Campiano, and the colonel was getting antsy.[39]

As dawn spread across the ridge, the fog settled in thicker than ever. All along the ridgeline soldiers dug into position and prepared for the attack. The Germans, apparently, were still safely tucked in bed, oblivious to what was accumulating around them.

Over on top of Mount Cappel Buso, porters dropped off the four .50-caliber machine guns for D Company's weapons platoon, which promptly began moving them toward Pizzo di Campiano. The wire between the two peaks was still out, so the transport team had no idea what to expect once they got there. Even before they arrived, they had to deal with problems of their own. As they moved along the ridge, a German machine gun opened up on their advance patrol, wounding a lieutenant and his four men. Apparently, at least a handful of Germans had finally figured out that something was happening on the line between Mount Cappel Buso and Pizzo di Campiano. Forced to abandon the plan to take the guns to Pizzo di Campiano, the weapons team dug the guns in on Cappel Buso, where they could still fire at Rocca Corneta, albeit from farther away.

By 8:30 A.M., all across the ridge, the sun had begun to creep through the soup. Looking around his company's position, A Company's Captain Neidner was impressed. Even putting their position together in the dark, they had managed to place their machine guns almost perfectly; each one had a full range of fire over an unbroken field of hard-packed snow. Observation was excellent in all positions as well. Most amazing, however, was the absolute clarity with which he could see the movements of people and vehicles in the valley below. No wonder the Germans had been able to hold the ridge for so long. Come daylight, there would be no moving anywhere without attracting attention. Trying to attack the southeastern slope of the ridge would have been foolish, even suicidal, during the day. A few hours later a report, gleaned from a number of German prisoners, came in from regimental headquarters down in the valley. No one in the German command had had any idea they would be attacked on Riva Ridge. The surprise had been complete.[40]

Almost as soon as they were able to see anything at all, observers in A Company spotted a single man dressed in a white parka and carrying a single ski pole crossing a snowfield about five hundred yards away and two hundred feet downhill. Apparently unaware of what had happened while he had been asleep, the man seemed to be out for a stroll. His morning constitutional was soon interrupted. Every man in the company opened fire. The target scampered like a scared rabbit across the field and finally dived into a hole in the ground. A Company had found the bunker.

As Neidner watched, twelve Germans popped out of the hole and ran to what seemed to be prearranged positions. At first, they did not return A Company's fire, probably because they were unable to get a clear line of fire shooting uphill into a position far better than their own.

Platoon sergeant Torger Tokle, the greatest ski jumper in the world, led an assault on the bunker. Slipping away from the cliff, the platoon was well covered by the men back in the company's original position and remained invisible to the Germans below. As the platoon approached the bunker, supporting fire from the company rained down, keeping the Germans pinned down inside. Finally, with the platoon in position, the supporting fire stopped. After just fifteen minutes, the battle was over. Four Germans, including the ranking NCO, were killed, and eight more were captured. The bunker itself turned out to be a log cabin, large enough to house fifteen men, that had been completely buried in snow. Tokle grabbed a German pistol to commemorate the platoon's first assault. Other men wrestled over a lone pair of skis. Later, before turning them over as a gift for the mess sergeant back at the company command post, they tried the skis out on the slopes of Mancinello.[41]

The prisoners, all middle-aged men, seemed utterly stunned that they had been captured. They confessed to having heard a commotion in the valley the night before but thought nothing of it. The southeastern slope, they had been certain, was invulnerable to any force large enough for them to worry about.

WITH ALL OBJECTIVES on the ridge secured—and with surprisingly little resistance—all attention turned to Lieutenant Loose and his men climbing Pizzo di Campiano, the butt of the ridge closest to Mount Belvedere. Loose still had not reported in. Finally, at 5:45 A.M., just before daylight, Loose wired in from the top of the ridge. It had been a hell of a climb.

Throughout the night, the searchlights had bounced off the clouds and scattered eerie light along the ridge top. Whenever the team had stopped for a rest, each man had been ordered to turn around and tap the man behind him, to let him know when the climb was moving on. But in the darkness, the men had still gotten separated, and soon the team had been scattered up and down the trail. Up front, Loose's immediate team had been reduced to just twelve men. Worse, the fog had become so thick that the wire party, moving ahead of the rest of the men with a forward observer, had gotten lost. They wouldn't be found until the next day. At some point during the assault, a German patrol must have discovered the wire between Cappel Buso and Pizzo di Campiano, because suddenly all contact with the men on top of Campiano was lost.[42]

The climb was all the more frightening because the men still had no idea exactly what was waiting for them up there. Was it only an observation team, positioned to spot Mount Belvedere? Or was it a large unit, fully capable of defending Pizzo di Campiano itself? Every minute of the climb the men in the lead waited to be cut apart by machine-gun fire from above. These were fearful minutes. From the time they left camp until the time they reached the top, the Loose team climbed for nine hours.

Harry Reinig, climbing right next to Loose, helped the team negotiate the fixed ropes that had been placed around a fifty-yard patch of ice, formed over a natural spring. Shortly after this, they passed a small stone building that the team's medics would use as their aid station. Loose told Reinig to remember its location, in case anyone needed to find cover there in the dark.

Toward the top, Reinig and Loose hit a slope of scree—tennis ball–sized gravel difficult to negotiate and even harder to climb silently. Suddenly, a German "potato masher" grenade rolled down toward Loose's feet. He picked it up and threw it back into the fog before it exploded. The fight was on. From everywhere and nowhere came the pinging of small-arms fire and the explosion of German grenades. Loose ran through an entire clip from his carbine, at no one in particular. He just shot into the darkness and hoped for the best.

Luckily for Loose and Reinig, up high before the rest of their team, the Germans—as confused as they by the utter darkness—misjudged the location as well as the intention of the assault team. They clearly figured it was another small patrol, lost in the mist and now retreating. As quickly as it had begun, the German fire ceased. Loose later learned that the Germans had thought the assault team was lost and had turned back for the valley floor. Not worthy of their attention.

Around 4 A.M., Reinig and Loose hauled themselves over the top of the ridge and to their amazement found the Germans still sleeping soundly in foxholes and a four-person log lean-to. The advance team loaded up a bazooka and a light machine gun. A blast from the bazooka killed one German soldier inside the lean-to and brought another man running straight into a quick burst from the machine gun. For the moment, all was quiet on Pizzo di Campiano.[43]

By 6:30, the rest of the platoon, about thirty men, finally made it to the top. After manning the foxholes the Germans had prepared along the ridge, Loose and a small patrol began attacking the German gun emplacements. After a couple of brief skirmishes, Loose managed to capture two foxholes brimming with mortars and ammunition. They set them on fire, setting off an impromptu fireworks that let the Germans know their control of the ridgeline was now officially in dispute.

As happy as they were with the ease of the fight so far, Loose would tell the writer Flint Whitlock, he and his men realized that the ridge was far more heavily protected than they had imagined. Scouting along with another soldier, Sergeant James Germond, Loose told his companion to stay calm. He could sense an attack, even if he had no idea where the Germans were hiding.

"Watch it—I feel it," he said.

"So do I."

Suddenly, an American machine gun burst out to the left. Another of Loose's men had decided to trigger the ambush before the Germans were ready. To his right, Loose could see a German machine gun pointing out from underneath an evergreen, maybe thirty feet away. Too close, he thought. This is it. I'm done.

But Germond saw the gun, too, and opened fire. Frantically spraying his own weapon, Loose shot at the barrel sticking out from under the tree, killing the gunner, as Germond took out the loader. The German machine gun never even fired. Bewildered, Loose went in for a closer look. Incredible, he thought. The Germans had been so complacent about the possibility of an attack that as Loose and Germond approached they were caught cleaning their weapons in preparation for a later maneuver. Once they realized that the battle was joined, the loader had been so confused that he had inserted the bolt backward. No wonder it hadn't fired.

For Loose and his men, however, things changed very quickly. Private William Godwin took a bullet to the head and dropped like a stone. Spotting a rush of German soldiers 150 yards ahead, Germond shouted to a half-dozen members of his team to get into position and take aim. Germond's shooters took out the entire assault. At this very moment, a wounded German prisoner slipped away from his captors, dropped into a dugout, grabbed a burp gun, and fired a burst at Harry Reinig. Apparently the German's excitement at his good fortune ruined his aim, and all his shots missed. An American named Frank Fairweather sprayed his grease gun at the dugout and convinced the German to surrender for the second time that day.[44]

AS THE SUN ROSE HIGHER, Germans farther down the ridge began to emerge from their quarters. Only some seemed to realize that the end was at hand. Over by the intersection with Ridge X, the men in C Company looked up to see a group of German soldiers approaching; incredibly, they seemed to be waving. They still had no idea what had happened. The C men waved back. Then, before the rest of C Company knew what was happening, a man whose duties to this point had largely been limited to cooking the company's meals got nervous and fired. The ascending Germans were dumbstruck. Why would their own artillery observers be firing on them? Only then did they realize that the impossible had happened. Their men, so secure in their roosts atop the ridge, had somehow been routed out. As the rest of C Company opened fire, the Germans bolted. "Let's face it. This was our first baptism, so you can forgive him," Koch would say later of the cook. "We weren't really prepared, but if we had let them come, we might have gotten the whole bunch." An hour later, the remaining Germans tried to mount a counterattack but were pinned down by C Company's relentless fire from machine guns, artillery, and mortars.

By midafternoon, the Germans tried again. Again they were turned back. Not everything went C Company's way. Sometime later, an aid man, wearing a brightly painted Red Cross helmet, was out in the field attending to a wounded soldier when a German sniper shot him dead.

Indeed, the Germans seemed to make a habit of playing with the ethics of combat. Shortly after the death of the aid man, Lieutenant John

LIFE

MOUNTAIN TROOPER

NOVEMBER 9, 1942 **10** CENTS

YEARLY SUBSCRIPTION $4.50

Life magazine cover, November 9, 1942. The intense media coverage given to the mountain troops not only detailed their training but served as a remarkably effective recruiting tool.

Photo by J. R. Eyerman. Time Life Pictures / Getty Images.

Minnie Dole (center), a civilian skier from New England who became the driving force behind the mountain troops, flanked by Roger Langley (left), president of the National Ski Association, and Paul Lafferty, one of the division's earliest members.

Courtesy Denver Public Library, Western History Collection.

The First Battalion of the 87th Mountain Infantry Regiment, Paradise Valley, Washington, May 1942.

Photo by Charles C. Bradley. Courtesy Denver Public Library, Western History Collection.

John B. Woodward (foreground) and Peter Gabriel practice ice-climbing techniques on Nisqualli Glacier, Mt. Rainier, Washington, June 1942.

Courtesy Denver Public Library, Western History Collection.

Denis Nunan, from Short Hills, New Jersey. Before the war, Nunan said the highest he had ever climbed was "to the top of a Fifth Avenue bus."

Courtesy Denver Public Library, Western History Collection.

Torger Tokle, a Norwegian, held the world record in ski jumping before joining the mountain troops.

Photo courtesy of Bob Frauson.

Gene Hames, a rural Montanan before the war, led an amphibious assault on Mussolini's villa on the shore of Lake Garda.

Photo courtesy of Gene Hames.

Stuart Abbott, a soldier from Chicago, hoped for a life as a field naturalist after the war.

Photo courtesy of Abbie Kealy.

Camp Hale from above. Situated at 9,200 feet, the camp was surrounded by mountains that offered both excellent ski training and inescapable smog from locomotives and furnaces.

Photo by David B. Allen. Courtesy Denver Public Library, Western History Collection.

Mountain soldiers field training with skis and poles on their backs.

Photo by Curt Kreiser. Denver Public Library, Western History Collection.

Practicing a traverse near Camp Hale, May 1943. Advanced climbing and rescue techniques became one of the division's lasting postwar legacies.

Photo by C. M. Molenaar. Courtesy Denver Public Library, Western History Collection.

Dick Wilson, an expert skier from New England, in a shelter made of pine boughs near Camp Hale.

Photo courtesy of Dick Wilson.

A destroyed Japanese
submarine base on the
Aleutian island of Kiska,
site of one of the war's
eeriest encounters,
September 7, 1943.
U.S. Army photograph.
Courtesy Denver Public Library,
Western History Collection.

Unloading supplies after
the ill-fated assault on
Kiska Beach. Mountain
troops remained on the
island for four months,
learning to survive in
Arctic conditions.
Courtesy Denver Public Library,
Western History Collection.

Mules at Camp Hale occasionally had to maneuver through shoulder-deep trenches.

Photo by C. M. Molenaar. Courtesy Denver Public Library, Western History Collection.

Hugh Evans, a prep school boy from California, drying socks during the infamous D Series, considered one of the most rigorous exercises in military history. Evans would later win a Silver Star in Italy.
Courtesy Denver Public Library, Western History Collection.

Famous Arctic explorer Vilhjalmur Stefansson instructed the mountain troops in winter survival techniques, including igloo construction at Camp Hale, September 1943. *Courtesy Denver Public Library, Western History Collection.*

Dan Kennerly (second from left) and his machine-gun squad. Before the war, the Georgia native thought skiers treated their boards with beeswax.

Photo courtesy of Dan Kennerly.

Riva Ridge, February 1945.

Courtesy Denver Public Library, Western History Collection.

The rescue tramline set up to relieve soldiers on Riva Ridge, built by a company of specially trained engineers, mirrored techniques learned from civilian mountaineers. *Photo courtesy of Bob Frauson.*

The summit of Mt. Belvedere, after the first day of fighting, February 19, 1945.

Photo by Richard Rocker. Courtesy Denver Public Library, Western History Collection.

**Explosion near
Mt. Della Spe,
April 14, 1945.**

*Photo by Roy O. Bingham.
Courtesy Denver Public Library,
Western History Collection.*

Returning from the front along the supply route for Mt. Belvedere, February 22, 1945.

Courtesy Denver Public Library, Western History Collection.

**Mules and troops
resting during a
break in battle,
February 1945.**

*Photo by Roy O. Bingham.
Courtesy Denver Public Library,
Western History Collection.*

Ruins of town of Castel d'Aiano, March 5, 1945.

Photo by Richard Rocker. Courtesy Denver Public Library, Western History Collection.

Italian Alpini mule train near Pietra Colera.

Photo by Richard Rocker. Courtesy Denver Public Library, Western History Collection.

General Mark W. Clark, commander of the Allied 15th Army Group, and General George P. Hays, commander of the 10th Mountain Division, confer before the spring offensive, April 1945.

*Photo by Roy O. Bingham.
Courtesy Denver Public Library,
Western History Collection.*

Crossing the Po River, April 24, 1945.

*Courtesy Denver Public Library,
Western History Collection.*

Soldiers and artillery
inside tunnel on Lake
Garda, where the
mountain troops ended
the war in Italy.
Photo by Richard Rocker.
Courtesy Denver Public Library,
Western History Collection.

Taps at American cemetery
at Castel Fiorentino near
Florence, April 6, 1945,
a week before the
division's worst losses.
Photo by Roy O. Bingham.
Courtesy Denver Public Library,
Western History Collection.

McCown, a member of the American Alpine Club, a friend of Howard Koch's, and the man who had discovered the route up Serrasiccia, was leading a patrol toward a forward position along Ridge X. Suddenly a group of Germans, waving the Red Cross flag and shouting "Friend," stood up with their hands in the air as if to surrender. As McCown's team approached, the Germans suddenly dropped to their knees and began firing, killing the lieutenant and two of his men and wounding six others. Aid men trying to help the wounded were also shot. A heavy American counterattack, with mortars, artillery, and machine guns, took control of the area, but the losses—and C Company's rage—were nonetheless deep. "McCown would always take you at your word; that may have been his undoing," Koch said. "He believed in the Geneva Conventions, but the Germans apparently didn't adhere to this."

To help C Company care for its dead and wounded, Bob Frauson and several others from A Company moved over from Mancinello to serve as litter bearers. "You could hardly tell the living from the dead, their shock was so bad," Frauson would say. Just getting to the men was dangerous; as he carried an empty litter over to Ridge X, German machine-gun fire cut the litter in half.

When Frauson arrived at C Company's position, he found that one of the injured was a soldier named Orville Bjorge, a Norwegian from Hot Springs, Montana, whom he had befriended back at Camp Hale. Bjorge was "white as a sheet of paper." Frauson loaded him into an abandoned German litter and helped carry him over to the top of Mount Cappel Buso, where the engineering company was busy stringing a tramway from the summit all the way to the valley floor. Bjorge would be one of the first to make the trip.

After McCown's death, C Company attacked Ridge X in earnest. With 30-caliber light machine guns and 60-mm mortars clearing their path, two rifle platoons performed what Koch considered a "perfect problem." They just walked right in and captured any Germans who hadn't already fled back down the hill.

With Ridge X now secure, C Company turned its attention to the German prisoners, whom they had been told to send back to A Company once it had moved over to Serrasiccia. One was a German officer who had been badly wounded in the groin and seemed to be bleeding to death. Koch spoke a bit of German and quickly discovered that the officer, even as he expired, was mean as a snake. Koch asked two mortar men to take the German back to A Company for interrogation. Even with his mortal wound and his arms draped over the shoulders of two American soldiers, the officer refused to stop fighting. He kept trying to kick the wire leading back to A Company with his hobnailed boots. A few moments later, Jacques Parker heard a crack and figured the German had been shot. Koch later heard that somebody had kicked the German down the ridge the men had come up. However the German met his end, A Company had one less POW to worry about.[45]

The importance of Riva Ridge to the Germans became evident by the intensity of the counterattack on Loose's position on Pizzo di Campiano. A little after 3 P.M., Loose's men began receiving sporadic bursts of sniper fire. From then on, all through the night, some forty German soldiers pecked away, creeping closer and closer with each volley. For the next thirty-six hours, hunkered down inside the well-fortified former German bunkers, Loose and his men withstood the worst pounding on all of Riva Ridge. Inside one foxhole, Harry Reinig could hear a soldier named Leon Mermet firing an automatic weapon. When Mermet was killed, the weapon kept firing, then became strangely muffled as Mermet fell face first into the snow.

When a burst from a German burp gun hit two soldiers named Al Fernandez and Stanley Milanowski, Reinig was ordered to climb five hundred yards back down the ridge to the stone building where medics had set up an impromptu aid station. Milanowski had been hit in the back of the neck, though since the bullets had somehow missed his bones and major blood vessels he was able to evacuate himself. Fernandez, hit in the chest, was less lucky. Reinig and two of the aid men managed to belay him three hundred yards down the ridge, where two other medics were able to take him in.[46]

As the second night wore on, Loose's team had run out of grenades and were almost out of ammunition. Loose and a forward observer named Frank Gorham decided to make a radical call: in addition to ordering relief from B Company on Mount Cappel Buso, they asked for artillery gunners to bring their fire in tight, within twenty-five yards of his unit's positions. At first the artillery men were reluctant to fire so close to their own men; what if they overshot? They would not only kill their own men, they might jeopardize the entire mission. Over and over, Loose called for the artillery fire; he had already lost one of his own men, he reported, and had five more wounded. Those who were left were running dangerously low on food and were forced to melt snow for water.

Finally, when the Germans had gotten close enough to lob grenades into their positions, Loose radioed down again, this time demanding artillery fire in a tight, unbroken ring around his bunkers. Again, the artillery gunners were reluctant to fire so close to Loose's team's fragile position. Lieutenant Loose bellowed into the radio, "Where's that artillery support? If it doesn't get here soon, you'll have nothing to support!"[47]

Finally the shells started to fall, and fall precisely. When a friendly round dropped just five yards from his men's position, Loose told the artillery men they had come close enough. Finally, the Germans backed off. As night fell after two days of relentless fighting, Loose looked up to see an American walking toward him. "You stupid ass," he yelled, "get your head down if you want to keep it on your shoulders!" The man was Henry Hampton himself, the battalion commander, personally leading a relief party. Given what he could see around Loose and his men, Hampton was relieved to find any members of Loose's battered platoon alive. Around the grounds where the battle had raged, twenty-six Germans lay dead. For their efforts on Pizzo di Campiano, Loose, Gorham, Fairweather, and Hampton received Silver Stars; every man in Loose's platoon received a Bronze.[48]

Riva Ridge was now secure. Not only had the five teams survived without suffering 90 percent casualties, not a single man of the thousand involved had been lost during the actual climbs of the ridge. During the counterattacks only twenty-one men had been killed, fifty-two wounded, and three taken prisoner.. Three more men were reported missing.

GETTING THE DEAD and wounded off the ridge proved significantly more difficult than anyone had expected. Hand-carrying a wounded soldier down the rocky slopes took more than twelve hours and risked turning rescues into funeral processions. Soon after the ridge was secured, however, division engineers from the 126th Engineers Company performed a remarkable feat. After building a road a mile and a half long to Farne at the base of Mount Cappel Buso, they constructed—in one eleven-hour day—a 1,500-foot aerial tramway that dramatically improved medical relief and food supplies for the men on top. Carrying seventy-pound loads on their backs, the engineers managed to string cable to a plateau three quarters of the way up the face; a pair of climbers had to tie quarter-inch wire cable around their waists to free their hands for the final climb. With a pair of eight-foot litters hung like cocoons from the wire, which itself ran through a winch at the boot, the tram cut the evacuation time from half a day to a matter of minutes and released three full crews of litter bearers—including Bob Frauson—from their arduous duties. Writing home to Minnie Dole, Lieutenant Bill McGuckin expressed the amazement felt by most of the foot soldiers. "The guys who built the Brooklyn Bridge better come over and see this one."[49]

On the first day of the operation, thirty wounded soldiers were evacuated and five tons of supplies delivered to the ridge top; by the twenty-first, some eleven tons of food and ammunition had been hauled up on the wire. Casualties weren't the only things sent down the mountain; C Company's Jacques Parker, who was also an artist, sent sketches down in an old mortar shell case. Five decades later, veterans would return to the spot where the tram had hit solid ground at Farno and place a plaque dedicated to the engineers: an etching of a beaver with a branch in its mouth and the Latin phrase *Aedificamus et Destruimus:* Build and destroy.[50]

Even with the fighting over, not all the needed supplies made it up to the men on the ridge. As the men from A Company settled in for their second night on Mount Serrasiccia, they learned that once again they would be without their bedrolls. The pack teams, overloaded with ammunition and food, had been too exhausted to bring up the company's personal gear, and the trail was far too steep for a mule train. The gear would travel by mechanized Weasel from Vidiciatico to Poggiolforato and be backpacked up from there.

At least as disappointing as the prospect of another cold night on the mountain, the men of A Company found that the darkness and fog would prevent them from watching the Big Show across the valley: the assault on Mount Belvedere.[51]

CHAPTER ELEVEN

MOUNT BELVEDERE

SEVERAL HOURS BEFORE DAWN on February 19, Dan Kennerly woke up cold. He and his platoon in the 85th's D Company were bunkered down in some woods below the slopes of Mount Belvedere, in an area known as Vaie di Sapre. At the front edge of the woods, engineers had strung tape to prevent soldiers from moving outside the protection of the trees. With Germans high on the ridge, the slightest movement in the open could be disastrous.

Apparently, the runaway kitchen mule that had caused so much ruckus the day before had been caught, since the mess was now open for business. The men ate in shifts. After breakfast, they got a look at a map that located German positions on the Belvedere ridgeline, each position marked in red. To Kennerly, it looked as though the "whole damn map was red."[1]

Hugh Evans, in the 85th's C Company, had his spirits briefly bolstered by a trip back to a rear supply route, where he picked up a load of white phosphorous grenades. Field after field along the entire two-mile route was filled with ammunition—the clearest sign yet that the 10th's assault would get the support it needed. The massive arms cache also brought home to Evans the fact about which he and his comrades were proudest—and most scared: at this late stage of the Italian campaign, they were the sharp point on the tip of this American spear.[2]

The 3rd Battalion of the 85th was to take the summit of Belvedere itself, with two battalions of the 87th attacking the mountain's west slope before moving up behind the summit. The 3rd Battalion of the 86th would attack the southeast slope of Mount Gorgolesco and offer protection for the assault's right flank.

Evans and his company huddled together for their last few hours of sleep. In the blackness, Evans saw a platoon runner sprinting through the low brush and trees toward company headquarters. Time to go. The men rolled up their blankets, stuffed them in their rucksacks, and laid their gear for the Italian Alpine forces and their mules to carry up after the attack. They dressed in wool and combat boots and stuffed their mountain jackets with grenades, ammunition, and extra K rations. Evans carried one of the platoon's two machine pistols, known as "grease guns" from their shape; the others carried M-1 rifles. In twenty minutes, C Company was ready to go. They moved up Mount Gaggio, a high point on the route toward Mount Gorgolesco that the Germans had heavily protected with artillery and machine guns.

As the men trudged along the road to Querciola on the skirt of Belvedere, their loads seemed to grow heavier as they drew closer to the German positions. Conversation stopped. Ahead, the thick beams of American searchlights coming up from the valley floor doused the ridgeline in brilliant white light, a hand in the face of the German observation posts.

At 4 P.M., the men were ordered to throw all their packs, filled with their personal letters and anything else not essential for battle, into a big pile to be left in the valley. Dan Kennerly checked his ammunition: two boxes of machine-gun belts, fifty-four rounds for his carbine, and four hand grenades. He became a walking stockpile. He needed to be. Units from the German 114th Jaeger Division, the 232nd Infantry Division, and the 4th Mountain Battalion were uphill, waiting to pour down the boiling oil.

At 6 P.M., Kennerly and his men were called together for the final attack order. At 11 P.M., they were to cross the road running along the base of Mount Belvedere. The attack would be made with two companies abreast, Hugh Evans's C Company on the left and B Company on the right, with A Company in reserve. Kennerly's machine-gun platoon would follow C Company straight into the center of the German position on the saddle between Mount Belvedere and Mount Gorgolesco. B Company would assault the summit of Mount Gorgolesco itself. By the time the sun rose, all companies would be in position for the assault on the saddle, at which point A Company would also be committed to the fight, with D Company in support, moving northeast along the base of the ridge toward Mount della Torraccia. By the time this was accomplished, the 2nd Battalion would take over the fight for the summit of Mount della Torraccia. Once taken, every peak must be held at all costs.

Before they left, all soldiers were told to do something that ran against all their instincts for self-defense, something akin to being told to remove their boots and assault the mountains in bare feet: they were ordered to remove the ammunition from their weapons. No shots were to be fired under any circumstances. If they saw a flash, they would know it was the enemy. That was where they were to throw the grenades. Since there would be absolutely no artillery support for the men assaulting the slopes, utter silence would be the most effective means not only of reaching the summits but of staying alive on the way past German positions on the way up. Any German soldiers who could not be avoided were to be silenced with bayonets, knives, or grenades.

After they had heard their orders, Kennerly and his men were asked if they had any questions. Looking around at his companions, who appeared to be scared into silence, Kennerly spoke up.

"Man alive," he said. "We are to make an assault with five battalions against the strongest German positions in Italy and not a goddam loaded gun in the entire outfit. That's a large order, Sarge. I hope the general knows what he's doing."[3]

Just before the attack was to begin, Kennerly checked his gear for the hundredth time. Carbine. Machine-gun ammunition. Packboard. Knife. Water. C rations. First-aid pack. Above, blacking out the horizon, loomed Mount Belvedere. The night was crisp and clear, the moon just rising above the mountain. As they stood around on the frozen mud nervously waiting for C Company to pass and their own orders to move out, the men in Kennerly's unit felt the cold begin to seep under their clothing. No one spoke. Finally, whisper by whisper, the order to move out passed through the waiting troops. Did the Germans have any idea that the men were there? Had they heard the commotion on Riva Ridge? Were they waiting in ambush?

Kennerly and his men emerged from the woods, quickly crossed the road, and moved through the shadows thrown by the moon. Early in the march, Kennerly's guide lost his way; the men were stranded in the darkness, lost. Kennerly began to think of home.

The guide figured out his course, and the men were once again on the move. Sometime after midnight, Kennerly heard a German burp gun—a 9-mm Schmeisser machine pistol—on his left flank.

They know we're here, he thought, now shivering with fear as well as the cold. With mortar fire starting to fall around them, the men took cover in a stand of trees. They got their feet soaked sloshing across a small creek, adding to their misery. Shards of shrapnel whizzed by their ears, each piece whining at a different pitch. Kennerly found it odd how several pieces of shrapnel actually seemed to harmonize. Musical shrapnel.

A small moon gave just enough light for the men to move in a thin line, each man able to see only the soldier marching five yards ahead. Suddenly, another German burp gun rang out, but no one could tell where it came from. Kennerly's reverie was cut short by a burst of German machine-gun fire, its tracers cutting streaks across the sky. A flare went up, and suddenly burp guns and grenades were barking all around them. For C Company, up ahead, the fight had begun.

Uphill from Kennerly, the men of C Company hit the ground. Lying in the dark, Hugh Evans could see only the man ahead of him, in the silvered shadow of a tree. Crawling up to him, Evans realized that the soldier by the tree had lost sight of the man in front of him and the rest of the column had moved on. The line had broken. Only a handful of soldiers were up ahead, and now they were cut off from the battalion behind. Evans took off into the darkness at a trot, German fire coming from his left.

He quickly came to another man, also lying on the ground, who had maintained contact with the line. The two of them moved forward and joined the men up ahead. German shells started screaming in, apparently from all sides. Had the Germans heard them? They were laying down artillery in a very mechanical pattern: up one ridge and "laddering" down another. Maybe they hadn't yet figured out C Company's exact position, but they were covering the entire slope just in case, and eventually their sweep would hit Evans and his team.

Sure enough, the barrage came with a fury, shells landing below and rapidly working up the slope behind them. Evans hit the ground, the muscles in his buttocks and shoulders so tight he thought they would rip apart. Shells fell everywhere, filling the air with dirt, rocks, powder, and smoke so thick it became difficult to breathe. Shrapnel sang out. A burst erupted right next to the man just ahead of Evans. Sure the man was dead, Evans crawled up to him and found him alive, paralyzed by the shock of the explosion, his fingers dug into the frozen ground.[4]

After quietly picking their way up the mountain, Dick Wilson's mortar platoon had nearly made the summit when it took a barrage of mortar and artillery fire that lit up the entire slope. Artillery fire was always the worst, psychologically. Somehow rifle fire seemed pestering, an annoyance that never went away. Artillery fire, shockingly loud, dismembering in its violence, made you want to pull your helmet down over your knees. Wilson, lying down, was one of the first men hit. A shell burst just three feet away, lifting the New England skier ten feet into the air. He landed and started somersaulting down the slope. Men who had been standing next to him were killed instantly. Such was the force of the explosion that Wilson felt no pain at first; all he could figure out, there in the darkness, was that he couldn't feel his right hand. When he looked down, he saw two bones sticking out of his forearm, his wrist hanging from the arm by nothing more than an inch of skin.

Surprised at his own calm, Wilson called for a section medic named Neil Dearborn standing just ten yards away. The medic wrapped a tourniquet around the two halves of Wilson's arm and shot him up with morphine. He wanted Wilson to wait for a litter, but Wilson, seeing men with shattered legs, refused. He began hiking down Belvedere, holding the floppy packet of his right arm in his left hand. Wandering off the course he had ascended, he soon realized he was lost and, worse, had veered into a pocket of German resistance that had somehow survived the initial assault. Sniper bullets began pecking at the trees and ground around him, but once again the darkness served him well.

Finally, Wilson stumbled across a battalion aid station in an old farmhouse, where heavy German shelling forced him to stay for twelve excruciating hours. He was strapped to the back of a jeep and driven several hours to an evacuation hospital, then moved through a series of field hospitals. Twice doctors decided to amputate his arm and twice, finding the tiniest pulse still trickling through his hand, they decided to wait.[5]

MOVING UP BEHIND C Company, Dan Kennerly and his men in D Company found their own rhythm, based on the sound of enemy gunfire: stop at machine guns, go after grenades.

They passed into a meadow, which quickly revealed itself to be a minefield littered with American bodies, probably from C Company or the engineers. The current path through the minefield was marked with engineer's tape; Kennerly felt his way by running his hand along the tape. The route got steeper and harder to climb as the men progressed, and matters got worse when Kennerly's unit bumped up against C Company. The units were getting mixed up.

Kennerly's platoon sergeant said he couldn't figure out where the rest of his men were. Maybe they were up ahead. Nervously, the sergeant took out a cigarette and began to light it. Like a flash, a sergeant from C Company held a carbine to his head. "If you light that match," he growled, "I'll blow your goddamn brains out."

In the darkness, Kennerly heard shells falling and cries for medics. Uphill, he could just make out the huge rocks and trees perched on the slope of the mountain, men from the confused companies scattered among them. Peering around, he couldn't recognize anyone. The chill had left him with no feeling in his hands or feet, yet sweat ran down his forehead. The two boxes of ammunition strapped to his packboard pressed hard into his back. Loud explosions echoed up from behind; A Company, moving up in support, had started taking it as well.[6]

Hugh Evans, who had risen once again to noncommissioned officer status in his new company, continued to lead his men up Mount Gaggio. Pausing in the woods just two hundred yards below the German position, he began to hear word trickling in that a platoon from the 3rd Battalion had been crushed by the incessant shelling—two dead, a half-dozen wounded. Shouts of "Medic!" rang out through the darkness. German tracer bullets from automatic weapons seared the sky; Evans thought they looked like rocket-propelled fireflies.

Evans's company commander, Captain C. Page Smith, gathered the platoon leaders together and gave the order to keep moving forward. But the darkness continued to cause confusion; platoons kept crisscrossing one another, and once again Evans lost contact with the men in his unit ahead of him. Clear on his orders, he led the men he could still recognize up the slope, hitting the dirt whenever he heard a shell coming. Nearing the summit, he passed an injured soldier, who pointed the way toward a silhouetted hill up ahead. Sixty yards later, Evans ran into his platoon leader, Lieutenant Merle Decker, who ordered him to join a group of men up ahead on a reverse slope and have them dig in. Once this was done, Evans shuttled up and down the slope with his company commander, pointing out routes for the battalion's heavy .30-caliber machine guns. Dawn was coming—and with it the real beginning of the fight.[7]

AS THE SUN'S RAYS flowed over the misty ridge top, bathing the snow in orange, the restrictions on returning fire were finally lifted. Dan Kennerly had just begun to make out the saddle of the ridge—with Hugh Evans's C Company pinned down beneath it—when he heard the sound of American machine-gun fire. It was beautiful. He never heard an order to assault, but suddenly everyone was jumping up and rushing forward. Men were running, screaming, and falling. Shells fell everywhere. The *pop-pop* of small-arms fire sounded like a million firecrackers. German machine guns opened up, kicking up snow and dirt all over the slope.

Still not seeing anyone from his own squad, Kennerly followed a couple of men from C Company on their way forward. A German machine gun opened up, and the two men in front of Kennerly went down, their legs broken by the slugs. Kennerly stopped to help, then remembered General Hays's admonishment to keep pushing forward and left the men to the medics. He dropped into a shallow ditch and lifted his eyes to see if he could figure out where the machine-gun fire had come from. Far up the saddle, he saw a lone figure standing up, apparently directing others. His upper body was exposed, and he seemed to be wearing a ski cap instead of a helmet, along with a light tan jacket. Kennerly lined him up, but his vision grew blurry. Was he a German or an American? It was hard to tell. Kennerly crawled to his right for a better view, but by the time he looked again the man was gone. At least the machine gun had stopped firing.

At last, up ahead, Kennerly recognized some men from his platoon moving through a patch of trees. Suddenly, the ground beneath them started exploding: a minefield. Men were falling everywhere, their lower halves torn apart. An aid man, a young man known as "Rosey" because of his peach-colored complexion, moved forward to help. As he sat down to assist one of the wounded, a mine exploded right beneath him. Ignoring the frantic waves of his men, Kennerly picked his way through the minefield to get to Rosey. He was dead, his body a mass of torn clothing and flesh.[8]

AS THE BLACKNESS of night began to seep away, Evans could see the big machine guns moving into place about 150 yards to his right. Soon they were laying down a heavy barrage on what seemed to be the last German position up ahead. Evans left his position and moved toward the guns. Looking ahead through the dim morning light, he could see his platoon sergeant, a good friend named Bob Fischer whose girlfriend Evans had known back in Texas. He signaled, hoping for an indication of where to go next. Fischer did not signal back. Perhaps he had not understood Evans's signal. Evans crawled forward to speak to Fischer directly, but when he came upon his friend he found him lying across the lap of another soldier, Mac Mackenzie. Fischer had been riddled with machine-gun bullets; one bullet had penetrated his lungs, leaving a sucking wound that hissed and wheezed as he fought for breath. Fischer begged Mackenzie not to let him die. "Oh God, please not now. Please not now."

Evans and Mackenzie did their best to plug the wound. Evans used his bayonet to hack off a piece of Mackenzie's jacket to create a makeshift bandage, but his efforts were in vain. Fischer died in Evans's arms. He was twenty years old.

For Hugh Evans, the quiet former Exeter student Bob Bates had so worried about, time suddenly slowed. The battlefield ahead of him became quiet, vivid. He moved forward to a pocket of C Company machine gunners and asked where the fire that killed Fischer had come from. The men pointed. After checking back with his squad just below the top of Gorgolesco, Evans asked a BAR gunner to cover him and began crawling on his stomach—under heavy fire, just as in training—toward the top of the ridge, following another GI he had spotted ahead of him. Evans launched a pair of rifle grenades in the direction of the German machine gunners, but both fell short. Silently, the other GI jerked his thumb toward a bunker. Evans rolled a grenade. After it exploded, he jumped into the bunker, brandishing his machine pistol. Standing over a pair of soldiers killed by the grenade, Evans took three more Germans prisoner. As he handed them over to other advancing soldiers, Evans heard the words of General Hays in his head: Keep moving. Always keep moving.

Still in a rage, he went over the top of Gorgolesco. Now in an area barren of trees, he was terribly exposed. Mortar shells instantly started falling around him, pocking the earth. Evans bolted down the back side of the ridge. A German soldier popped his head up from a slit trench. With a burst from his machine pistol, Evans dropped him and jumped into the trench, where he found three other Germans, their backs turned as they fired a machine gun. Wrestling the gun from them, he killed them as well and kept moving. Amazingly, it seemed that the rest of the German defenses, terrified by this sudden turnabout, were fleeing down the ridge. The last German soldiers Evans encountered he took prisoner with an empty gun.

When he finally looked up and took in his surroundings, Evans counted some thirty German gun positions, each fully capable of covering the path he had traveled. How he had survived, he had no idea. Why the Germans turned heel was also a mystery. Perhaps they figured that no American soldier would advance as furiously as Evans had unless he had a crushing amount of support behind him. It hardly mattered. All he knew was that Sergeant Fisher had died about three that morning, and when Evans finally caught his breath, having killed eight men and helped capture nearly two dozen in an effort that would earn him a Silver Star, it was just daylight. On the way back to his unit, Evans met a man from C Company named Eugene Savage walking in the same direction. As the two passed a dead American lying on the dirt with the top of his head blown off, Savage turned to Evans. "That's my brother," he said.

Back with the rest of the company, Evans found Captain Smith sitting with a blanket covering two broken legs. Evans told him the mountain had been taken and walked away weeping.[9]

FOR MUCH OF THE NIGHT, Stuart Abbott's platoon in the 86th's L Company made its way up Mount Gorgolesco with little trouble. Abbott's cohorts had to keep reminding the gangly young naturalist to keep his head down; whenever he moved across a field or had a few minutes to himself in a foxhole, Abbott's lanky frame would unfold itself to look out over the Italian landscape. It was as if he were never fully there, in the maelstrom. You could tell just by looking at his eyes that he was more interested in cataloguing chestnut trees than in shooting Germans. As dawn arrived on the twentieth, Abbott's company, spearheading the assault, came under heavy machine-gun and mortar fire. With the Germans still hidden along the mountain ridges, their gun positions were impossible to make out. Abbott's platoon had no choice but to bolt to a nearby valley about noontime and dig in. The platoon leader, Staff Sergeant Paul Anderson, who had first befriended Abbott during an orientation course at Camp Hale in 1943, could see German gunners close by, but they didn't seem to be the problem; their guns were pointed elsewhere. Anderson, once again, warned his tall friend to keep his head down; Abbott had "a tendency to stay standing up quite a bit, though. He didn't seem to worry much about being hit."

Anderson's words were not enough to protect his men or himself; soon after his warning, a shell fragment cut a gash in his arm. Abbott and two other soldiers had just finished digging their hole when a shell exploded nearby. Abbott, the twenty-year-old naturalist who throughout his training in Colorado had routinely dropped out of line to inspect an interesting piece of granite, who kept field journals chronicling minute weather changes and bird migrations, who wanted nothing more than to go back to Chicago and take his sister Molly to the zoo, never knew what hit him.[10]

Staff Sergeant Ben Duke of the 86th's L Company had been a friend of Abbott's since Camp Hale and had moved practically alongside him during the assault on Gorgolesco. Writing home to Abbott's family, he said his friend's death "was as merciful as death can be." Abbott was buried by a Protestant chaplain in a cemetery near Florence, with full military honors.[11]

AS THE DAY WORE ON, all objectives on Belvedere and Gorgolesco were secured. The air corps arrived late, its P-47s flying over the valley to the north. As the German prisoners were being assembled in the lower part of the saddle, a German shell landed among them, killing one and wounding three; among the remaining prisoners, several men, reputed to be members of the SS, were separated from the rest. Dan Kennerly figured they would be shot.

Dealing with prisoners captured in the midst of a battle presented opportunities for securing both intelligence and, in some cases, insight into the minds of the German soldier. A great many admitted to having despaired over their country's prospects in the war but had been so afraid of being shot by their superior officers that they had not deserted. When some men in the 87th captured a German company commander, the lieutenant refused to talk until someone told him they would mark his Red Cross card "deserted." German officials were known to threaten the families of anyone who dared flee from the front.

As the sun rose higher, Kennerly's unit followed A Company through the saddle. The bodies of men from C Company were everywhere, some with arms or legs sticking straight into the air. They all had a pale yellow, waxy color about them that reminded Kennerly of artificial fruit. They also contributed to a smell that took Kennerly a few moments to recognize: a slaughterhouse. What he was smelling was blood. In one spot, eleven bodies from B Company were lined up in a row—probably the site of the last German defensive position. Their bodies were more grotesque than any Kennerly had seen; the top of one's head blown off, its brains spilling out on the ground. Kennerly could see the stump of the spinal cord inside the cavity, which reminded him of a watermelon with all of the meat scooped out.[12]

The sight of the carnage hit Kennerly in the belly. The man who had been fearless on the football field felt himself trembling, beginning to panic. He wanted, with everything he had, to drop his gear and run.

Once again German shells began falling on the saddle. Kennerly ran up a steep slope and hit the ground. If he could have, he would have crawled inside his helmet. Shrapnel was flying everywhere. When the shelling stopped, Kennerly lifted his eyes and saw a dead German immediately in front of him. His older, Mongolian features made Kennerly wonder if he wasn't a Russian conscript. Kennerly reached out to touch the man's cheek, then recoiled with a jerk, as if his hand had somehow been contaminated by death.

Incredibly, the valley beyond the ridgeline looked bucolic; Kennerly could actually see a farmer plowing his fields, oblivious to the carnage on the mountain. Finally, the shelling stopped. Colonel Barlow, commander of the 85th, strode by and told an aide in a dark voice to get the bodies collected at once.

Kennerly, who seemed to be the only member of his unit present, was ordered to get ready for the next move, over to the snowy ridge leading to Mount della Torraccia, the last promontory along the Belvedere ridgeline. With the snow-covered fields between Belvedere and della Torraccia still under constant fire, the men were ordered to move one at a time. When his turn came, Kennerly began sprinting across, only to lose his footing on an icy patch. He rolled down the slope to his right, his carbine and ammunition coming loose from his packboard, and began sliding farther on his belly. His first reaction was embarrassment; he felt the entire Fifth Army had seen his fall. Then he sat up. A 75-mm German shell landed just two feet away, scattering the snow. Kennerly froze and watched as the shell skipped to a square of ice and began spinning like a top. A heartbeat later, the shell stopped spinning and came to rest, steaming in the snow. A dud.

Kennerly gathered his gear and climbed back up the path. He finally found his squad on the other side of the field and learned the plan: they were to dig in and cover A Company's flank. As he began digging through the snow with his spade, Kennerly saw an American soldier sitting peacefully beside the path, looking ahead with his eyes wide and his hands folded in his lap. His lower right side had been blown away. His intestines had spilled out onto the snow. There was vapor rising from them. A soldier named Casamino Polizzi from A Company was lying nearby, wounded in his lower back and begging to be taken back to the aid station. A medic gave Polizzi some morphine, but it wore off quickly. Kennerly and another man offered to take him back, but their squad leader refused. A few moments later, a pair of German prisoners walked by. Ordering one of them to remove his overcoat, Kennerly used it to make a stretcher. Laying Polizzi on the coat, the Germans carried him toward the rear.

Ahead, Kennerly could tell that A Company was in a hell of a firefight. The noise from the shelling was incredible; every time a shell hit, Kennerly would start to tremble. He began to feel sharp pains in his eardrums and his rectum. As the walking wounded began filing past on their way to an aid station, an errant P-47 dropped a five-hundred-pounder in the middle of the line. Miraculously, no one was hurt.

As American planes reappeared, and with German troops in sight just eight hundred yards away on A Company's left, Kennerly took control of his unit's machine gun. His tracers fell right among the Germans, so Kennerly ran through an entire belt. He saw a number of Germans drop and others scatter. He reloaded and, with no visible targets, fired a stream of tracers along the draw. When two Germans ran out, a mortar crew took them out. Three more P-47s flew at tree level over the west slope of Belvedere, well below Kennerly's positions, and strafed the entire slope.

Gradually, Kennerly and his unit moved two hundred yards farther along the ridge, the noise of the battle growing louder with every step. Loaded with ammunition and apparently indifferent to all that was happening around them, a line of pack mules filed by, led by Italian partisans; later they returned with the bodies of the dead lashed across their saddles. The battle on top of della Torraccia had been apocalyptic; Kennerly wondered how anyone up there could have survived. A soldier from A Company ran back and collected ammunition from the dead; he also delivered the news that Sergeant Walter Hall, a gregarious friend of Kennerly whose father had been a history professor at Princeton, had rushed a German burp gun and taken a burst in the chest.

As the P-47s flew off, German artillery opened up again. Once more, Kennerly crawled into a hole. As he did, a grenade popped loose from his belt and fell to the bottom of the trench. Kennerly sat on it, right between his legs, just as several other soldiers dropped down on top of him. Kennerly held his breath, praying that the pin hadn't come loose. When the shelling finally stopped and the men crawled out, Kennerly let out a yell: "All you sons of bitches go dig your own damn hole!"[13]

Finally word came that A Company had secured its position and had been ordered to hold the line until replacements arrived from the 2nd Battalion. Kennerly's D Company retraced its steps back across the saddle. The bodies from the battle had already been removed. By the time the Belvedere ridge was secured, four hundred Germans had been taken prisoner.[14]

On Wednesday, February 21, Kennerly woke before dawn, threw back some breakfast and washed it down with a shot of cognac and a cup of black coffee, and waited for news about the rest of his unit. All night long, the Germans had fired machine guns into the trees over the heads of the men of the 2nd Battalion, many of whom had been unable to cover their shallow trenches. A number of men had been killed or injured. There were a few casualties in Kennerly's platoon as well, but no one had been killed. Jim Snell, the section leader, had taken a bullet to the center of his helmet, but by some miracle the bullet had traveled between the helmet and the liner and fallen down the back of his neck.[15]

Hugh Evans's C Company, which had taken the hardest hit the day before, would be held in reserve for today's battle. Kennerly's unit would be kept in regimental reserve but would follow the 2nd Battalion's attack on the ridge. By the time they had climbed back up to the saddle, where the previous day's battle had raged, all of the bodies had been removed. Strewn all over the hills was an enormous amount of broken equipment, from rifles and shattered helmets to piles of bloody bandages; in places, patches of snow had been stained red. But there was also evidence of the day's victory: news teams had arrived, looking for interviews. Kennerly put on his most rugged face as he walked by the cameras.

Moving past the hole where he had straddled the grenade, Kennerly saw another soldier in residence; he wished he could kick him out and carry the hole with him. Instead, he kept marching down the trail along the south side of the ridge leading to Mount della Torraccia, past the deep crater caused by the bomb dropped on A Company by their own plane.

A lieutenant ordered Kennerly to move off to the top of the ridge to help protect the assault's flank. In the woods, Kennerly paused for a moment to look at the trees, which reminded him of the white pines of home. Glancing down at his feet, his heart jumped. There, inches from his boots, was the three-pronged trigger mechanism of a land mine. They were everywhere. He had absentmindedly wandered into the middle of a minefield. Picking his steps carefully, he moved back the way he had come when it occurred to him to look more closely at the mines. They weren't triggers after all; they were clusters of pine needles. No wonder he had been confused. These weren't white pines. White pines have clusters of five needles, not three.

All along the ridge to della Torraccia, trees were bursting into flame. Jumping behind a stone wall, Kennerly heard someone scream for a medic. Looking over, he saw an aid man named Mike Lombardi lying in the middle of a meadow, his leg a bloody mess from a shell. Kennerly and two others jumped the wall, sprinted to Lombardi, and half dragged, half carried him back behind the wall. Looking at the wound, Kennerly could see that the main artery had not been cut, and suddenly his worry turned to envy. Binding up the leg, Kennerly looked at Lombardi. "Mike, you lucky bastard," he said, "you have a million-dollar wound. In three weeks' time you'll be on the big boat home."

Hunkered down among the burned-out trees, Kennerly learned that plans had changed. His company was to hold its position, then work up Mount Gorgolesco to a small hill leading to the summit of Mount della Torraccia. The Germans, they heard, were planning an attack for that night, so the GIs needed to dig in deep and cover their holes with logs. They were also to take two-hour watches on the gun; the password for the night was "Betty." Countersign "Grable."

As Kennerly scouted around looking for wood, he stumbled across a dead German soldier. Searching his pockets, he found a wallet with some Italian lire and a picture of two soldiers and two women standing by a road: the man's family. The soldier wore a gold wedding band. One of Kennerly's platoon mates tried to pull the ring off his finger. When he couldn't, he asked for Kennerly's knife.

"Damn," Kennerly said. "You aren't going to cut his finger off, are you?"

"Damn right I am," the soldier replied. The ring had an inscription on the inside. Another member of the platoon called the man with the knife "a damn grave robber."

The next day, the 2nd Battalion continued the attack on della Torraccia with heavy strafing support from the American P-47s. Kennerly and his men, gearing up for battle, once again began throwing away all nonessentials. The shucking put Kennerly in mind of Stonewall Jackson, whose foot cavalry had fought with nothing but muskets and the clothes on their backs. Men in battle, he decided, become expert in their reliance on instinctive action. If a soldier could survive his first twenty-four hours in battle, he figured, his chances of surviving the war increased dramatically. This thought improved a mood soured by the incredible filth he and his men were living in. It had been ten days since their last shower or change of socks and underwear. Ringworm, jock itch, and an unspeakable stench had begun to take hold of the men; to make himself feel better, or perhaps to go completely native, Kennerly decided to hell with shaving.

With the Allied tanks and bulldozers blown to rubble by countless mines, engineer companies used TNT and bangalore torpedoes to clear the road. To Belvedere's northeast, Edward Nickerson, in the 85th's G Company, was busy digging a trench near the top of Mount della Torraccia. Though partially protected by tall hardwood trees, the men still felt vulnerable to incoming artillery fire. Sure enough, a German shell exploded fifty feet downhill from Nickerson, right among three of his companions, Tom Brooks, Tony Ragazzine, and Jack Doyle. Brooks stood up, stunned by the explosion. He was covered with blood from the waist down, but the blood was not his. Doyle and Ragazzine were dead. Several others were wounded, including Clyde Soeder, the youngest man in the company, whose chest and stomach were "a bloody confusion." Soeder had developed a lighthearted reputation for complaining about his "aching back" whenever he was ordered to dig a trench or pick up the pace on a march. Now, lying in the dirt, dying, he said it again: "My aching back."

The rest of the company scrambled to dig in, terrified of tree bursts. Tom Brooks continued to stand, covered in his friends' blood. Soeder lay in his own blood as a couple of medics tried to administer a bottle of plasma. One of the medics, a battalion medical officer named Morton Levitan, had trouble with the plasma, since the frigid weather had made the fluid too cold for Soeder's body to accept. "My aching back," Soeder repeated softly and died. Tom Brooks was so shaken he could barely move. Just to get him moving again, his platoon sergeant, Andrew Lopez, grabbed a large entrenching shovel and put it into Brooks's hand. "You dig in over here," Lopez said.

Captain Levitan, meanwhile, perhaps from the unimaginable strain of administering aid to the shattered bodies of his friends, wandered away from the rest of the company and found himself in some woods, where he was quickly captured. After defiantly informing his captors he was Jewish, Levitan was taken to a German command post, the only officer in the entire division taken prisoner. Over the next few weeks, he would be marched behind German lines, ordered onto a train leading to a concentration camp, and, with the train grinding to a halt to make sure everyone on board saw it, shown Dachau. The day the war in Europe ended, Levitan was rescued from a train by Allied soldiers and sent home.[16]

As the attack on della Torraccia continued, Kennerly stumbled on German propaganda littering the fields. "Men of the 10th Mountain Division: Welcome to Italy. You have come a great distance from Colorado to die." Another pamphlet showed a cartoon of a Jew with a big nose and thick glasses trying to seduce a pretty blond girl; the caption read, "American soldiers are dying while the Jews are seducing their wives and sweethearts at home." Where the leaflets had come from was a mystery. Perhaps they had flown in with the artillery shells.[17]

Finally, late in the day, word came that the men from the 86th had taken Mount della Torraccia. Although its 3rd Battalion was cut up pretty badly, another critical objective was secure. With momentum shifting in its favor, the division for the first time began using psychological warfare of its own, boomed over loudspeakers mounted above the town of Montese: "Austrians and Bavarians—you have suffered for seven years under German domination. After the war, Austria will be free! Shorten your time of serfdom. Many of your comrades are already here in American hands. They are well treated. Surrender! Come across to our lines. Come without weapons. Leave your equipment and belts. Come across in groups of not more than three with your hands up and hail our outposts."

The broadcasts always followed heavy American mortar fire and were usually followed by a heavy German response. Once quiet returned, however, the messages were replayed. The Germans seemed to be listening. Within a few hours a small handful of Germans had given themselves up. Few Americans believed the broadcasts would cut too deeply into the enemy ranks; Hitler's command to fight to the death was well known. "It is an awfully difficult thing for a German to desert," one American lieutenant said. "He has to worry about getting shot not only by the Americans but by his own men as well. If he is able to get away from his men he still has mine fields and wire to cross, and he has to sweat out the possibility of reprisals against his family if the Germans find out he has deserted."[18]

As the men of the 10th Mountain Division came down from Belvedere, news of their victories began to fuel a new burst of excitement in the American press. A March 3 story, originally published in the *Seattle Post-Intelligencer* and picked by other newspapers, appeared with a Rome dateline—and a number of misspellings that irritated the men in Italy. The article reported that the men had whooped "Ski Hail!" as they made "spectacular gains on precipitous Mount Velvedere. Only recently disclosed to be in Italy, the ski-riding, rock-climbing, mule-packing mountaineers made their presence known to the Germans long before the home front heard about it. This spectacular outfit of Schussboomers is chock-full of famous American and European skiers and mountaineers known from Mount Rainier to Tuckerman's Ravine."

If the rhetoric used to extoll their training in Colorado had seemed excessive, this new round of prose, given the carnage the men had just experienced, seemed almost grotesque. The fight for control of the Mount Belvedere–Mount della Torraccia ridge had cost the division 926 casualties. Yet the division had performed with a speed that Fifth Army brass considered remarkable. Even the most optimistic generals had hoped the mountain troops would take Riva Ridge and the Belvedere massif in two weeks. They had done it in five days.[19]

CHAPTER TWELVE

MOUNTAIN OF HOPE

THE DIVISION'S ASTONISHING SUCCESS on Belvedere shifted the entire Allied plan for the spring offensive on the Po River valley. Before Belvedere, the plan had called for II Corps, some parts of which were just six miles from Bologna, to spearhead the push north. After Belvedere, General Truscott, in charge of the Fifth Army, realized that the best chance for breaking through the German mountain defenses was with his mountain troops.

Truscott gave the 10th Mountain Division its next assignment: a patchwork of peaks constituting the last German defenses before the Po—notably Mount della Spe, the "Mountain of Hope"—and the mountain village of Castel d'Aiano. In a panic to plug the holes the mountain troops had blown in their defensive line, the Germans were scrambling for reinforcements from the 114th Jaeger and 29th Panzer-Grenadier Divisions, and Truscott wanted to drive the Allied victory home before the line could be retrenched.

If Truscott's confidence in the mountain troops ran high, he was not willing to release their leash just yet. Once the sector surrounding della Spe had been secured, he ordered, the division must hold up and wait for the rest of Mark Clark's Fifteenth Army Group to launch the final offensive. Truscott's decision did not sit well with the men of the 10th, especially given their impressive performance on Belvedere. With the Germans reeling, why not push straight on through to the

Po River valley? Stopping at della Spe would only allow the Germans to regroup, lay mines, and fix defensive positions where none had yet been set up. After all the false starts and halting advances that had cursed the Italian campaign from the start, after all the bloody ambivalence, here was a chance to end the thing once and for all. Why wait?[1]

General Hays laid out the plan. On the right flank, and out on the raw edge of the assault, the 85th Regiment would attack the knob of della Spe. Running up the middle of the hills, the 87th would try to seize the town of Castel d'Aiano. On the left flank, the 86th would work to capture Mount Terminale and the town of Iola. Della Spe dominated the north end of a ridge that overlooked a road leading along its base. The tiny village of Canolle, where a battalion aid station had been set up, lay at its upper end, a mile and a half away. The town of Castel d'Aiano sat at the mouth of the valley at the north end of the hills. Taking Mount della Spe in particular would cut the main German line of communication and supply to the Po Valley and give Allied troops control of Route 64 to within fifteen miles of the valley itself.

There was one main difference between this assault and the successes on Riva Ridge and Mount Belvedere: this attack would take place in full sunlight, against fully prepared and heavily armed German soldiers. As extraordinary as the earlier successes had been, the protection of darkness and surprise had been the division's greatest asset. Neither would be available this time around. The time had come for an old-fashioned, grinding ground attack.

Intelligence sources assured the men that della Spe was not strongly held and would yield easily to attack. "We will have a grand and glorious turkey shoot," they said.

"Don't bet your life on that," someone in Dan Kennerly's platoon muttered under his breath.

AT 6 A.M. ON SATURDAY, MARCH 3, Britain's 178th Lowland Medium Artillery Regiment, one of the best such units in the world, opened the assault on della Spe with a punishing shower of shells. P-47s streaked overhead, and the mountain troops' 86th and 87th moved out. Near Iola, a rifleman from the 86th's E Company named Albert Ejem reported the

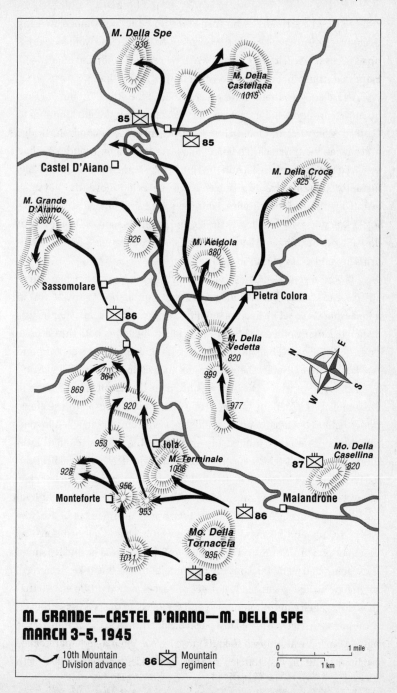

M. Della Spe
930

M. Della
Castellana
1015

85 ⊠

⊠ 85

Castel D'Aiano □

M. Della Croce
925

M. Grande
D'Aiano
860

926

M. Acidola
880

Sassomolare □

□ Pietra Colora

⊠ 86

M. Della
Vedetta
820

N
E
S
W

864

869

999

920

977

953

□ Iola

M. Terminale
1008

Mo. Della
Casellina
820

87 ⊠

928

956

Monteforte □

953

⊠ 86

Malandrone □

Mo. Della
Tornaccia
935

1011

⊠ 86

M. GRANDE—CASTEL D'AIANO—M. DELLA SPE
MARCH 3-5, 1945

10th Mountain
Division advance

86 ⊠ Mountain
regiment

0   1 mile

0   1 km

killing of two "Germans" who turned out to be Italian women wearing German uniforms; apparently the Germans had forced the women to dress up as decoys. "We felt sorry as hell when we realized what had happened," Ejam said, "but what can you do when they fight like that?"[2]

Art Delaney's battalion was ordered to lead the attack. About 7:15, as he moved around a hill in a steep valley leading from Gaggio Montano to Castel d'Aiano, Delaney looked out over a field near the Malandrone Bridge and saw only a haystack. The baseball player from Long Island, who had survived the fiasco on Kiska and the Homestake Maneuvers at Camp Hale, instantly knew he was in trouble. Before he could move, the haystack erupted with machine-gun fire. Four men were shot immediately, including Delaney, who took bullets to the leg and groin. As soon as Delaney went down, a private named Allen Schauffler sprinted through a hail of small-arms fire and dragged him to safety.

"If you're gonna get shot, get shot early in the morning, when you're still close to the medics," Delaney would say. Half an hour later, he was in a makeshift clinic set up inside a building away from the front. After he was evacuated, many others in his unit were killed, including both the Catholic and the Protestant chaplains. Delaney's L Company lost its captain and two lieutenants. Delaney spent the rest of the war in a hospital in Livorno.[3]

Not far from where Delaney was hit, near the heavily mined town of Sassomolare, Lieutenant Colonel Henry Hampton, one of the strategic minds behind the assault on Riva Ridge, was reading a map when incoming shrapnel seriously injured his arm. Hampton was evacuated. Even more devastating to the division's morale was the death of a soldier who for two years had become a figurehead for the entire division: Torger Tokle, the world champion ski jumper from Norway. In a wooded area near Iola, a soldier named Lyle Munson, a superb ski jumper and member of the Norway Ski Club, and his close friend Tokle were suddenly pinned down by machine-gun fire. Munson crawled over to Tokle and said he and his squad were going to try and take out the machine gunners, but Tokle disagreed, saying he would go instead and get a bazooka man to do it. At that moment, a shell came screaming in and exploded, in the process setting off some bazooka shells strapped to a packboard. Thrown to the ground by the blast, Munson was amazed to find himself alive. Then a lieutenant called for him. Lying on his stomach nearby was Tokle, his body riddled with

shrapnel. Nearby was the bazooka man, also dead. Moments later the lieutenant was shot through the legs. The next day Munson himself was hit by
a mortar, and he spent the next seven months in a hospital.[4]

Tokle's death stunned the rest of the division. The record-setting ski
jumper had seemed invulnerable, so strong in body and mind that enemy
fire seemed almost insulting to him. The fact that such a man's life would
end in a war that by all accounts was within weeks of its conclusion
seemed galling, pointless, a symbol of the insanity of continuing this
obsessive attack up the Italian peninsula. Bob Frauson, who had first met
Tokle when he was a fifteen-year-old boy learning to ski on New York's
Bear Mountain, considered Tokle's death "the worst day of the war."[5]

Over on della Spe, the going was getting worse. The men had awakened
well before daylight, with platoons moving out toward the southeast along
a road with three-foot dirt banks on either side. In the distance, artillery
and small-arms fire opened up around 8 A.M., but nothing seemed too serious. The 85th moved out in squads, following a road littered with abandoned German vehicles shattered by Allied warplanes, smoking in the
morning sun. They found a German ambulance filled with artillery shells.
They passed a house where some American officers were interrogating a
belligerent German prisoner; Dan Kennerly heard the men tell the soldier
that the Allies had just launched a thousand-plane attack that had virtually destroyed Berlin. The prisoner didn't believe them.[6]

Along the road, tanks from the 1st Armored Division rolled past. At 9
A.M., the 85th was ordered to move out across the fields to the northeast of
the road. The idea struck Kennerly as foolish: the men on foot would lose
the protection of the tanks, and nearby haystacks—as Arthur Delaney
found—offered perfect cover for German snipers. Suddenly the sounds of A
Company's attack echoed through the valley. Kennerly turned toward his
own unit's objective, moving through a swamp as bullets from somewhere
up in the hills began to streak down among them. As B Company emerged
from the fields, they came out just below Upper Canolle into an area with
absolutely no protection. Kennerly thought of the Twenty-third Psalm. He
figured the guy who had written about walking fearlessly through the valley of the shadow of death hadn't had Germans firing on him.

As he entered and then passed through Upper Canolle, Kennerly followed the woods toward the crest of the ridge. After two hundred yards, he

heard the sound of gunfire ahead and stopped. A Company was in a hell of a firefight, pinned down in the saddle just below their objective. Anyone trying to move beyond that point was being cut down. The Germans were once again shooting American medics trying to get to the wounded. When one of B Company's medical teams moved forward to retrieve a wounded man, German snipers waited until they had loaded the man on a stretcher before opening fire, killing them all. On this day, Kennerly thought to himself, there would be no prisoners.

Someone from Kennerly's unit spotted a German ambulance up toward the north, a man in a white coat emerging and looking around the battlefield.

"Let's pot him," someone said.

"He's a medic!"

"Bullshit—you saw the ambulance back on the road loaded with shells, didn't you? I'll bet that bastard is an artillery observer looking for targets."

The squad agreed to shoot the German, and as the best marksman in the squad, Kennerly was chosen to be the executioner. He borrowed an M-1, slipped a tracer into the chamber, and estimated the range to be eight hundred yards. Kennerly set the proper elevation and windage, lay down prone, and squeezed off the round. The tracer shot straight and true. By God, I've got him, Kennerly thought, but the round started dropping fifty yards early and seemed to go right between the German's legs. The medic jumped into the air, bounded back into his ambulance, and drove away. "Damn," someone said, "if you'd had one more click of elevation you would have hit him right in his dick."

The next instant, the ground shook from a roar like the sound of a freight train flying through the air, and Castel d'Aiano exploded with what sounded like 170-mm German cannon fire, the largest shells the 10th had yet encountered. Every time a shell exploded, a house crumbled to the ground. The noise was tremendous, even to Kennerly's ears two thousand yards away. "See," someone said, "I told you that ambulance driver was an observer." Word came that A Company had finally secured its objective and that, just as Kennerly had predicted, several German prisoners had been shot. With the sun now just hanging over the tops of the mountains, B Company had little daylight left to move forward.

Through the noise of shells falling all around him, Kennerly could hear someone screaming. Looking ahead, he saw a sergeant from the battalion communications section holding one hand in the other. The back of the man's jacket was soaked in blood; when Kennerly went over and lifted up his shirt, he could see several angry shrapnel gashes along the man's back and shoulders, some extending all the way to his waist. Terrified, the man screamed at Kennerly, "It's my finger! It's my finger!" The first joint of his little finger had suffered a small cut, probably from a tiny piece of shrapnel. War does strange things, Kennerly thought. Here's a man with cuts on his back that will probably require two hundred stitches to close, yet all the pain is coming from his little finger.

As B Company moved up to the saddle secured by A Company, smoke wafted over a battlefield littered with bodies from both sides. On the far edge of the saddle, a lone figure sat in a shell-pocked foxhole, his head leaning forward, his body covered in dust. The walls of the foxhole had caved in, covering his legs in dirt. As Kennerly approached, the man looked up, his face, covered in dust and soot, reminding Kennerly of a minstrel in blackface. Peering closer, Kennerly recognized the soldier, Judson Decker, a sergeant from D Company. Kennerly kneeled down and asked what had happened. Decker said that shells had hit on both sides of his foxhole. A silly grin came over his face, the same grin a boxer displays after being stunned by a hard blow.

"Yeah, I'm okay," Decker said, "but I'll tell you one thing. Two shells may never hit in the same spot, but they can sure as hell overlap."

Kennerly's lieutenant came running down the hill in front and yelled for the men to move up, to secure their position before dark. B Company rushed forward toward the summit of della Spe, a rugged patch of ground covered with massive thrusts of granite and large oak and chestnut trees. B Company moved along the south side of the summit, then split into squads and dug in in case of a counterattack. Kennerly, now in total darkness, grabbed his D-handled spade and dug into the steepest slope he could find. He had always wondered about the best way to dig a foxhole—should the long or the short side be at a right angle to the path of enemy shells? He had always favored the long side, so he dug a good deep hole six feet long, with a three-foot sleeping cave dug into the wall at the bottom. At least now he might survive a direct hit.

Some distance from the hole, Kennerly helped set up the gun position, which he pointed north. If he felt a moment's relief at having his shelter and defense established, it was quickly upset when he tried to swallow. He hadn't had a sip of water all day, and there was no water to be had anywhere.

Moments later, German fire started coming in, most of it back along the ridge where A Company was dug in. Kennerly felt lucky—the Germans must not have realized his company had moved so far forward. At about 10 P.M., heavy fire erupted on the eastern side of the mountain, and B Company briefly opened up with its artillery. Then silence. Kennerly was afraid to go to sleep. The Germans were coming.

When Kennerly's time came to man the gun, he heard Germans close by yelling and throwing grenades, and realized to his horror that he had set the gun up pointing in the wrong direction. He grabbed it, tripod and all, and ran down the slope to the left, firing off two short bursts as he went. In the momentary light of the muzzle blast he caught a glimpse of his foxhole and moved toward it. Jumping in, he landed on top of another soldier, and ordered him to go get more ammunition. Kennerly set up the gun to fire down the slope to the left and loosened the traverse and elevation knobs. He took his grenades off his belt and laid them on the edge of the foxhole. Once again there were German shouts and grenades flying through the air. An American lookout fell to the ground right in front of Kennerly's gun and began shouting for a medic. Kennerly shouted for him to get the hell behind the gun.

The ammunition arrived. The German assault intensified. Another soldier in Kennerly's unit told him he was supposed to hold his fire, to wait until the Germans got closer. Kennerly was getting nervous, though, and frightened. Grenades were exploding all over the place. Finally the call came to fire. His machine gun set to free traverse and rapid fire, Kennerly aimed low, hoping for ricochets. He swept the gun in a steady arc, from left to right and back again, his tracers slicing through the darkness. He fired until his belt ran out and reloaded. By now the Germans knew where he was.

A bright blue light flashed just in front of his position—a grenade—blinding Kennerly and knocking his machine gun sideways. With white spots still blurring his vision, Kennerly ran through another ammo belt, reloaded, and began firing again.

A machine gun behind him opened up. "Where the hell have you been?" Kennerly grumbled. Someone standing over his foxhole yelled, "Hey, I'm an American! I want to come in!"

"What's the password?"

"I forget."

Kennerly couldn't remember either. When the man said he was from B Company, Kennerly invited him in. He told him Kennerly's first blast from the machine gun had cut right through the middle of the German assault; Kennerly gave one more sweep, threw the last of his grenades, and, in a cracking voice, asked about water. He was so parched he couldn't even spit. His tongue had begun to swell. Finally a canteen materialized and Kennerly took a long draft.

The shelling continued unabated. Outside his foxhole, Kennerly heard a man whimpering, saying he couldn't take any more. Someone shouted for him to go back to the aid station by Upper Canolle; a little while later the same voice shouted, "Get up and walk! You can't crawl the whole way!"

When the morning of March 6 finally arrived, Kennerly, still desperately thirsty, popped out of his hole to look around. Not two feet away from the lip of his gun position was the body of the soldier who had crawled up asking for a medic the night before. Kennerly had been firing all night and had never known the man was there. Other bodies lay across the field, most likely outposts who had tried to push the perimeter of the front line. Kennerly stood up and went looking for water. A couple hundred yards down he found a house with a well and asked the terrified owner for a couple of eggs. Before he could offer to pay, the man slammed the door in his face. With no way to cook them, Kennerly mixed the eggs with water and lemon powder and swallowed them.

Back in his position, Kennerly learned that B Company was stuck on top of Mount della Spe with German positions entrenched on three sides and only a narrow corridor open from the rear. Supplies were thin, the wounded were having a hard time getting back to the aid station, and the communications wires had been knocked out. Digging himself another foxhole, Kennerly decided that a root the size of his wrist that protruded into his sleeping cave needed to go; he pulled out his carbine and tried to shoot it out. The root held. He changed positions and shot again. Suddenly, he felt a sharp pain in his calf, as if someone had hit him with a baseball bat. Too afraid—and embarrassed—to look, he asked another soldier to tell him how it looked. Incredibly, there was no hole in the calf, not even any blood. There was just a welt the exact size and shape of a carbine round. The bullet must have hit his leg sideways. With replacement troops arriving and the fighting for della Spe beginning to tail off at last, Kennerly went to see a medic about the blood blister. His boots looked as though he had been standing in shit for a week, and his helmet was dented and scarred. Arriving at the aid station, he was told to wait. The doctor was busy pulling a piece of shrapnel from the rear end of a farmer's ox.[7]

ONCE DELLA SPE had been captured, the 85th's L Company was ordered to hold it. For three weeks, the men dug in deep and put up with only sporadic artillery fire from the Germans below. Bill Putnam, who had once distinguished himself in Colorado by walking the seventy-five miles from Camp Hale to Glenwood Springs in twenty-four hours, found himself tying bundles of TNT to the trunks of ragged chestnut trees. Though the trees had been badly damaged by the battle for the hill, their crowns still offered Germans ripe targets for tree bursts, and Putnam, by pruning the trees with explosives, effectively eliminated that problem.

With della Spe secure, Putnam and L Company began probing the German defenses on a nearby mound to the north that American planners had named Hill 913, for its altitude in meters. The Germans continued to defend their line furiously, laying land mines along the road between della Spe and the town of Castel d'Aiano—which itself had been badly damaged during the run-up to the initial battle for della Spe—and firing mortars at the men on della Spe. As he would later recount in his memoir *Green Cognac*, Putnam was asked to lead a patrol to Hill 913, to see what he could find out about a small group of houses known as Pra del Bianco. Putnam agreed, and was quickly approached by a young private first class named Lorenz Kohler, who eagerly asked to join the patrol. The son of German immigrants who had suffered at the hands of the Nazis, Kohler could not be dissuaded from joining the mission; he had, he said, personal reasons for taking the fight straight to the people who had forced his family to leave their homeland. Following the wisdom of Giuseppe Garibaldi, to say nothing of General Hays, Lorenz had carved the stock of his submachine gun with an Italian motto that became the unofficial motto of the regiment: *Sempre avanti*—always forward.

After midnight, the ten-man patrol moved out. Slipping along behind the hedges that lined the battered roadway, the team, with Putnam leading on the left and Kohler on the right, crept toward the houses at Pra del Bianco. When they were so close to the village that the only remaining cover was a solitary tree, Kohler whispered to Putnam that he would go ahead with a couple of others if the rest of the team would provide cover. Only as far as the tree, Putnam whispered back. Kohler moved ahead, and disappeared over a small rise in the road.

Within seconds, Putnam heard three short bursts from a German burp gun, and saw Kohler jump and collapse. Another man, next to Kohler, had also been hit. Frozen and unsure where the fire had come from, Putnam did not know what to do. "Go back! Go back!" Kohler yelped. "The village is strong!"

Putnam ordered the rest of the team to retreat but inched forward himself. Lifting his head, he could see the village and his companions lying in the road fifteen yards ahead, motionless. A tommy gun opened up behind him and Putnam, caught in a cross fire, had to find cover. Retreating, he discovered to his horror that fifty yards behind him two of the men he had sent back had been killed by their own rear guard. The devastated team, with four men dead, returned to the lower slopes of della Spe.

The next day, Putnam received a call from an artillery observer asking him to come look through the binoculars at something down in the valley, near where the previous night's disaster had occurred. There, hanging from the beams of a roofless building to the left of Hill 913, was the body of Larry Kohler. "Those dirty bastards!" Putnam cried. "They couldn't just kill him, they had to hang him out for us all to see."

The next day Putnam plotted his revenge. He would take a dozen men and a couple of *Panzerfaust* weapons his men had captured from the Germans. A *Panzerfaust*—literally an "armor punch" or "chain-mailed fist"—was similar to the American bazooka. Designed as an antitank weapon, it could accurately fire a five-kilogram load of TNT at a target forty yards away. Putnam wanted to drive a mailed fist right into the heart of Pra del Bianco.

That night he split his team into two units. Four men with *Panzerfäuste* moved along the road the men had taken the night before; the rest, moving along the side, took positions on a hillside overlooking the town. The hill teams would do their best to prevent a counterattack from any Germans that might be camped above the village, and a small litter team would do its best to retrieve the four lost bodies. Up on the hill, one of Putnam's men found a communications wire and severed it with his bayonet. The village below was now cut off from the rest of the German army.

Down below, the fireworks began. The mailed fist, Putnam could see, was perfectly delivered, and with no return fire. Among the dead Germans was an unexpected prize: an *Oberfeldwebel*, or master sergeant, who for some reason had been carrying a satchel filled with a copy of the dispositions of all the German forces in the region.[8]

Other booty had less strategic significance but perhaps, once made public, more power. In mid-March, the division's newspaper, *The Blizzard*, published the translation of a captured German officer's diary, written in a bunker shortly after the capture of Belvedere. "A terrible explosion and fire all around me," the diary read. "A human being cried for help. This war is terrible. Whoever has not gone through it as a frontline infantryman cannot possibly picture it. What human beings can do to one another. They are hurling death and destruction-bringing material at each other. Damned humanity, what insanity are you committing? We all, whether young or old, whether officer or enlisted man, are subject to the laws of this embittered war. Its iron fist forces us into the smallest hole when the splinters start flying around. When the Yankees pull the lanyard, we become animals."[9]

OVER NEAR CASTEL D'AIANO, the constant strain of ducking artillery shells was beginning to take its toll on Denis Nunan as well. One night, asleep in a muddy foxhole, Nunan dreamed that he was back home, lying on a beach on the New Jersey shore with the tide coming in. When he awoke, he found that he had urinated in his sleeping bag.

"Although spring is in the air and 'tis warmer, one finds himself still trembling like a leaf when caught in an artillery barrage," he wrote home. "There is less ducking however, 'cause when you hear a shell from an 88 sing overhead, it has already passed you—you don't hear the one that scores a direct hit on you; and the one that gets you with shrapnel sings in the distance and explodes in your ear. War is more of a mental strain, I believe, than physical, 'cause the enemy is always trying his darndest to kill you no matter if you are in a foxhole or tending to the call of nature."

As lucky as Nunan felt to still be alive after so much bloodshed, he had his share of close calls. One of his companions seemed to follow every battle with an obsessive search for souvenirs, to the point that for a time he carried around a small grandfather clock. Nunan felt obliged to warn him about the booby traps the Germans had rigged in so many of the houses, but the soldier wouldn't quit. One day Nunan watched as the man, chirping with delight, bent over to pick up another trinket and was blown to pieces by a trip-wire explosive.

"Thanks to the failure of the press, and to the stupidity of Hollywood, the Home Front has no real conception of war, and only by doggies' true fact letters home can the truth be made known," he wrote home. "One digs into the earth's surface every time he is halted for any period of time—he digs with all the speed and strength he can summon. He sweats and prays as he digs—sweats out the 88s and mortars and prays for soft digging. Prayer has loosened more than one rock for your youngest!"[10]

After the initial intensity of the fight for della Spe had passed, the mountain troops reluctantly hunkered down to wait for the final spring offensive, a six-week halt in the fighting that few soldiers seemed to support. By the time della Spe and Castel d'Aiano were secure, the Allies controlled a six-mile stretch from Mount Grande d'Aiano to Highway 64. Though Major General Willis Crittenberger, in charge of IV Corps, seemed ready to push through to the Po River valley and take Bologna, Truscott ordered the division to wait and consolidate the ground already taken. For the first time in nearly six weeks, the soldiers could breathe a little easier. *The Blizzard* printed another Pin-Up Mountain of the Week, this time of La Nuda, the snowcapped massif visible to the south of Riva Ridge. The mountain, the editors couldn't help noting, had been given its name because from certain angles it looked like a reclining woman ("quit tilting the paper," the caption advised, "this isn't one of them").

Atop the summits of della Spe and its neighboring hills, the 10th Mountain Division could imagine its ultimate objective, the Po valley to the north. The intensity of the German desire to keep control of the valley was nowhere more evident than in their refusal to withdraw to the safety of the Alps, on the valley's northern fringe. They needed the Po's resources too much. "As the Krauts are driven back on both the eastern and western fronts, as bombs rain on their home industries, the Po becomes even more important," *The Blizzard* reported in an editorial on March 15. "With the fall of Berlin and the loss of Germany's northern provinces, the industrial heart of Italy with its slave labor and vast factories becomes a priceless source of food and supplies needed to continue this struggle.

"That is our target," the editorial continued. "Smash the Kraut's hold on the valley, and we smash at their dwindling resources. From the heights we hold today we look down on more than a river valley. We look down on one of the Krauts' last, forlorn hopes."[11]

To the American public, the mountain troops had become so popular after their early victories that they once again became media darlings, a camera-ready backdrop for exhibitions of national pride. Showing up at the front one day was Congresswoman Clare Boothe Luce, who, *The Blizzard* reported, arrived "looking more like a star of a USO show than a member of the House of Representatives." Luce even joined a gun section, mugging for the cameras as she fired on a couple of German-held homesteads. "A few of the boys were a little uneasy at chatting with a prominent legislator while the movie cameras ground and the flash bulbs popped, but it didn't take long for the representative's charm to thaw them out," the newspaper reported. After pulling the lanyard on a cannon, Luce boasted that she "had pulled the lanyard on guns on the Yellow River front in China, and in the Maginot Line, but they didn't pull half as hard." Later, she surprised a sunbathing private named Rudolph Heins, who "had a little trouble deciding whether to put on his shoes or his shirt first." When she jumped back into her jeep, an advance detail rushed ahead to tell the boys at a curbside shower unit to get dressed.[12]

With the fighting at a temporary lull, the mountain troops had a few moments to contemplate their dead. In an editorial marking Memorial Day, *The Blizzard* described a funeral service twenty-nine miles outside of Florence. Protestant, Catholic, and Jewish chaplains prayed silently. General

Hays said a few words about the sacred soil and the dignity of the dead. A band played "Semper Fidelis" and "Shenandoah" while a large wreath was placed at the base of the flagpole, inscribed to the memory of the division's fallen soldiers. The Reverend W. J. Moran, division chaplain, prayed, and an eight-man squad fired three volleys. As the bugler blew taps, the flag was lowered from half-mast. The troops marched out of the cemetery to the tune of "Washington Post."[13]

By the end of March, blossoms were popping out on the torn trees all over the countryside and flowers were sprouting among the shell holes. Tanks and transport trucks had worn the roads to dust. For three quiet weeks, armored artillery, heavy equipment, and supply dumps dotted the countless greening valleys. On March 18, Nunan and some companions rigged up an altar on a hillside studded with shell craters, a ruined church in the background. With the sound of cannons banging away in the distance, the little group invited a group of hungry, dirty, and ragged locals to join in a mass, complete with communion. "As we advance through the rubble of the war-torn villages," Nunan wrote, "one can't help wonder how this country will ever be the same again."[14]

CHAPTER THIRTEEN

THE CRUELEST MONTH

DURING THE FIRST WEEK OF APRIL, Fifth Army commanders put the final touches on plans for the final push for the Po River valley, dubbed Operation Grapeshot. Though the Germans were clearly reeling from the breakthrough at Belvedere, they still managed to mass troops from the 19th, 334th, and 94th Divisions, the last of which had fought stubbornly at Cassino. The curtain was dropping on the Italian campaign, but the German army remained determined to leave plenty of blood on the stage.

The Allies planned to get to the valley with tens of thousands of men from IV Corps, an artillery barrage of two thousand guns, and, perhaps most critically, a massive air attack. In the center of it all, the mountain troops would pour off the northern slopes of Mount della Spe and its surrounding hills, spreading their attack like a fan. The 85th would move down the western slope of della Spe, then attack the two hills to the west of Pra del Bianco. The 87th and 86th Regiments would push forward on the 85th's right flank, through Torre Iussi and Rocco Roffeno, respectively. The terrain would be exceedingly difficult to negotiate, the hills steeper than any the division had seen since Riva Ridge itself. Forests of chestnut trees offered some protection, and the men hoped to move from peak to peak along the precipitous draws that lay between them. Roads were oiled to prevent the inevitable clouds of dust that gave away troop movements. Countless trucks, field guns, and crates of supplies littered the valleys, along with small mountains of gas cans and ammunition. The 87th alone hauled in 500,000 rounds for its .30- and .50-caliber machine guns. They would need them all. With no night cover and no surprise, the assault would prove to be the division's bloodiest day yet.

On April 13, the day before the offensive, Denis Nunan heard dark news that made the spring leave the air. President Roosevelt had died of a cerebral hemorrhage. If the death of their commander in chief left the men reeling, they had little time to contemplate its repercussions. The very next day, the division began the final push to dislodge the Germans from the hills leading to the Po valley.[1]

Dan Kennerly could see that something big was about to happen. At last the leash was being pulled from the neck of the 10th. Had the leash been pulled a month ago, he felt, the division could have been in Austria by now. About nine in the morning, four-plane waves of Thunderbolt fighter-bombers pounded Hill 913 with five-hundred-pound bombs, then swung around to fire rockets and strafe the hill with machine-gun fire. Artillery gunners followed, hammering away with more than thirty-three thousand shells. After forty minutes, the shelling stopped, and nothing but smoke and silence hung over the battered hillside.

Houses seemed to disintegrate spontaneously, sending billows of smoke and dust hundreds of feet into the air. Soon there were no individual sounds, just a hellish cacophony. Kennerly had a grandstand view. Looking over the incredible display of American military hardware, he turned to his squad. "Man, the taxpayers are sure catching hell today." The bombardment was so intense, he wondered if even rabbits and squirrels could survive. Finally the dust in the valley began to settle. Through the haze Kennerly saw one of the most inspiring things he had ever seen: the men of the 2nd and 3rd Battalions moving down the north slope of Mount della Spe. With a flourish, he and his men opened up their machine guns in support, firing well above the heads of the advancing units. Even as they did, German mines began exploding around them and enemy machine-gun fire began pecking away. The mines were particularly nasty and hard to avoid; the division's engineers said they were the worst they had ever seen. Some mines had high trip wires, some had low trip wires, some had trip wires on the side; some were designed to blow under pressure even after their wires were cut. Glass-topped Topf mines, made not of plastic but of asphalt-impregnated cardboard, eluded detection devices. Holes six feet deep had been filled with dynamite and capped off with mines. Working around the clock, mine-clearing teams dismantled three thousand mines in thirty-six hours.[2]

Stepping gingerly through the field, Kennerly aimed as close as he could to the source of the fire and ran through his ammunition as fast as the gun could spend it. Even with a soldier pouring water over the barrel, within minutes the gun was so hot it stopped firing. Kennerly and his team quickly broke it down and found that the firing pin had seized on the bolt— a highly unusual malfunction that, by temporarily breaking Kennerly's concentration, ended up saving lives. Taking time to find another bolt, Kennerly looked up to see a jittery young engineer from a unit outside the 10th firing on a column of men that Kennerly could clearly see were his own.

"You dumb son of a bitch! Those are our men!" he shouted at the frightened engineer. Kennerly decided he no longer trusted anyone not part of the 10th. He just wished everyone would leave them alone and let them fight this war their own way.

A new box of bolts arrived, and Kennerly renewed his fire on the crest of the mountains ahead. He opened another box of ammunition, the hundredth for his gun alone. Word arrived that the 2nd and 3rd Battalions, though banged up, had made good progress. Tanks appeared on the road as the sun began setting and disappeared behind della Spe. B Company, Kennerly learned, would enter the attack on the left flank of the 3rd Battalion and try to relieve some of the pressure they had been under. They would also support the 85th's A Company in its attack on Hill 883—the nose projecting off Hill 913 toward the southwest—which had been the 3rd's initial objective.

As darkness fell, Kennerly's unit leader, Lieutenant Martin D'Ooge (pronounced, in Kennerly's thick Georgia accent, "Lieutenant Dogie") ordered his men to move quickly; there were German snipers everywhere, and they had already taken a heavy toll. He reminded the men to stick to clear paths through the ubiquitous minefields. The men moved out and picked their way through Castel d'Aiano. Past the town, they moved along the valley floor past wrecked tanks, abandoned jeeps, and horribly mangled bodies. Kennerly and his men crept along through a massive section of mines resting on sticks two feet off the ground. Kennerly saw one man whose abdomen had been blown open, trailing several feet of pale intestines. He must have run a few feet before falling. His liver, dark and bloated, lay drying on the ground. It reminded Kennerly of a bloated basketball with its rubber bladder protruding out.

Near one smoking shell of a tank, Kennerly saw something that took the edge off the carnage: a pretty American girl in a pin-striped Red Cross dress standing beside the road, smiling and waving. How in the hell did she get here? Kennerly asked himself. She's pretty and nice to look at, but whoever let her up here is crazy as hell. People are getting killed up here. What is she trying to prove? The Red Cross girl was almost certainly Debbie Bankart, who had been the first female ski instructor in New England and had helped the great mountain filmmaker John Jay recruit men for the 87th. Bankart had been with the IV Corps since Rome. She would later marry a captain from the 87th named Roger Eddy.[3]

Kennerly's reverie was broken by sniper fire and a mortar barrage. He ran for a low stone wall and waited. The next moment, without hearing a thing, he felt a strange and sudden change in air pressure around him. He had fallen to his knees. A mortar shell had exploded in the trees above. Incredibly, no one had been hurt, though when he removed his pack, Kennerly found it full of shrapnel. The men moved on, toward the top of the ridge, keeping their guns pointed toward the north.

As the troops advanced up the hill to inspect the damage, they were surprised by ferocious machine-gun fire, mortars, and artillery. A captured German diary revealed that the German soldiers were certain that the mountain troops would not take any prisoners. "This undoubtedly accounted for the fanatical resistance that our troops encountered, which often meant digging the Germans out of their well-prepared bunkers," an American field report said.[4]

If many of the German prisoners had lost their belligerence this late in the war, many others continued to sneer at their captors. Once, while escorting some thirty-five prisoners to the rear off Hill 909 on April 14, Edward Nickerson and his fellow guard ducked away from a German shell that killed fully twenty of the captured German soldiers. Nonetheless, one of the surviving men told Nickerson that despite the Americans' numerical superiority, it was still "impossible" that the Allies would take Berlin.[5]

To Denis Nunan, recently made a platoon sergeant, the sight of German prisoners marching past was almost more than he could stand. "To see them marching to our rear and safety, after killing and maiming our men, made one want to kill them in cold blood," he wrote. "As I have always felt it my duty to take care of my men and bring them back safely, the loss of men was a great shock to me. Wounded men are one thing, but the passing of men who you have lived with since Ft. Lewis days is something else again. The cries of the wounded and the stillness of the dead finally broke my heart." Nunan's rage found a terrifying outlet when an officer ordered him to take a group of six German prisoners out behind a haystack and shoot them with his service revolver. He followed the orders and suffered for the rest of his life.[6]

Flying over all this was Conrad Brown, the former ambulance driver now assigned, despite his nearsightedness, to be an airborne observer for the division's artillery units. Brown and a pilot circled over the battlefields in a yellow Piper Cub, which had been commandeered so recently it hadn't even been retouched with a military insignia, and called in enemy positions over the radio. Brown's eyesight was not improved by his army-issue glasses; whenever the pilot would tip his wings and ask if Brown could see a gun emplacement, Brown would demur; he could see nothing but green rolling hills and scattered farmhouses. Nothing, that is, but the long strings of tracer bullets coming straight at him, which the pilot rather casually dodged around by flying an erratic course, continuously turning and changing altitude.[7]

As the day wore on, Hugh Evans, whose 85th's C Company was in reserve, looked up to see Allied planes bombing "the holy bejeezus" out of hills 903 and 913, behind the towns of Pra del Bianco and Torre Iussi. The main attack had been launched from Mount della Spe, and after thirty minutes of intense bombing, the slopes around these new targets were fields of burning fire. When the planes swept away, Evans heard the heavy artillery attack begin; for the next thirty minutes, the big guns hammered away at 903 and 913. Finally, after an hour of unimaginable noise, the troops advanced. The roads were littered with dead and wounded mules and men split open by machine-gun and sniper fire. A single medical section within an 87th battalion lost three medics to artillery fire. Friedl Pfeiffer, one of the division's most famous skiers, went down with a serious wound. Brigadier General Robinson Duff, arriving on the top of Hill 903, assisted in dressing a machine gunner's wounds, noting that there wasn't an unoccupied medic for forty miles.[8]

Evans, who had taken his winning the Silver Star on Belvedere with a grain of salt, had nonetheless learned a thing or two about surviving in battle. "Sometimes intelligence is an advantage. In battle is one of those times when it doesn't mean much," he would write home. "If you think and realize what is going on around you, and what could easily happen to you at any second, your fear will get the best of you. You have to forget, be impersonal, and get angry to really fight. It's worst if you go at it halfhearted. Fear steps in and you are much more liable to get hurt. However you can be careful about certain things. That's mostly instinct: move fast, stay low and keep your eyes open. But you can't get around bullets, stop shells, or miss all mines."[9]

This time, from his perch on a hill overlooking the battlefield, Evans may have let his guard down. He stood above his trench, watching the attack. His moment's respite was understandable. He was not directly involved in the attack; he was just waiting and watching. To a German mortar crew, however, Evans was just another American soldier and might well have been a forward observer, radioing German positions back to the 10th's gunners. In any case, Evans heard the shell almost as soon as it had been launched, and dived, too late, for his foxhole. The shell burst in the crown of a tree four feet above his head, blasting fragments into Evans's forehead. He fell into his trench, blood pouring down his face.

Terrified, Evans ran his fingers over his face and found, to his amazement, that the wounds were superficial. His limbs were intact, and his torso had escaped the blast altogether. When he realized he wasn't dead or even seriously wounded, he popped out of the trench and made his way over to his platoon. It was then that he realized he couldn't hear anything. The explosion of the shell had blown an eardrum.

Over the next three days, as Evans tried to continue leading his platoon, his ear grew increasingly painful, infected, and full of fluid, to the point that he could no longer keep his balance or even get to his feet. Finally he was sent back to a field hospital, where he promptly contracted hepatitis from a dirty needle. Weeks later, still in the hospital, he contracted polio, underwent a spinal tap, and lost the use of his legs. Though he would eventually recover from all of these ills, his time at the front was over.[10]

EDWARD NICKERSON and the rest of the 85th's G Company moved down the slope of Mount della Spe and then picked their way up the heavily mined Hill 909. Men were dropping all over from small-arms fire, mortars, and artillery fire. Above them, the hill's summit was in chaos. Pulling up in front of a stone farmhouse, Nickerson was astonished to see a German machine gunner firing away at troops on a far-off flank; the noise from the bombing was so loud the German didn't even see G Company on his front lawn, thirty yards away.

Nickerson's platoon sergeant, Andrew Lopez, ran forward and lobbed a grenade inside, and the rest of the squad opened fire. One of the men firing his M-1 on that hilltop nearby was twenty-year-old John Magrath, a Boy Scout leader and Episcopal church acolyte from East Norwalk, Connecticut.

As the rest of the company dug into the hill, with mortar shells wounding men every few seconds, Magrath ran forward, moving from the house to a machine-gun nest near the summit of Hill 909. At first Magrath seemed to run between the bullets that sprayed all around him. In less than a minute, he had killed two Germans, wounded several others, and commandeered the machine gun, which jammed almost as soon as Magrath fired it. In a whirl his companions found astonishing, Magrath somehow managed to change the gun's barrel and get it working again. Where he had learned how to operate a German machine gun, no one knew. Now more heavily armed, Magrath continued his rampage, killing or wounding five more Germans and capturing several more. In his frenzy, Magrath almost seemed to burst with power. When a German soldier came upon him from the window of the shattered house, Magrath whirled on him and yelled "Surrender!" The German spontaneously dropped his weapon and raised his hands. Magrath moved out again, well in front of the rest of his company.

A short time later, Edward Nickerson was ordered to go up and corral

Magrath and tell him to report back to the lieutenant in charge because he was needed for radio work. G Company needed to regroup.

Nickerson took off to find Magrath. For seventy-five yards, moving along the hilltop, Nickerson was alone. Then he spotted Magrath, lying prone, the German machine gun against his shoulder, a long ammunition belt feeding the gun from the right. Seeing Nickerson approach, Magrath uttered a greeting that Nickerson would never forget: "I've been having fun!"

Nickerson told Magrath about the orders to return back down the hill. He told him he would take his place with the machine gun. Magrath gave Nickerson a forty-five-second tutorial on firing the German gun and left him there.

Some time later, when Nickerson was relieved, he grabbed some of the many prisoners Magrath and others had captured and ordered them to carry an unconscious soldier named Richard Condo down the hill. Lying on a blanket, Condo died on the way. Such was the intensity of the German artillery shelling that at least twenty German prisoners and one American guard were killed just during the descent. At one point Nickerson and the four prisoners carrying his comrade dived into a hole with Nickerson on the bottom, the others on top like pancakes. "Just get me safely to the rear," said the oldest prisoner, who had six silver wound bars on his chest.

By the time he had made his way back to the top of Hill 909, Nickerson learned that Magrath had been killed in one of the many furious artillery and mortar bursts that reduced their company by two thirds in a single day. Later, when his body was returned to East Norwalk, Magrath was buried in a Revolutionary War cemetery in the middle of town. He was the only man in the 10th Mountain Division awarded a Congressional Medal of Honor. During Magrath's burial ceremony, "Taps" was played by a blind thirteen-year-old boy whom Magrath had mentored as a young Boy Scout.[11]

JUST TWO WEEKS AFTER avenging the death of Larry Kohler, Bill Putnam and the rest of the 85th's L Company were ordered to take Hill 913 for good. The little town of Pra del Bianco had been destroyed by the *Panzerfäuste*, Putnam would write in his memoir *Green Cognac*, but land mines and clusters of machine guns still pocked the hill itself. Putnam and two companions, Staff Sergeant Mike Mitkowski and Platoon Guide Jim Palmer, began moving up the hill where they had found the *Oberfeldwebel* with the satchel full of German strategy. When they came to an open draw bordered by a small group of houses to which the German had apparently been trying to escape, Putnam and Mitkowski moved ahead with Palmer providing cover with his Browning automatic rifle. Jumping from chestnut tree to chestnut tree, Putnam and Mitkowski drew only light enemy fire. Ahead they could see a crumbling wall and, to its left, a small house. Mitkowski bolted for the wall and Putnam for the house, where—if the place did not turn out to be a hornet's nest of Germans—he figured he'd be able to see around the wall.

As he threw himself through the doorway, Putnam saw its wooden frame splinter from German machine-gun fire—from outside the house, luckily, and from the other side of the wall protecting Mitkowski. Peering out, Putnam could see the gunner, preparing to lob a "potato masher"—a German grenade with a long wooden handle used for long-distance throwing—toward Mitkowski. "Look out, Mike! Above you!" Putnam yelled. Mitkowski looked up and saw the grenade coming. Incredibly, he managed to smack it back over the wall, where it exploded thirty feet above his head.

As Mitkowski prepared to lob his own grenade, Putnam took aim from the house with his .45, shot, and missed. The German, distracted by Putnam, raked the house with one burst of machine-gun fire, then another. Mitkowski threw his grenade, which destroyed the machine gun and sufficiently stunned the gunner that he was no longer able to resist. Putnam, Mitkowski, and Palmer all ran toward the downed man. Shouting in broken German for the man to tell if others were nearby, Putnam got the man to point toward a doorless entrance to what seemed to be a cellar leading into a nearby building. Resigned to his plight—and those of the men hiding in the cellar—the German agreed to draw them out. One by one, ten men popped out into the daylight, their hands over their heads. Though some still had weapons slung over their backs, all seemed relieved, at this late stage of the war, to give up.[12]

Down in a deep valley beneath Hill 913, a platoon led by a young replacement officer named Bob Dole was pinned down behind a four-foot hedgerow facing an open field about two hundred yards square. The hill itself rose steeply on the far side, occluded by the smoke of the astonishing bombing raids. Dole had enlisted in the army in December 1942 while a student at the University of Kansas. Called into active duty in June 1943, he had done basic medical corps training at Camp Barkley near Abilene, Texas, then transferred to the Army Specialized Training Program (ASTP) in Brooklyn, where he had studied engineering. After moving to bases in Louisiana and Kentucky, he had been accepted into OCS at Fort Benning, Georgia, emerging as a second lieutenant in the fall of 1944. Soon afterward, he had boarded a ship for Italy and been sent to the 24th Replacement Depot near Rome. Finally, in late February, he had been assigned to I Company of the 85th Regiment and sent to the Apennine front, where, at the age of twenty-one, he had taken over a platoon for an officer who had been killed in action. From the beginning, I Company had had a particularly bad time of it; of the two hundred members of the original company into which Dole was assigned, only eighty-eight would emerge from the war alive and unhurt.[13]

As a Kansas native and war rookie, Dole knew better than to try to pull rank among a bunch of mountain troopers; even among his men, he kept his profile low. A twenty-year-old skier from Utah named Devereaux Jennings, who would compete in the 1948 Olympics and later be inducted into the Ski Hall of Fame, accompanied Dole on a number of night patrols during the March campaign. "Dole was a pretty cool, fair guy who handled himself with dignity," Jennings said. "He asked what we thought and I was happy to work with him because not all officers were like that. He wasn't an outspoken person. He just quietly did his job. I liked him. He wasn't out there to prove anything. I thought he was the best officer I'd seen."[14]

As his men moved up Hill 913, Dole's platoon watched as a sergeant led another group of soldiers straight into a minefield and a deadly barrage of machine-gun fire from a nearby stone house. Outraged, the I Company commander ordered Dole's platoon to flank the house and take out the machine gunners with their Browning automatics.

As Dole led his men into a narrow, grassy dip that opened into a ravine, his unit again met with fierce fire from machine guns and mortars. Jennings, on the platoon's far right, saw the Germans haul out and use a mobile rocket launcher he had never seen before; the enemy, he decided quickly, did not intend to give up this hill. The shell from this strange new weapon killed a number of the men in Dole's platoon, including the radio operator. Dole grabbed the radioman and dragged him into a foxhole. Moving forward, he threw a grenade toward the farmhouse. Too short. One of Dole's scouts reached for a grenade but was mauled by machine guns before he could pull the pin. As Dole scrambled from his foxhole, he felt something—a bullet or a shell fragment—slam into his right shoulder. He collapsed facedown in the dirt. He could not feel either of his arms; only later would he learn that they had been stretched out over his head. Over and over, lying out in the open field, he yelled for help. A couple of medics tried to reach him but were themselves gunned down. Finally, a half hour later, a terrified Sergeant Edward Carafa crawled across the body-strewn battlefield and grabbed his lieutenant, who was now barely able to moan. He folded Dole's right arm over his chest and dragged him to safety behind the hedgerow.

Dole was gray, "the way they got before they died," Sergeant Stanley Kuschick would later recall. Although the standing orders were to leave fallen soldiers for medics to attend, the German practice of picking off men with red crosses on their helmets gave Kuschik pause. Reaching for a dose of morphine he had taken off the body of a dead medic, Kuschik gave Dole an injection; dipping his finger in Dole's own blood, he wrote a scarlet "M" on his forehead to ensure that the wounded man would not be given another, possibly deadly dose of the opiate later on. Other soldiers managed to get Dole away from the front, but he still spent the entire afternoon stretched out on a litter.

Dole's I Company lost so many men on Hill 913 that Company K had to move up and assist in the final, successful assault late that afternoon and the next day. Including the dead and injured on nearby Hill 909, the 85th suffered 462 casualties, including 98 men killed, in the two-day fight. In surgery the next day, a terrible wound to the back of Dole's shoulder—officially diagnosed as the result of an exploding shell—was cleaned and dressed, the surgeon removing a number of bone fragments but pronouncing the arteries and nerves in good shape.

Two days later, Dole was transferred to a military hospital in Casablanca, Morocco, where doctors discovered something far more frightening: Dole was paralyzed. The shell had apparently not only shattered his shoulder and collarbone but damaged his spine as well. Dole was placed in a cast from his hips to his chin. Back in the United States, Dole once ran a temperature of 108.9 degrees, and doctors told his mother he might only live a few hours. Although he survived this, he then developed a kidney infection that forced doctors to remove one of his kidneys; six months later, after being bedridden for so long—and having lost 70 of his original 194 pounds—he suffered a blood clot in his chest that nearly killed him.

After seven surgeries on his shoulder—all performed by an Armenian-born neurosurgeon named Hampar Keikian—that included transplanting tendons from his leg, Dole recovered most of the use of his arm. Fifty years to the day later, during Dole's campaign for the presidency of the United States, the residents of Castel d'Aiano would place a memorial near the spot where he had been injured. "On this site, theater of the atrocities of the Second World War, Lt. Robert Dole, member of the 10th Mountain Division, was seriously wounded while fighting for the freedom of our town," the sign reads. "The citizens of Castel d'Aiano, as a token of their eternal gratitude, dedicate this plaque in recognition of his valor and of the sacrifices of all the soldiers and civilians who fell fighting for freedom. 14 April 1995."[15]

By the second day of the assault, the 86th and 87th Regiments had opened a serious break between the German 94th and 334th Divisions, and the German general Bernhard Steinmetz was rushing in reserves. His move was thwarted by the 85th, however, and Steinmetz, realizing his troops were being outflanked, ordered a retreat. It was too late. The 86th and 87th had already cut off the roads leading from that sector, and Steinmetz's units were forced to flee in the night, abandoning all their heavy equipment.

Sometime in the early hours of April 15, Dan Kennerly heard a scream that sounded as if it had come from the throat of a terrified woman. Someone said it sounded "like someone de-nutted a dinosaur and turned him loose." Again and again the terrible shrieks pierced the darkness. Finally the men learned they came from German rockets known as "Screaming Mimis." They were landing around Castel d'Aiano. B Company moved forward, under heavy mortar fire, and occupied a hill to the left of the 3rd Battalion. The Screaming Mimis were replaced by cries for medics. Stretchers with wounded men from the 10th passed Kennerly's men on their way up the ridgeline.

As the day grew warm, Kennerly realized he was again running low on water. He remembered a spring he had passed on his way up—now several hundred yards behind him—and set out to fill up his squad's canteens. Looking up after filling them, Kennerly saw, standing beside him, a German soldier. He had not heard him approach and had been caught with his arms full of water bottles. His carbine was back with his squad.

The German did not want to kill Kennerly, he wanted to surrender. He pointed down the path and tried to tell Kennerly something; Kennerly motioned for him to follow him up the hill. Back with his unit, Kennerly shouted for someone who could speak German to come and translate. A medic he had never seen before trotted over and translated the German's story. Another German soldier, badly wounded with shrapnel in his chest and stomach, was back by the spring. The two men had been hiding in a bunker for two days, unnoticed by hundreds of 10th Mountain troops. They had been afraid to surrender, because they had been told that the 10th did not take prisoners. When the uninjured soldier had seen Kennerly appear without a gun, he had taken a chance on surrendering.

Kennerly ordered the wounded man taken to the rear, with the healthy German walking alongside. Kennerly caught a breath. If the German surprising him at the spring had been in a different mood, he could have taken another life for the Führer.

Moving forward, Kennerly's unit came to the top of the ridge. Bombed-out houses and German bodies lay strewn across the summit. They came across an unmanned bunker ten feet square and eight feet deep and big enough for the whole squad to mount their guns and spend the day.

Word arrived that the 3rd Battalion had jumped off in its effort to take its final objective. Kennerly and his men prepared to move out. The terrain around them was desolate, covered in scrub oak and protruding rock. To the right Kennerly could hear heavy action, and sure enough, by 2 P.M., he learned that the 3rd Battalion, despite very heavy losses, had at last taken its objective. The German defenses were collapsing, their soldiers on the run. The 10th had finally broken through.

All efforts now shifted to supporting the 86th and 87th as they hammered through the last small hills to the sweeping agricultural valley formed by the Po River, which ran some four hundred miles west to east before pouring into the Adriatic. Along the main road in the valley, troops and vehicles raced past on their way to the fight. Others, the wounded and those guarding prisoners, followed more slowly. Kennerly saw one prisoner being pushed in a two-wheeled cart; he was sitting up, smoking a cigarette. Both his legs had been cut off at the knees. Some men with bandages over their eyes walked by, their hands on the shoulders of men in front. Kennerly learned of a friend from A Company who had been shot in the thighs by an Italian woman as he tried to enter her house. In response, he had blown the woman "all over the mountainside."

Bodies from both sides were scattered all along the shoulders of the road, their skin blackened, so bloated that their uniforms were pulling at the buttons. Flies covered their faces. On top of a ditch bank, Kennerly saw a dead German soldier, lying with his arms folded. He must have been brought here when he was still alive. He was a young man, maybe eighteen, and handsome, his rifle so new it gleamed. Kennerly took the rifle and covered the young man with a blanket. He couldn't stand to see flies eating a dead man. And there were plenty of dead men. The battles of April 14 and the couple of days following were more costly than any of the division's fighting. In all, the mountain troops suffered nearly 1,800 casualties: 370 dead and 1,427 wounded.[16]

Among the badly wounded was Wilson Ware, whose patrolling and intelligence expertise had been so critical to the Riva Ridge climb. And among the dead was a young replacement officer named Lieutenant William F. Callahan, the son of a former chairman of the Massachusetts Turnpike Authority, whose name was later attached to the tunnel leading from Boston to Logan International Airport.

But the victory, after all the carnage, was complete. The German 94th and 334th Divisions had been virtually destroyed, and 2,200 prisoners had been taken. By April 20, the Allies' air superiority was such that planes were dropping bombs on the XIV Panzer Corps's command post itself. A house right next door to General Frido von Senger's headquarters went up in flames, scattering cattle and blowing the general's laundry into the trees. That same day, the 86th Regiment marked Adolf Hitler's fifty-sixth birthday by breaking through to the Po River valley. They were quickly followed by the rest of the division. The cracking of the German hold in the mountains sent German troops running as fast as they could to the Po River; in their desperation, they left abandoned equipment strewn all over the roads north.[17]

As the worst of the fighting wore down, Conrad Brown, who had watched it all from his Piper Cub, searched out a place to stay near a makeshift airstrip, out of range of all German artillery except for a lone "Big Bertha," which had reportedly been seen mounted on a German railcar. He and another enlisted man quickly turned up a little hilltop farmhouse, where they were shown a room with a couple of beds all made up with clean white sheets. One thing puzzled Brown; he asked the farmer what the enormous round hunk of metal was sticking out of the ground a few feet from the house. "Bomba," the man said, gesturing to show how it had come down out of the sky. To Brown, this was no bomba. It was a dud shell from the Big Bertha.

That night, as he lay in bed, Brown was pleased to discover that his bedroom door opened onto a chamber occupied by the farmer's three lovely young daughters. Brown contentedly drifted off. Sometime later, he jerked awake to the rapid *whish-whish-whish* of what sounded like an incoming artillery shell. Strangely, the sound did not pass, and Brown, hearing a few final dribbles, realized it was only one of the daughters in the room next door using the enameled chamber pot under her bed.[18]

Marching their way north through the last of the hills, Dan Kennerly and his men loaded their gear into jeeps and moved out, passing through woods for a while before hitting a paved road and turning north into a wide valley. They passed through the ruined town of Montepastore, jumped out of their jeeps, and continued on foot. To the northeast, their objective was already under attack by P-47s.

As the men marched along, a stray cow walked up to inspect the commotion. Kennerly got someone to hold her and, removing his helmet, filled it to the brim with the first milk he had seen since leaving the United States. Leaning forward, he took a deep swallow and passed the helmet around. Someone from A Company walked by and sniffed that the milk was not fit for drinking. It hadn't been pasteurized, he said. The men could get undulant fever.

Kennerly turned to his squadmate J. T. Kindred. "What the hell is undulant fever?"

Kindred had never heard of it either. Kennerly and his men moved on and took the cow with them. Every time they stopped for a rest, Kennerly milked her and drank the milk as fast as she could make it.[19]

CHAPTER FOURTEEN

ACROSS THE PO

AND INTO THE ALPS

THEIR WORK IN THE MOUNTAINS COMPLETE, the division now ran a foot race to catch the Germans in the Po River valley before they could reach the Alps. Assigned by General Hays to lead a platoon of tank destroyers, the 86th's 2nd Battalion, and a team of bridge-building engineers, General Robinson Duff pushed the men to keep up the pace, roaming the advancing column like a nervous sheepdog. Apparently, his coaching worked. Running ahead of thirty other Allied divisions, the advancing mountain troops sometimes arrived in towns just three hours after the Germans had left. So quickly did they cover the fifty miles from Mount della Spe to the Po that German general Frido von Senger had to decide whether to run or give himself up. By the time he reached the bridgeless river—just hours before the mountain troops arrived—Allied planes were already so ubiquitous that crossing by ferry was impossible. At dawn he decided to swim.

"I no longer entertained any hope of again having a combat-ready force at my disposal south of the Po," he would write. "I had tried repeatedly to drive such stragglers back to their units still fighting at the front. These were only ineffective, isolated measures, however, since the commanders were themselves physically exhausted and could no longer see the utility of this. It was demonstrated here that after catastrophes of this sort, when whole major units have been disbanded and the infantry troops are exhausted from long marches, swimming across rivers, and sleepless nights, there remains for psychological reasons but one alternative: to act in accordance with the instincts of the ordinary soldier and order the units to withdraw."[1]

Fast in pursuit, Dan Kennerly's unit moved forward from village to village, skirting artillery attacks and sniper fire. Through his binoculars, Kennerly could see C Company up ahead, filing down a slope into a gorge right in the path of his own men's fire. He ordered a cease-fire. Almost instantly, German sniper fire began peppering Kennerly's position. He also got some troubling news: C Company's commander, Captain Herbert Wright, had been wounded, and his men had commandeered a tank to try to get him off the front. Glassing the area, Kennerly could see that Wright's back was very bloody; he hoped his kidneys had not been hit.

Lieutenant D'Ooge ordered his men to retrieve a pile of ammo boxes. For the first time in his career, Kennerly questioned the order. Couldn't the lieutenant hear the sniper fire? It made no sense getting someone shot to save a couple of empty ammo boxes. The lieutenant said the orders had come from battalion headquarters, and they had been emphatic. Kennerly had heard enough.

"We're going to get someone killed because some fat-ass rear echelon colonel thinks up a hare-brained idea because he's got nothing else to do?" Turning to his men, he said, "Let's go get those boxes." As one of Kennerly's men tossed his gun into a trailer, a live round exploded out of the chamber, tore through the side of the trailer, and passed between Kennerly and the lieutenant. The two men looked each other in the eye. The lieutenant spoke for both: "Everybody in the jeep. Let's get the hell out of here."

They turned left on the main road and dropped sharply toward the river. Along the way, they passed a group of beautiful Belgian horses lying dead and bloated, their feet stretching toward the sky. The sight shocked Kennerly, a farm boy who had always felt a deep empathy for animals caught up in warfare.

Once on the floor of the valley, Kennerly's unit turned left on a dirt road and came upon a courtyard with a well in its center, surrounded by a house and a barn. Drawing water from the well to slake their thirst, the men looked up to see the farm's owner emerging with a stack of bread and cheese. His wife and two teenage daughters followed, their rustic beauty and shy giggles doing more to lift the men's spirits than the food. After an hour, they loaded themselves back into the jeep and started up a mountain slope toward their next position. As they moved out, they met a German prisoner in an SS uniform being led past in the opposite direction. Kennerly figured he must have been the sniper. The man smiled as he walked past, revealing a mouthful of large yellow teeth. Kennerly smelled what he had come to recognize as the emblematic odor of the German soldier—a mix between damp earth and a new puppy—that he was sure he could notice from thirty yards away. As riflemen from the 10th pushed the soldier along, the Italian farmer walked over and kicked the man in the seat of his pants. Kennerly figured the man would be lucky to leave the stockades alive. Few SS did.

Once on top of the hill, Kennerly once again took out his binoculars. To the east he could see the towers of Bologna; to the north, he could see the flat Po River valley stretching off toward the horizon. This was the prize they had been striving for since February. Moses, Kennerly thought, never got to the promised land; General Hays would surely not deny his men the pleasure.

Kennerly's vision was fleeting; the next day, April 20, proved so hazy that he could no longer see Bologna or the Po River valley. What he could see, down in the gorge below, was a group of 10th Mountain Cavalry Reconnaissance troops flying along on the backs of beautiful horses they had commandeered from the Italians. Kennerly, a student of heroes such as Light-Horse Harry Lee, Jeb Stuart, and Nathan Bedford Forrest, suspected this might be the last horse cavalry action in the history of the U.S. Army.

Driving toward the river in jeeps, Kennerly's unit passed the wrecks of innumerable German vehicles, among them monstrous 170-mm cannons, their forty-foot-long barrels mounted on steel tires; these were likely the guns used on Castel d'Aiano and Mount della Spe. Crosses, marking German graves, also lined the road. Why do Europeans bury their dead where they fall? Kennerly wondered. It seemed so impersonal. Soon no one will know where they are. In a few years, no one will give a damn.[2]

For meals, the soldiers would stop in at a farmhouse and ask for some bread and cheese, a piece of sausage, a cup of wine. At one stop, a Catholic priest blessed the men in Kennerly's platoon. There was no way Kennerly was going to tell the priest he wasn't Catholic; in war, he figured, you could use all the help you could get. At one crossroads, a large group of 10th soldiers had gathered to await their next orders. Emerging out into the yard of a stone house, an old woman said she would prepare a roast made from a German horse for supper. Kennerly asked the woman if she had seen any German soldiers. *"Tedeschi tutti via,"* she said. The Germans have all gone.

Almost on cue, German gunfire sounded to the west. Kennerly grabbed his gun and jumped for cover. Since Lieutenant D'Ooge had joined the unit on Belvedere, Kennerly's team had not lost a single man. It would be a shame to get it so close to the end. As suddenly as it began, the shooting stopped. In the distance, a group of Americans stood over a German soldier lying on the ground with a bullet hole over his still-blinking left eye. Every few seconds, his lips moved and his arms and legs twitched. He had apparently tried to run the roadblock. You dumb sonofabitch, Kennerly thought. Why didn't you surrender? Don't you realize the war is almost over?

As Kennerly and his team prepared to make their way down to the river, a motorcycle with two German soldiers aboard came roaring down the road, apparently oblivious to the arrival of the Americans. Under a barrage of rifle fire, the motorcycle spun out and crashed, its driver tumbling off to the side with a bullet in his thigh and a surprised look on his face. A crate of eggs that had been lashed to the rear of the motorcycle had landed in a ditch by the side of the road. Apparently the soldiers had been sent to Bologna on a shopping run for their company mess and were unaware that in their brief absence their fortunes had changed dramatically. As medics patched up the German soldiers, Kennerly and his men commandeered their motorcycle, pistols, and what was left intact inside the crate and went off to cook up the first fresh eggs they had had since arriving in Italy.

The Germans seemed now to be in full retreat. The 10th's foot soldiers continued to move forward, using any vehicles they could find: abandoned German trucks, Volkswagen jeeps, Italian sports cars, motorcycles, bicycles, horse-drawn wagons, a school bus, even an old 1936 Ford. To Kennerly, they looked like a band of heavily armed gypsies.

As they advanced along the flat bottomlands to the Po River, the chalky roads weaving through an endless chain of irrigation canals threw up a fine dust that turned everything white. Dust got into their pores, their eyes. In places, the dust was so thick, the truck drivers were having a hard time keeping their vehicles on the road. At one point a dust-covered jeep driven by a fearless, sandy-haired, and completely grimy soldier nicknamed Nellie came screaming up the road toward Kennerly, who couldn't help but notice the dents in the jeep's chassis, apparently the result of Nellie plowing into the rear of a six-by the day before.

"Why don't you slow down?" Kennerly asked.

"If I slow down," he said, "I can't get to where I'm a-goin'."

Getting killed by Germans was one thing, Kennerly thought; getting killed in a wreck would be damn stupid.

As the men moved on, hundreds of demoralized German prisoners, unguarded, marched in the opposite direction. They must have known the war was almost over, Kennerly figured; besides, there was nowhere else for them to go. By the time the division reached the river, some four thousand prisoners would be captured, disarmed, and taken in trucks to the rear.[3]

GENERAL ROBINSON DUFF'S advance task force reached the banks of the Po River on April 22. On its shores, willows were beginning to leaf out. The south bank of the river was low and flat, broken by three high dikes a hundred yards apart. Two hundred yards across (about the width of the Colorado River where the men had once practiced river crossings), sandy beaches lined the north bank. As the 87th Regiment approached from the south, the main blacktop road to a ferry landing ran atop one of the dikes, which offered some shelter to the men as they waited to load up. They needed it. As the trucks were delivering boats to the riverside, the Germans were wasting no time battering the American position with artillery shells. Just 2,500 yards to the west, they had set up two crescents of 20-mm anti-aircraft guns.

Only an hour before the task force reached San Benedetto Po, the primary point of departure, General Duff saw an antitank mine lying in the path of one of his own advancing tanks. When his warning shouts went unnoticed by the tank's driver, the general ran forward to get the tank to stop. Just as he arrived, the tank hit the mine. The explosion wounded Duff badly. Determined to complete the push, General Hays took command of the spearhead himself.[4]

Given more time, division commanders would likely have decided that a crossing farther east would have lessened the army's vulnerability to German antiaircraft artillery. But the sheer speed of the division's advance meant that no aerial reconnaissance photos had been taken of the river, and the German position on the north bank had been noted too late for thorough reconnaissance. Though some artillery protection arrived before the crossing, it was far from the air support and heavy artillery the men needed. In fact, the division had moved so quickly that there weren't any vehicles available. Worse, almost no bridge-building material had arrived, nor were power boats or amphibious vehicles available. The men would have to paddle themselves across. They didn't even have a telephone cable sturdy enough to withstand the river's strong current. There were no maps. General Hays had concocted the plan only the night before; at 6 P.M. on the twenty-second, he dispatched an engineer to Bomporto to round up fifty assault boats. Twelve hours later, the "assault boats" arrived south of San Benedetto Po on the back of five 2½-ton trucks. Hays could hardly have been impressed. The boats were little paddleboats that could hold just four oarsmen and six soldiers. Moving an entire division across in these things would be a trick.

As D Company of the 87th set up machine guns and 81-mm mortars on the left side of the road, the 85th's 3rd Battalion did the same on the right.[5]

The night before the crossing, the Germans strafed the south side of the river; the next day their antiaircraft batteries chased Allied planes away, then leveled the same guns on the mountain troops. When Kennerly arrived, he could see, far down the river, a bridge that had been blown out. He dug a gun pit and hunkered down—just in time to see General Hays and a couple of colonels arrive with their aides. Snapping to attention, Kennerly saluted.

"At ease," Hays said. "How you boys doin'?"

"Fine, sir," Kennerly replied. "We've been giving the Germans a good ass-kicking."

The general grinned. "We sure have."

Hays told his men that he was looking for some large rowboats to help get across the river but that German warplanes had been creating some problems upriver. He advised the men to put covers over their foxholes.

Later on, word came down that the 87th would be crossing the river that same afternoon, a couple of hundred yards to Kennerly's left. To cover the crossing, the 85th would lay down a barrage aimed at the other side of the river and would only lift it when the boats arrived on the opposite bank. As soon as the 87th established a defensive perimeter, the 85th would cross. The prospect of crossing the Po made many of the men nervous. They had never made such a move before, except in training, and the idea of rowing across two hundred yards of open water under marauding German warplanes hardly improved the prospect. Kennerly, who had started his military career as a swimming instructor, didn't even know how many of his men could swim. He told them to put their packs in the bottom of the boat; if the boat capsized, they were to hold on to the upturned bottom of the boat and kick their way across. The boat would not sink, and the men would not drown—unless they wasted their energy trying to flip the boat right side up and climb back in.[6]

As the 87th loaded up on April 23, German artillery shells began splashing all around them. Small-arms fire popped everywhere. In Denis Nunan's boat, men who hadn't been given paddles dug in with the butts of their rifles, trying to push their boat across as fast as they could. Pausing for a moment to catch his breath, Nunan raised a camera to capture the scene and the camera was shot right out of his hands. Bullets tore into men right next to him, but once again Nunan survived without a scratch.[7]

As Dan Kennerly watched, the lead boats made it halfway across the river; then German artillery opened fire, their initial shells exploding in the air and pounding into the river. My God, he thought, they are going to be slaughtered. Where in the hell were the American airplanes? Kennerly's platoon strafed the opposite bank with their machine guns, spraying the spot where the boats hoped to hit the beach. As the first men made it ashore, a rifleman fired on a German-occupied house on the bank above. From the south side, an Allied tank destroyer dropped two shells on the upper story of the house, finally convincing five Germans to come out with their hands above their heads. At last the Allied planes arrived, and the German artillery stopped. The first boats made it ashore, the men scrambling up the banks and disappearing over the top of the dike. The landing was so swift that some six hundred German soldiers, including a corps commander, were taken prisoner before they could make it to their foxholes.

At 4 P.M., Kennerly's battalion was ordered into the boats. Kennerly had his men lay their gun pack and equipment in first, then pile in on top. At first the anxious soldiers started rowing at will, sending the boat spinning erratically rather than forward in a straight line; Kennerly, like a giant coxswain, ordered his men to paddle only on his count. Stroke. Stroke. Stroke. Halfway across the river, their oars hit the sandy bottom. The men could probably wade in from here; instead, they leaned more heavily still into their oars and moments later struck the riverbank, climbed out, and hustled over the dike. Off in the distance to the north lay a sight the men had waited to see since leaving Camp Hale: the snowy peaks of the Alps.

For the next several days, as engineers built a treadway and a pontoon bridge across the Po, the sleepless men of the 10th Mountain Division, moving with the speed and excitement of the victorious, cleared the roads north of the river to make way for a column of tanks. The intense fear of the previous weeks was beginning to drift away. Kennerly spent one afternoon pulling up and eating the hottest onions he had ever tasted from a farm field; later, a soldier with a more sensitive nose told him he had been eating giant bulbs of garlic. Guess I won't have to shoot any Germans today, Kennerly thought to himself. I'll just breathe and they'll run like rabbits.[8]

What the men in the mountain troops couldn't see was a stream of German soldiers running for the Alps. "This might have been regarded as a sign of imminent disintegration, had we not long since become accustomed to the sight," General von Senger would write. "Every man questioned insisted that his unit had been 'rolled up,' or 'outflanked,' had fought its way out, and was assembling 'in accordance with orders' in its rear service area. The possibility of grouping the stragglers in units other than their own directly behind a newly occupied line of defense did not exist, for the soldiers were too fearful of being cut off from their mail, their field kitchens, and their familiar military surroundings."[9]

With the war in Europe coming to an end and word of liberated concentration camps beginning to reach the division, the ghastliness of what the men had been fighting became all too clear. Most of the men, throughout their training and first months in Italy, had considered Hitler's expansionism their only enemy. Only after news of the wide-reaching Nazi genocide became public did they realize the full stake of their commitment to the war. Like the rest of the world, the mountain troops at first had trouble finding words to express their horror. In a caustically sarcastic editorial, *The Blizzard* recommended that American soldiers become "buddies" with their German counterparts:

> Dachau the unspeakable? Forget it. Forget the freight cars stacked with whip-scarred dead, the smooth efficiency of the crematory. Forget Dachau's compound, swarming with 32,000 lice-ridden, typhus infected beings so hysterical at freedom they tore themselves heedlessly getting through the barbed wire to touch their liberators.
>
> Forget the wholesale slaughter of prisoners at Buchenwald, prisoners who smelled like nothing else on earth. The chute below which SS guards waited to strangle them with garrotes, the hooks on which they hung until their turn at the furnaces. (They had to wait. The furnaces only handled 400 daily.) Forget Erla, whose SS guards, unable to carry their prisoners with them when Leipzig fell, jammed 295 of them into one barracks, doused prisoners and buildings with acetate, and ignited a roaring inferno. Forget the screams of terror, the bursting hand grenades tossed in the doorways, the crazed human torches mowed down with machine pistols and bazookas, clubbed to death as they tried to douse the flames in the filth of the latrine. And Belsen, where 17,000 died of starvation in March alone, where the scattered dead lay in thousands under the miles of pipes, their clothes torn off by the living to build fires for cooking roots, their hearts and livers cut out by the starving.
>
> Oh no. Don't embarrass these fine people, who are very sentimental about flowers and adore little children. Give them a sportsmanlike pat on the back and wish them better luck next time. Otherwise you might discourage them. The sons of bitches are terribly sensitive.[10]

Even with the Germans in retreat, the mountain troops were still jumpy. The roads were littered with abandoned vehicles and dead German soldiers. Here was one young man sitting upright, his face blown away, revealing a hideous smile; there were two others inside a truck, their arms and feet and chest muscles completely burned away. A German plane sat smoking on a makeshift airfield. One afternoon an unmarked sedan came screaming down the road, moving Kennerly's platoon to follow it with their machine guns. Hold your fire, Kennerly said, and good thing: the car was being driven by a group of drunk Italian partisans, laughing and holding aloft bottles of wine. Those crazy bastards better show some discretion, Kennerly thought, or someone is going to get nervous and blow their asses away.

The soldiers' vigilance would prove well advised. After a couple of days marching north, the men came to a number of well-to-do villages laced through with leaf-lined avenues, large estates, and carriage houses. Removing their shirts and shoes to soak up some sunshine one afternoon, a column of men from the 85th suddenly heard the *whoosh*, boom, and whine of an exploding artillery shell releasing its shrapnel. Silent, and terrified, the men jumped into bunkers and waited. Ten minutes later, Kennerly looked out to see medics stuffing the body of a dead American soldier into a mattress cover, his blood already staining the sheets. That poor bastard, Kennerly thought. He was lying in the sun just like the rest of us, without a worry, thinking he was miles from any action, the war was almost over, and he's made it. Now he's dead because some sorry sonofabitch decided to fire one last round before he abandoned his gun. What lousy rotten luck.[11]

CHAPTER FIFTEEN

SLEEPING IN MUSSOLINI'S BED

W

ITH ONLY FLATLAND REMAINING between the Po and the Alps, the mountain troops pushed the pace to the shores of Lake Garda, a magnificent lobe of deep mountain water that had inspired Goethe, Shelley, and D. H. Lawrence. Before the First World War, the lake's eastern shore had served as a border between Italy and Austro-Hungary; more recently, it had become the final redoubt for Germany's XIV Panzer Corps, commanded by General von Senger. The regional center of the German army was centered in the towns of Riva and Torbole, on the lake's north end. Other prizes, on the lake's western shore, were the headquarters of Mussolini's puppet government in Gargnano and, just to the town's south, an opulent thirty-seven-room mansion known as Villa Feltrinelli that Il Duce had used as a retreat. Once again, the division made its objective in a remarkably swift fashion. Some units covered the last eighteen miles in four hours.

The water of Lake Garda was a remarkable deep blue, its shores evolving from broad, flat plains in the south to dramatic, Yosemite-like crags to the north. Along the western shoreline were villas and hotels catering to Europe's elite, their windows gazing up at the gray granite and snow of the Alps to the north. To Dan Kennerly, the lake was the most beautiful place he had ever seen.[1]

On April 26, General Hays announced the final plan for the

assault on Lake Garda. The entire division would move along a single narrow road up the lake's eastern shore, with one regiment up front marching hard for eight hours while the other two regiments rested. At the end of each shift, a rested regiment would move to the front in transport trucks. The 87th would take the point first, followed by the 85th, then the 86th. With no German opposition, Hays figured the division could cover the lake's sixty-mile shoreline in twenty-four hours.

The next day, the 87th's K Company led and moved out as far as Bardolino, a third of the way up the eastern shore, without opposition, other than streets crowded with cheering Italians offering sprays of flowers and jugs of wine. All along the south end of the lake, church bells heralded the division's approach. To the north, things were far more ominous. The Germans had taken control of the lake's north end, where the towns of Riva and Torbole were protected by enormous mountain walls.

Well-armed German patrols also controlled the road leading north from at least the town of Garda, just north of Bardolino, where American scouts had reported seeing SS troops with self-propelled guns and artillery. After the lowlands of the lake's southern lobe, the terrain leading to Garda also became dramatically more hilly, the road pinched between a rising butte to the right and the lakeshore hard on the left. Once again, the Germans had taken advantage of the landscape's natural defenses.

As the 87th advanced on Garda, a platoon encountered a roadblock just to the south of the town. When a party took some heavy machine-gun fire while marching up the road, one platoon hopped over a stone retaining wall to the left of the road and continued the assault along the water's edge. Another platoon climbed up the steep butte to the right of the road. A third stayed on the road, in a staggered column. Under artillery support from the rear, the teams managed to silence the machine gun inside the roadblock. The unit moving along the water's edge soon ran out of dry land and had to hop back up onto the road, where it emerged right in front of the roadblock and instantly drew a storm of high-velocity, armor-piercing shells, which smashed into the road and rock outcroppings, sending forth waves of stone shards. An engineer was killed, and American bodies lay all over the road.

Under fire from antiaircraft guns, a sergeant named Robert Manchester and thirteen of his men rushed forward to occupy a building in the

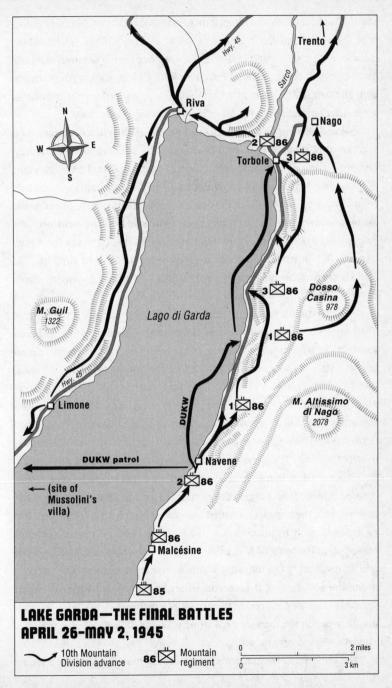

Trento

Hwy. 45

Sarco

Riva

Nago

2 ⊠ 86

Torbole

3 ⊠ 86

N
W E
S

3 ⊠ 86

Dosso
Casina
978

M. Guil
1322

Lago di Garda

1 ⊠ 86

Hwy. 45

1 ⊠ 86

M. Altissimo
di Nago
2078

Limone

DUKW

DUKW patrol

Navene

(site of
Mussolini's
villa)

2 ⊠ 86

⊠ 86
Malcésine

⊠ 85

**LAKE GARDA—THE FINAL BATTLES
APRIL 26–MAY 2, 1945**

⌇ 10th Mountain
Division advance

86 ⊠ Mountain
regiment

0 _____ 2 miles
0 _____ 3 km

town of Garda, where they hoped to get a line of sight on the ack-ack gunmen. Moving from the Terminal Hotel to other buildings nearby, Manchester, a BAR team, and two riflemen drew fire from a German machine gun. The BAR man, Private First Class John Clenin, took a round in the arm and, while the others attended to him, took a shard from a grenade as well. After patching him up, Manchester decided to withdraw.

Meanwhile, on the butte to the right of the road, a first lieutenant and veteran mountaineer named John Hunter was pushing less experienced climbers over a series of massive boulders to get a look at the German gun emplacements. As they came over a small ridge, they could see another road leading to the lake from the east. Along it, about two thousand yards away, was a column of a hundred German soldiers, two field artillery pieces, two trucks, and a tank. Hunter scrambled back down the butte, found a British artillery colonel, and asked for some rapid support. The shells landed precisely, flipping over one of the trucks and destroying a pair of 88s. The column of German soldiers scattered.

At 7:30 P.M. on the twenty-seventh, the 87th pulled up in the town of Torri del Benaco, one town north of Garda, and allowed the 85th, and then the 86th, to pass through. Through the night, Edward Nickerson's squad in the 85th's G Company, out in front of the entire rest of the division, hiked seventeen miles on the two-lane road between the lake and the towering mountains before giving over to the 86th; at one point, General Hays himself drove up in a jeep to check on their progress. Sometime before daylight, the lead companies of the 86th came to the first of five road tunnels north of Navene. The Germans had destroyed them all.[2]

The next day, Dan Kennerly's platoon set up camp on a large, grass-covered athletic field. Large stone buildings, apparently dormitories, stood nearby. The townspeople seemed friendly, Kennerly thought, but not nearly as friendly as those back in the Po River valley. Kennerly's platoon moved on to the town of Malcesine, south of Navene, famous for its castle and for impressing Goethe. They would wait there until the 86th took control of the north end of the lake; once they had succeeded, the 85th would complete its drive for Trento, twenty miles northeast of the lake. Unloading their packs, the men sat on a stone wall and looked out over the lake. The war seemed very far away.

Not for long. German convoys were already moving along the western edge of the lake, about two miles from where the 85th had set up. Almost instantly, Allied M-10 tanks and British 5.5-inch howitzers started blasting away at the convoy. Grabbing his binoculars, Kennerly looked over at the convoy and could see a number of trucks in flames, their passengers scurrying for cover. A group of P-47s coursed overhead and completed the job. The convoy was destroyed.

Walking down to the docks, Kennerly couldn't believe his eyes: some British artillerymen were trying to load their massive 5.5-inch howitzers onto a pair of lashed-together fishing boats. That rig is gonna sink sure as hell, he thought, and if it does, that major is going to be sent to an outpost in deep dark Africa for the rest of his life. But he sure had guts, you had to give him that.

Up ahead, as division engineers tried to get the tunnels cleared, units from the 86th had decided to skirt the demolished roads by commandeering amphibious military vehicles, brought north from the Po, and Italian fishing boats. The 2½-ton amphibious boats were known by their initials, DUKWs, given by General Motors to indicate their body type and four-wheel-drive capacity, but were called "ducks," as in "sitting ducks," by the men. The boats could move only six miles per hour.

Though General Hays had ordered fourteen DUKWs, only seven arrived; by the time the men packed themselves into half the space expected, with all their weapons and gear, the boats had barely enough freeboard to stay afloat. Though the men had no life jackets, the company commander directed the boat drivers to move out into open water rather than hug the shore, as Hays had ordered. As the boats moved up the shore, with Hays watching "in horror," the men in the boats were hammered by 88s, which sent up geysers of water fifty feet high. Hays immediately ordered three 105-mm howitzers directed at the big German guns. Finally the boats moved back closer to shore, and the 88s quit. The mission, General Hays would write, "was one of the most daring operations I have ever witnessed."[3]

"The shells were coming close, so we headed for shore, established our own beach-head, and ran for the nearest tunnel," wrote a soldier named Merrill Pollack. "Many men leaped into the water when we approached shore. They got wet up to their waists in their scramble for the steep, shale cliff. I got wet up to the tops of my combat boots, lost my helmet."

With the air corps strafing German positions and swerving to avoid antiaircraft fire, artillery fire from both sides made the lakeside ring and echo; bigger shells blew out the windows of shoreside houses. As the Germans tried to blow up a road between the fourth and fifth tunnels, their explosives went off prematurely, killing at least fifteen of their own soldiers. Body parts and torn clothing were everywhere.

In a last-ditch effort to defend the north end of the lake, the Germans launched another round of 88s from Riva. "For the Germans it was a one in a million shot, and they tried it," Pollack wrote. "The first two landed on either side of the tunnel, the third went ten yards inside, then exploded. The explosion was terrific; a great deal of pressure was built up in the confined space, and the blast ripped out of both ends of the tunnel. Shell fragments ricocheted off the walls; the blast set off rock fragments that were as deadly as the shrapnel. Men who weren't hit were dazed. Amid the smoke and the dust the agonized screams of wounded men filled the air. Cries of 'help, help!' echoed through the tunnel. Men crawled out on their hands and knees over the bodies of dead Germans . . . many thought the explosion was a mine, hesitated to go in immediately after the wounded." The concussive blast wounded fifty men and killed five in the 86th's H Company, including Captain Lawrence Ely. A soldier named Bob Carlson had to "walk over the arms and legs and dismembered bodies of these people who had just been blown to bits."[4]

Not long after this, another DUKW, carrying twenty-five members of the 605th Field Artillery Battalion, flipped over in heavy winds up near the north end of the lake; all hands but one, a soldier named Thomas E. Hough, were drowned.[5]

AS THE MOUNTAIN TROOPS advanced up the lake, Daniel Petruzzi, who had spent the war acting as a liaison officer between the Allies and the partisans before being attached to the 10th, was driving through Milan when he came upon a mob roiling around an Esso service station in Loreto Square, just off the autostrada. Stopping to see what the noise was all about, he saw a string of bodies hanging upside down, riddled by machine-gun bullets. Among them, wearing a bloody white shirt, was Benito Mussolini. Next to him, her skirt hanging around her face, was his mistress,

Clara Petacci. Throughout the crowd, people were spitting on the bodies and cursing. Jumping from his jeep, Petruzzi, the first American officer to arrive at the scene, shouted at the crowd in Italian, "*Vergogna!* [Shame!] You should be ashamed of yourselves! You have barely been liberated from barbarism and already you are acting worse than your oppressors . . . already you dishonor your country." His disgust spent, Petruzzi asked his driver to get moving before the two got shot themselves.[6]

On the first day of May, word began to spread south that the north end of Lake Garda had finally fallen. This news was quickly followed by word that the Germans planned to surrender Italy at 6 P.M. the following day. There was no shouting, no firing of guns. Dan Kennerly was overwhelmed with relief that he and his men had made it through the war alive, and would not have to chase the Germans into the Alps. The men were also washed over with grief for their comrades who had not been so lucky.

Indeed, rumors of the impending surrender were subdued by news that one of the division's highest-ranking officers had been killed by a random shell up in Torbole, at the lake's north end. It was Colonel William Darby, the legendary founder of the Army Rangers who had won the Distinguished Service Cross in Sicily. Darby had just been made the division's assistant commander, replacing Brigadier General Robinson Duff, who had been wounded just before the crossing of the Po. Darby had been meeting with General David Ruffner and several other officers in a hotel in Torbole that had become the 86th's command post. Just minutes before the meeting broke up, the officers heard a German 88-mm shell explode nearby. Ruffner told Darby he would have his jeep driver take them up to the front to have a look at the troops. When Ruffner's assistant, Bud Warner, started to get into his usual seat on the jeep's rear passenger side, Ruffner asked him to remain in town and give his seat to Darby instead. Just as Darby hoisted himself into the jeep's backseat, another shell from an 88 tore into the adjacent building. Pieces of shrapnel ripped into Darby's chest, killing him and Sergeant Major Tim Evans instantly.[7]

ON MAY 4, A GROUP of generals including Truscott and Benjamin Chidlaw, who oversaw the air forces in Italy, arrived at Mark Clark's headquarters in Florence, removed their sidearms, and, before a throng of reporters, awaited the arrival of German officers, who would officially declare the surrender of Italy. General Heinrich von Vietinghof, the commander of all German armies in southwestern Europe, was holed up in the Alps near the Brenner Pass, afraid that partisans would kill him if he tried to make the trip south. In his place came General von Senger, the commander of the XIV Panzer Corps, who had spent the day before in Verona discussing the terms of surrender with the mountain troops' commander, General George Hays. Senger considered his trip from the mountains to Florence one of his most dangerous assignments of the war; his caravan had been attacked repeatedly by partisans, and he would have been killed had not a group of American officers intervened.

In sunnier times for the German army, Senger had participated in the French surrender, so he knew what he was in for. He arrived at Clark's office wearing a green uniform with an Iron Cross hanging from a ribbon around his neck. He still seemed to be shaking from his near capture by the partisans and hardly felt at home after Clark's cocker spaniel bit him through his boot. "General Clark," Senger said with an Oxford accent he had picked up as a Rhodes Scholar. "As representative of the German commander in chief, southwest, I report to you as commander of the Fifteenth Army Group for your orders for the surrendered German land forces."

Clark ordered his staff to pull some papers together. Senger saluted, turned, and made for the door. Only then did a reporter notice that the German had never removed a small pistol attached to a holster on his belt. Standing in the doorway, Clark called Senger back. "Get rid of that gun," he said. The German took off the leather belt, turned, and flung it toward the foot of a tree.[8]

By the end of the campaign in Italy, Allied forces had taken 160,000 prisoners of war. The Allies had suffered 312,000 killed, wounded, or captured—189,000 of them from the ranks of the American Fifth Army. In the 602 days since it had landed at Salerno, the Fifth Army alone had seen 32,000 soldiers killed, 134,000 wounded, and 22,000 missing in action. The German losses in Italy have been hard to accurately estimate, but army casualties have been placed at 435,000, including 48,000 men killed in action and 214,000 missing.

Over the course of its mission in Italy, the 19,000 men of the 10th Mountain Division (14,000 of whom shipped out from Virginia, plus

5,000 replacements) faced a total of some 100,000 German soldiers. Though 978 soldiers died, 3,882 were wounded, and 28 were taken prisoner, the mountain troops effectively destroyed five full divisions. Senger, a veteran of fronts in Russia and France as well as throughout Italy, told Hays that the 10th was the most impressive opposing force he had ever faced.[9]

Praise streamed into Italy from the highest echelons of the Allied forces. Mark Clark called the division's action "one of the most vital and brilliant of the campaign." Major General Crittenberger said, "Seldom has a division contributed more effectively to an offensive which has so decisively thrown German forces completely off balance."[10]

For the men of the 10th Mountain Division, however, most warming was the praise given by their own leader, General George P. Hays. "I am proud indeed that the knockout thrust has been spearheaded by the 10th Mountain Division," Hays told them. "When you go home, no one will believe you when you start telling of the spectacular things you have done. There have been more heroic deeds and experiences crammed into these days than I have ever heard of. Many times we stuck our neck out with exposed flanks. At one time we were 45 miles in advance with both our flanks exposed. The Lord had us by the hand."[11]

Hays ended the campaign in Italy in style: on a tip, he investigated a small building in a mountain village where the Germans were rumored to have stored a vast collection of art stolen from Florence. He found the building, marked with a red cross, completely stuffed with paintings and guarded by a German professor. Hays posted a platoon of mountain troops to guard the paintings until a unit from the 88th Infantry Division could take over the postwar transfer of the art.[12]

Dan Kennerly spent his last days in Italy as he had spent his first days in the army: as a lifeguard, keeping watch as the exhausted men of the 10th swam from the beaches of the lake. Hugh Evans ended the war in a military hospital in the Po River valley. Miraculously, the hepatitis, the polio, and the paralysis in his legs dissipated, and he managed to rejoin his company for their return to the United States. "When all this waste of time is through, I have a million and one things I want to do: college, travel, work, sing, think, travel, marry and have children," Evans wrote home. "Mother, I'm afraid I still have stardust in my eyes. Did you ever notice how a star winks, mother; mine always seems to wink and twinkle. The only thing to do is to sneak up on it and grab it. Of course you don't know what I'm talking about. You probably have guessed by now that I have had a beer today. It's true but the music has had the main effect on me."[13]

For Dick Wilson, the end of the war meant being transported from one hospital to another. The nerves in his hand were slow in healing, but the doctors told Wilson he would eventually get the feeling in his fingers back. He eventually did—but only after three years in the hospital and twenty-eight operations.[14]

Denis Nunan rediscovered peacetime in a tiny hamlet barely clinging to the side of Lake Garda, and it was here that the Irish romantic finally fell in love with a beautiful Italian girl. While washing the road dirt from his face at a community watering trough near a tiny chapel, Nunan picked his head up to find himself surrounded by a pack of Italian children. A handful of candy bars made quick friends of the youngsters, and soon Nunan was tossing a ball around with a boy and chasing others, threatening to toss them in the watering trough. The children quickly realized their strength in numbers, and soon every kid in town was throwing water on their new American friend. Parents poured out of their houses to watch Nunan get soaked to the skin.

As Nunan looked out from the water streaming down his face, his eye settled on a girl, her dark face framed by black braids tied with dirty ribbons. She flashed Nunan a perfect smile, and Nunan took the cue. He chased her down, held her over the trough, and was just about to give her a dunking when his heart melted and he let her go. That night, Nunan and the girl sat down after dark for a meal. Although Nunan hadn't eaten since three the previous morning, he was plainly in better shape than the girl. He gave her his rations, and as the townspeople watched in envy, she wolfed them down. After supper, Nunan took the girl home, his heart dancing, and handed her an armload of rations and a few bars of soap for her mother. After securing a promise to share breakfast the next morning, Nunan returned to his billet, elated.

During the night, however, orders came through to move out, Nunan and his men left before dawn. "'Twas hard to go by my girl's house without being able to say good-bye," Nunan remembered. "All day long I wondered what she thought when she woke and burst out of her door to find no soldiers in town." The girl who had so captured Nunan's fancy was ten years old.[15]

Perhaps no one ended the war in more dramatic fashion than Gene Hames. In the last days of April, Hames, part of the 85th's 3rd Battalion, watched from Lake Garda's eastern shore as Germans appeared and disappeared between the long tunnels on the opposite side. On the rainy evening of April 30, Hames found himself walking so late into the night that he almost fell asleep on his feet. Halfway up the lakeshore, Hames was called into a battalion command post for an intelligence briefing. He was ordered to pile ten of his men into a small motorboat, cross the lake, and capture Villa Feltrinelli, where Mussolini had been spending quite a bit of time. The villa was south of Gargnano, where Il Duce had run his puppet government after the Italian capitulation.

Hames didn't like the assault idea. He could tell just by looking through his binoculars that his platoon would be vastly outnumbered. A handful of men in a small boat would be easy pickings for even a lone man with a sniper rifle. As Hames and his men, teeth clenched, were getting their automatic weapons together for the mission, a jeep drove up. A colonel whom Hames had never seen before jumped out. When he spotted the "chicken" on his shoulder and a 10th Mountain patch, Hames walked over and saluted. The man turned out to be Colonel Darby, the assistant division commander who would be killed two days later. When Hames told Darby what he had been ordered to do, Darby said he didn't like the plan. Hames said he didn't like it either. Darby canceled the mission.

Instead, on Darby's orders, the crossing would be made by a company-sized special task force. Platoons would be loaded into amphibious DUKWs. If the DUKWs would make the crossing a bit more pleasant than the skiffs the 10th had used to cross the Po, the granite walls rising above Lake Garda's eastern shore would amplify the noise from their heavy engines into a cacophony. To Hames, crossing the lake in these clumsy boats would be like hunting pheasants from the back of a Ford tractor. There would be absolutely no chance for surprise.

The plan was to pull up north of Gargnano, climb up a series of short terraces, move south along the access road, occupy the town, and storm the villa. At 1:30 A.M. on April 30, as he and the two hundred men of K Company packed themselves into a half-dozen DUKWs, Hames discovered that his boat—the lead boat—had a .50-caliber machine gun mounted to the left of the driver's seat. Besides Hames, no one in his platoon had ever fired such a big gun, and he had done so only at OCS, shooting at targets towed by small planes. While the rest of the platoon hunkered down in the boat, Hames stood by the gun all the way across the lake. Behind him, the rest of K Company growled along in a staggered formation, their engines plainly audible under the night sky.

As Hames and his platoon approached the shore, braced for a firefight, they were surprised and heartened by the quiet. Surely, even if the Germans had held off firing during the crossing, they must be waiting to hammer the men as they emerged from the boats. Pulling up to the terraced shoreline, Hames kept the machine gun trained on the rising slope; still no noise. With some of his replacement troops reluctant to leave the landing area, Hames felt his anger rising. He cursed them to get moving.

Strangely, the first man Hames came across was an elderly Italian man riding a bicycle through the early-morning darkness. He was lucky he wasn't shot. The man told Hames that the Germans had left that morning. Sure enough, the rest of K Company moved into Gargnano's government buildings and town square with no resistance. Hames took a group of riflemen and a machine gun up a series of steep switchbacks above the town and set up a roadblock along the road leading into town.

Down they went to the villa, an elegant, two-story affair with three dozen rooms. By the waterfront they discovered a dock and, sunk beneath it, what until quite recently had been a very nice motorboat. Behind the main building they discovered a cement-floored bomb shelter. Inside the garage were two large limousines, their engines apparently blown apart by phosphorous grenades. Like the motorboat, the cars seemed to have been sabotaged.

The villa itself was filled with the trappings of a dictator who had not only fallen but had been seriously ill, including a room Hames dubbed The Pharmacy, stuffed with pills and medicinal powders. There was an enormous kitchen, which the men quickly had humming for a feast of fish, vegetables, and eggs. Upstairs in the thirty-seven-room mansion, Hames found a number of well-appointed bedrooms, which he assigned to every member of his platoon. For himself, as the leader of the amphibious assault, he chose the largest bedroom of all, which for appearances' sake he dubbed Platoon

Headquarters. Two days later, on the night the war in Europe ended, a night on which he and everyone else got roaring drunk on grappa, wine, beer, and "anything that would run down hill," Gene Hames, the boy who had grown up in a house with no running water and no electricity, who had had to ride his horse to school in the middle of Montana winters, curled up and slept in Mussolini's bed.[16]

N LATE MARCH, SIX WEEKS BEFORE the end of the war, Minnie Dole received a series of letters from Washington stating that despite "services of inestimable value," the relationship between the army and the National Ski Patrol would officially end in late June. Dole was plainly heartbroken. "From my civilian way of thinking, if a specialized division such as the 10th is not fed with the proper replacements, it will soon, due to normal combat attrition, become purely another division of flatland character," he wrote to General Hays. Just six months later, the 10th Mountain Division was deactivated. It was re-formed in 1948, and for a decade would train soldiers for missions in Korea and Europe. By the time it was reorganized in 1985, the division had been moved to Fort Drum, New York, where it remains today.[1]

Minnie Dole had spent so much time volunteering for the war effort that by the time the war ended, he owed his employer $10,000 and had to leave his position at the head of the ski patrol and return to work full-time. As a token of his gratitude for Dole's remarkable contribution to the mountain troops, General Hays gave Dole an Ethiopian sword he had removed from the wall above an armchair in Mussolini's Lake Garda headquarters.[2]

After the war, Dan Kennerly returned to life as a high school science teacher, football coach, and athletic director in Atlanta. Denis

Nunan, after a couple of years as a ranch hand in Colorado, returned to East Coast office work for IBM and other companies. Gene Hames became a trial lawyer in Denver and later served as president of the division's foundation of directors. Art Delaney and Hugh Evans recovered from their injuries and moved to Denver, Delaney as a hotel administrator and Coors beer distributor, Evans as a mining engineer and president of a coal company. Dick Wilson, finally recovered from more than two dozen operations on his arm, became public relations officer for the Disabled American Veterans and a longtime editor of both *The Blizzard* and civilian skiing publications. General Hays died peacefully in 1978 and was buried in Arlington National Cemetery. Up at Cooper Hill, the ski slope near Tennessee Pass, a memorial stone carries the names of the nearly one thousand mountain troops who died during the war, including both famous men such as Torger Tokle and unknown teenagers such as Stuart Abbott.

LOOKING BACK AT THE wartime history of the 10th Mountain Division, it's hard to overlook the fact that for all the remarkable attention they received during three years of training, the "ski troops" hardly ever skied during the war, and only a tiny fraction of the "mountain soldiers"—those who climbed Riva Ridge—ever used their technical mountain training. Even the equipment the men spent so many months testing in the highest mountains in North America never came into play during the war; much of it, in fact, never made it to the front at all. As for the fighting itself, Riva Ridge quickly became the only battle anyone outside the division ever talked about. Like the mountain troops themselves, Riva Ridge gradually accrued a mythical status that, given the rest of the war in Italy, seems out of proportion to its impact on the war.

For those following the exploits of the mountain troops—both before and after they left for Europe—Riva Ridge fit the division's public image perfectly. It was a terribly steep cliff and once again showed the brilliance of the men's extramilitary training. It wasn't marksmanship that won the day, it was mountaineering. But climbing the ridge took a matter of hours, and once the ridge was taken, the division's technical mountaineering skills—to say nothing of its expertise in skiing—were quickly made moot by terrain and spring weather. True, there were some preliminary ski patrols before the fighting got started in earnest, but by the time the men got to Italy the winter of 1945 was largely over. For all of Minnie Dole's remarkable contributions to the division, the ski training he had so adamantly advocated served the men less on the battlefield than their deep sense of camaraderie—stemming, in part, from their sense of a shared identity beyond that of soldiers—and their unprecedented physical fitness.

The fact that the men were kept at Camp Hale for so long, even as the American Fifth Army struggled for months in mountain chain after mountain chain, seems as odd today as it did to the men themselves. Had the division joined the fray at Cassino—as rough a patch of mountains as anything in the Apennines—the Italian campaign might have taken an entirely different turn. A decisive victory in southern Italy might have convinced the Germans to give up their hold on Italy and allowed Allied commanders to inject tens of thousands of experienced soldiers into France. As it in fact played out, the Italian campaign remains the subject of historical debate with one question at its center: Who tied up whom? Both the Allies and the Germans maintained they were in Italy to distract the enemy from other fronts; both sides succeeded—and failed—because of this.

On the other hand, if the mountain troops had arrived to fight at Cassino and had Kesselring still figured out how to escape, the 10th Mountain Division would have faced the same deadly slog up the peninsula that so tormented the rest of the Fifth and Eighth Armies and would doubtless have emerged from the war with an entirely different legacy. The American 34th Division, for example, fought in Italy for twenty months, suffered 16,000 casualties (more than the total number of mountain troopers arriving in Italy) and ended up fighting with 100 percent replacement soldiers. It is at least conceivable that had the mountain troops been inserted into the war at Salerno, every member of the original celebrated unit would likewise have ended up dead or injured.

To be sure, once they did arrive, the division gave the Germans a thumping that finally broke a string of ingenious defensive maneuvers by Kesselring's troops. The taking of Riva Ridge allowed for the taking of Mount Belvedere, which itself opened the way for a spring offensive that ended the war in Italy. The fact that the mountain troops arrived fresh to a campaign that had utterly worn out the armies on both sides served to enhance their strategic effectiveness and their postwar legacy itself.

Though the men were tired from their years of mountain training, this was nothing compared to the exhaustion and psychological horrors that the men of the Fifth Army had experienced since landing at Salerno in early September 1943. Again, soldiers reach their peak of efficiency after about ninety days in the field; for the mountain troops, the end of the war came just seventy-five days after their taking of Riva Ridge. By comparison, by the time the mountain troops even arrived in Italy, the men of the Fifth Army had already been on the front lines for sixteen months. Though the mountain troops had one of the campaign's highest casualty rates—more than 1,200 per month compared to 820 a month for the 34th—their four-month stint at the front nonetheless spared thousands of men who would undoubtedly have suffered injury or death had they trained less and fought more. And given their arrival so late in the war, it seems certain that by the time the mountain troops were inserted into the Apennines, the German armies there had already suffered the moral collapse that all armies suffer when confronted with inevitable defeat. If nothing else, the mountain troops executed one of the most important strategies of war: Arrive late, fight hard, leave early.[3]

THE 10TH MOUNTAIN DIVISION, then, was an unprecedented force of elite soldiers that the army didn't know how to recruit, train, or employ, and they were inserted into a campaign American strategists were never completely sure they wanted to fight. The men trained for an absurdly long time, fought for four short months, won some important battles, suffered their share of slaughter, and went home. The question then becomes why the 10th Mountain Division remains such a fixture in the American imagination, why, sixty years after the end of the war, do so many civilians with no particular interest in military history seem to know the division's story, or at least its reputation.

In addition to the burnishing nature of nostalgia, which has always gilded the memories of great soldiers, the country's romantic attachment to the mountain troopers is surely connected in part to the country's romantic vision of itself. To the great misery of human history, cultures have always used war as a way to develop, test, and honor their men; especially during their endless months of training, when the country was treated to a constant flurry of newspaper, magazine, and film treatments of soldiering in the Rockies, the mountain troops, for a brief time, seemed to offer a hint of something slightly more evolved, a "moral equivalent to war," to use an expression advanced by William James. The physical fitness, survival skills, and wilderness training embodied by the mountain soldiers transcended standard military preparation, turning out men with levels of competence and endurance that average citizens could only marvel at. Given a war that—especially as the century wore on—would stand out for its moral clarity, the mountain troops represented a fighting unit the popular imagination could celebrate for reasons that went far beyond fighting. Somehow, the mountain troopers' stature—in the war but not of it—appealed to the American public from the very beginning. They arrived in training camp as already fully realized heroes; all the army did was shape them into a fighting force. The ski troopers were rugged but irreverent, strong but smart, willing to fight but always aching to leave off fighting and head back into the mountains, which, after the war, they did in droves.

Indeed, by the time the war was over, the fact that the mountain troops had fought at all seemed less crucial to the division's reputation than the skills and raw enthusiasm for the mountains that the men brought back from Italy. If thousands of World War Two veterans contented themselves with a new home in a suburban Levittown, both the Americans and the Europeans who had fought in the mountain division dispersed deep into the country's mountain ranges, eager to put their training to work. In the years immediately following the war, the men employed their ski training and mountaineering skills to their fullest, and it is in this capacity that they have left their most indelible mark on American history and the American landscape. All across the continent, from New England to Colorado to the Tetons and the Cascades, hundreds of division veterans developed and ran more than sixty ski resorts, including Vail, just around the corner from Camp Hale, where a larger-than-life statue of a ski trooper, in full gear, stands watch over a mountain with trail names such as Riva Ridge and Minnie's Mile. Walter Prager became the head ski instructor at Squaw Valley; Alf Engen managed the resort at Alta, where another 10th Mountain vet, Montgomery Atwater, become the country's first expert in avalanche science and rescue. Friedl Pfeiffer (along with John Litchfield, Percy Rideout, and Fritz Benedict) founded Aspen, became coach of the U.S. Ski Team, and was one of thirty division veterans inducted into the U.S. Skiing Hall of Fame. Division veterans skied for the 1948 Olympic team and later helped construct the 10th Mountain Division Trail and Hut System, incorporating three hundred miles of huts and hiking and skiing trails near Camp Hale. John Jay became a world-famous mountain cinematographer; Bill Bowerman, a member of the 86th Regiment, became head track coach both at the University of Oregon and for the 1972 Olympic team in Munich; one of the many veterans who spent careers working for the National Park Service, Bob Frauson became one of the country's leading wilderness rescue experts. David Clark, a member of the 10th Cavalry Reconnaissance, recently became the oldest man to circumnavigate the globe alone under sail.

Paul Petzoldt's National Outdoor Leadership School remains one of the country's finest centers for mountain training and has turned out generations of men and women with not only remarkable wilderness skills but deeply ingrained respect for the wilderness they explore. David Brower, upon his return, eventually became the head of the Sierra Club and one of the century's most admired wilderness advocates. Bob Bates, though more an architect than a member of the division, continued to make remarkable ascents of the world's highest mountains and later became the first director of the Peace Corps chapter in Nepal. Likewise, Minnie Dole's National Ski Patrol not only transformed but sustained what has become a colossal winter sports industry. It is not too much to say that the conservation and exploration of American wilderness are as much a part of the division's history as its contribution to the war. Beyond the hype over their training, beyond even their wartime heroics, the 10th Mountain Division has left a legacy of spirited integrity that continues to do honor to the majestic American landscape.

Except where otherwise noted, all letters and correspondence consulted for this book can be found in the 10th Mountain Division Resource Center within the Department of Western History and Genealogy at the Denver Public Library (DPL). All additional documents from this collection, including official military documents, unpublished manuscripts, and Dan Kennerly's comprehensive oral history of the division, are noted "DPL."

Details denoted by "Imbrie chronology" are taken from the comprehensive list of relevant dates and facts compiled by John Imbrie, a 10th Mountain Division veteran and vice president for data acquisition and research for the National Association of the 10th Mountain Division, Inc., and his wife, Barbara. This chronology can be explored at the Web site http://10thmtndivassoc.org. All other sources are included in the bibliography.

PROLOGUE: THE NORTHERN APENNINES, WINTER 1944

1. "Why should we not": Samuel Hynes et al., eds., *Reporting World War Two. Part One: American Journalism 1938–1944* (New York: Library of America, 1995), 570.

2. "Nothing that the Fifth": *The New York Times*, September 25, 1944; Frido von Senger und Etterlin, *Neither Fear nor Hope: The Wartime Career of General Frido von Senger und Etterlin*, trans. George Malcolm (New York: E. P. Dutton, 1964), 276.

3. "It is awful": Hynes et al., *Part One*, 491, 496.

4. General Hays replied: Harris Dusenbery and Wilson P. Ware, *The North*

Apennines and Beyond with the 10th Mountain Division (Portland, Oreg.: Binford and Mort, 1998), 170.

5. Impossible, Truscott said: Henry Hampton, "The Riva Ridge Operation: Report of Lt. Col. Henry J. Hampton. Headquarters, 86th Mountain Infantry," 12, DPL; First Lieutenant Ian Francis, "The Assault of Riva Ridge: 1st Battalion, 86th Mountain Infantry Regiment, 19 February 1945. A Battle Analysis Submitted to the Infantry School Faculty for Completion of the Infantry Captain's Career Course in Military History, April 10, 1999," 12, DPL.

CHAPTER 1: SKIERS

1. In July 1942: Denis Nunan, letter to mother, July 6, 1942.

2. The first man to appear: Morten Lund, "Minot Dole, the Man Who . . . ," *Ski*, January 1966.

3. This history was well known: Frido von Senger und Etterlin, *Neither Fear nor Hope: The Wartime Career of General Frido von Senger und Etterlin*, trans. George Malcolm (New York: E. P. Dutton, 1964), 231.

4. Perhaps the most famous: Column by R. G. Lynch, *Milwaukee Journal*, March 18, 1945.

5. "When the time comes": Roderick M. Grant, "They'll Be Coming 'Round the Mountain," *Popular Mechanics*, December 1942, 50.

6. A headline over: Ralf Myers [*sic*], "Troops Training at Camp Hale Are Tough Triple-Threat Men; Must Be Able to Ski, Ride Mules, and Use Mountain Motorized Equipment; None But Real He-Men Need Apply," *The Denver Post*, January 13, 1943.

7. On a Saturday night: Charles Minot Dole, *Adventures in Skiing* (New York: Franklin and Watts, 1965), 90; Hal Burton, *The Ski Troops* (New York: Simon and Schuster, 1971), 19–23.

8. "No one can say": David Bradley, letter to Charles Minot Dole, February 18, 1941.

9. Dole knew the mountains: Dole, *Adventures*, 4–15.

10. The moniker could have stuck: Ibid., 18–29.

11. As traumatic as Dole's injury: Ibid., 53; Burton, *The Ski Troops*, 54–56.

12. So impressive was: Dole, *Adventures*, 67, 71; Burton, *The Ski Troops*, 58.

13. Dole and Roger Langley wrote: Major General E. S. Adams, letter to

Charles Minot Dole, September 16, 1940, DPL; George Marshall, letter to Charles Minot Dole, November 9, 1940.

CHAPTER 2: MOUNTAINEERS

1. In the fall of 1942: Author's interview with Robert Bates, January 4, 2002.
2. In July 1939: Ibid.
3. By the spring of 1940: Charles Minot Dole, *Adventures in Skiing* (New York: Franklin and Watts, 1965), 93–99.
4. On September 12: Ibid., 100.
5. Three months after: Robert Bates, *The Love of Mountains Is Best: Climbs and Travels from K2 to Kathmandu* (Portsmouth, N.H.: Peter E. Randall, Publisher, 1994), 165; Robert Bates, letters to Barbara Walton, July 16, 1998, and July 7, 1998.
6. Carter's first concern: Adams Carter, "Mountain Intelligence," unpublished manuscript, 1–4; Dole, *Adventures*, 107, DPL.
7. The extreme temperatures: Carter, "Mountain Intelligence," 5.
8. In the summer of 1941: Bates, *The Love of Mountains*, 167–181.
9. Searching for a warmer alternative: Ibid., 183–184, 186, 209.
10. Now that the army: Charles Minot Dole, letter to George Marshall, July 30, 1941.
11. On hearing this news: "Resolution of the National Volunteer Winter Defense Committee of the National Ski Association," October 8, 1941, DPL.
12. At long last: Hal Burton, *The Ski Troops* (New York: Simon and Schuster, 1971), 91–92.

CHAPTER 3: CASCADES AND ICE FIELDS

1. On the Soviet side: Larry Leseur, *Twelve Months That Changed the World* (New York: Alfred A. Knopf, 1943), 88–89.
2. On December 4, 1941: Williamson Murray, "Barbarossa," in *No End Save Victory: Perspectives on World War II*, ed. Robert Cowley et al. (New York: Putnam, 2001), 107–122.
3. In a May 5, 1942, notice: Charles Minot Dole, notice to National Ski

Patrol, May 5, 1942; author's interview with Robert Bates, January 4, 2002.

4. Three weeks after: J. A. Ulio, letter to officers of American Alpine Club, May 29, 1942.

5. As scores of skiers: Charles Minot Dole, letter to Captain John Woodward, August 18, 1943.

6. Others were more charitable: Paul Lafferty, letter to Charles Minot Dole, September 2, 1942.

7. Rolfe had graduated: Hal Burton, *The Ski Troops* (New York: Simon and Schuster, 1971), 93; "Onslow Rolfe Made General," *Colorado Springs Gazette*, December 20, 1942; "Norse-Speaking Soldiers Train at Pardo Camp," *The Denver Post*, December 20, 1942.

8. At first Rolfe was suspicious: Burton, *The Ski Troops*, 95, 99.

9. To be sure: Jim Briggs, letters to Charles Minot Dole, March 24, 1943, and April 7, 1943.

10. In the meantime: Burton, *The Ski Troops*, 122.

11. The repartee between Dole and Rolfe: Charles Minot Dole, *Adventures in Skiing* (New York: Franklin and Watts, 1965), 113.

12. By the spring of 1942: Denis Nunan, letter to mother, March 16, 1942; clipping enclosed with Nunan letter to mother, April 6, 1942.

13. While other recruits: Denis Nunan, letter to mother, August 16, 1942.

14. Nunan moved into: Denis Nunan, letter to Mim, January 13, 1943.

15. Once field training: Burton, *The Ski Troops*, 103.

16. As the general level: Robert Bates, "Mount McKinley in Wartime," unpublished manuscript, DPL; Lowell Thomas radio broadcast, October 13, 1942; Robert Bates, "Mt. McKinley, 1942," *The American Alpine Journal* 5, no. 1 (1943), 1–13.

17. Nine months after: Denis Nunan, letter to Mim, August 17, 1942.

18. Making matters worse: Ibid.

19. Mules themselves: Burton, *The Ski Troops*, 120–121.

20. So taken with the mules: Frank Harper, *Night Climb: The Story of the Skiing 10th* (New York: Longmans, Green, 1946), 97.

21. The men who trained: Burton, *The Ski Troops*, 120–121.

22. British prime minister: Major William D. Hackett, "87th Mountain Infantry Regiment Detachment Field Testing of Prototype Experimental Military

Oversnow Vehicles, Columbia Icefield Expedition, Alberta, Canada, 5 July 1942–7 November 1942," DPL; Burton, *The Ski Troops*, 102.

23. Over the next several weeks: Dan Kurzman, "Sabotaging Hitler's Bomb," in *No End Save Victory*, 362–378.

CHAPTER 4: THE LAND OF THE BLACK SNOW

1. When a skinny: Dick Wilson, letter to family, December 19, 1942; author's interview with Dick Wilson, June 27, 2001.

2. Except for the little: Charles Minot Dole, *Adventures in Skiing* (New York: Franklin and Watts, 1965), 107–108.

3. A spot near: "New Army Camp in Colorado Being Built Near Mountain," *Monte Vista Journal*, April 24, 1942; Tom Wood, "A Historical Study of Camp Hale, Colorado," unpublished thesis, 1974, DPL; "Five Miles New Highway Near Pardo Camp," *Glenwood Post*, April 23, 1942.

4. By May 1: Associated Press, June 24, 1942; Wood, "Historical Study."

5. A month after: Imbrie chronology.

6. Assigned to A Company: Dick Wilson, letter to family, December 25, 1942; Edward Nickerson, "John Magrath," paper presented at Eastern Regional Reunion of the 10th Mountain Division, Valley Forge, Pa., November 11, 2000.

7. Within a couple of days: Dick Wilson, letter to family, January 17, 1943.

8. Another expert-in-residence: Hal Burton, *The Ski Troops*, (New York: Simon and Schuster, 1971), 35; Dole, *Adventures*, 72.

9. If the downhillers brought: Carl Stenersen, letter to Minnie Dole, May 22, 1944.

10. If arguments over philosophies: Dole, *Adventures*, 120.

11. Far worse than: Dick Wilson, letter to family, undated (early January 1943).

12. Shortly before Dick Wilson: Dole, *Adventures*, 118.

13. Like many other: "Mountain Troops," *Life*, November 9, 1942; author's interview with Arthur Delaney, May 30, 2001.

14. Since the mountain troops: Denis Numan, letter to Mim, May 4, 1942.

15. In January 1943: Author's interview with Bob Frauson, April 23, 2002.

16. After two weeks: Burton, *The Ski Troops*, 129–130.

17. Not long after: William Johnson, "Phantoms of the Snow," *Sports Illustrated*, February 8, 1971, 55–67.

18. As Camp Hale began: "Jeeps, Mules and Toboggans Tote Camp Hale Guns in Snow," *The Denver Post*, December 29, 1942.

19. World-famous Arctic: Johnson, "Phantoms of the Snow."

20. When Warner Bros.: Warner Bros., *Mountain Fighters*, 1943.

21. Denis Nunan's opinion: Denis Nunan, letter to Mim, February 21, 1943; Nunan, letter to mother, February 22, 1943; Nunan, letter to Mim, February 15, 1943.

CHAPTER 5: CLIMBING AND FALLING

1. In May 1943: Anthony Beever, "Stalingrad," in *No End Save Victory: Perspectives on World War II*, ed. Robert Cowley et al. (New York: Putnam, 2001), 258.

2. The German general: Frido von Senger und Etterlin, *Neither Fear nor Hope: The Wartime Career of General Frido von Senger und Etterlin*, trans. George Malcolm (New York: E. P. Dutton, 1964), 78, 86, 106, 122.

3. With the steady: "Ski Troops Relax Requirements," *Rocky Mountain News*, January 11, 1943; "Outdoor Men May Ask for Induction into Army Mountain Corps," *Alamosa Daily Courier*, January 16, 1943.

4. Gene Hames was: Author's interview with Gene Hames, May 31, 2001; Eugene Hames, "From Gyppo to Topkick: A Rapid Transition," unpublished manuscript, 1998.

5. If Gene Hames stumbled: Author's interview with Hugh Evans, August 19, 2001.

6. By the time Evans: Hugh Evans, letter to Robert Bates, January 17, 1943.

7. Bates wrote back: Robert Bates, letter to Hugh Evans, February 2, 1943.

8. Privately, Bates was worried: Author's interview with Robert Bates, January 4, 2002.

9. Gene Hames and Hugh Evans arrived: Hugh Evans, letter to mother, January 12, 1944.

10. On July 15: Imbrie chronology; "Camp Hale Stars Are Naturalized," *The Denver Post*, May 2, 1943.

11. The Allies had a lot: Carlo D'Este, *World War II in the Mediterranean, 1942–1945* (Chapel Hill N.C.: Algonquin Books, 1990), 49.

12. Yet as would be the case: George Marshall, *Biennial Report of the Chief of Staff of the United States Army, July 1, 1943 to June 30, 1945* (Washington, D.C.: U.S. Government Printing Office, 1945), 14–18; George F. Botjer, *Sideshow War: The Italian Campaign, 1943–1945* (College Station, Tex.: Texas A&M University Press, 1996), 23–25.

13. Meanwhile, in August: First Lieutenant Ian Francis, "The Assault of Riva Ridge: 1st Battalion, 86th Mountain Infantry Regiment, 19 February 1945. A Battle Analysis Submitted to the Infantry School Faculty for Completion of the Infantry Captain's Career Course in Military History, April 10, 1999," 2, DPL; Albert Kesselring, *A Soldier's Record* (Westport, Conn.: Greenwood Press, 1953), 208; Botjer, *Sideshow War*, 26–27.

14. As the former: Douglas Orgill, *The Gothic Line* (New York: Zebra Books, 1986), 22.

15. The Allied push: Mark Clark, *Calculated Risk* (New York: Harper & Brothers, 1950), 2.

16. In the first four days: Marshall, *Biennial Report*, 18–20; Botjer, *Sideshow War*, 51–58.

17. With other American soldiers: Denis Nunan, letter to mother, May 14, 1943; Nunan, letter to mother, Mother's Day, 1943; Nunan, letter to Mim, May 10, 1943.

18. As the last of the snow: Robert Ellis, *See Naples and Die: A World War Two Memoir of a United States Army Ski Trooper in the Mountains of Italy* (Jefferson, N.C.: McFarland, 1996), 40–41.

19. The troops had become famous: "Proposed Manual for Mountain Troops," Mountain Training Center, October 1, 1943, DPL.

20. The climbing instruction: Raye C. Ringholz, *On Belay! The Life of Legendary Mountaineer Paul Petzoldt* (Seattle: The Mountaineers, 1997), 113–135.

21. Petzoldt had been busy: Ibid., 154–157.

CHAPTER 6: OPTICAL ALEUTIAN

1. Night was the worst: Denis Nunan, letter to mother, January 1, 1944.

2. "There is little doubt now": Corey Ford, *Short Cut to Tokyo: The Battle for the Aleutians* (New York: Charles Scribner's Sons, 1943), 1.

3. Worse, the 2,400 Japanese: Hal Burton, *The Ski Troops* (New York: Simon

and Schuster, 1971), 109–110; Brian Garfield, *The Thousand Mile War: World War Two in Alaska and the Aleutians* (New York: Doubleday, 1969), 256; John Morgan, letter to Charles Minot Dole, April 20, 1944.

4. "All around were cliff-walled shores": Fern Chandonnet, ed., *Alaska at War, 1941–1945: The Forgotten War Remembered: Papers from the Alaska at War Symposium, Anchorage, Alaska, November 11–13, 1993* (Anchorage: Alaska at War Committee, 1995), 104.

5. The suicidal intensity: Garfield, *The Thousand Mile War*, 273.

6. At Fort Ord: Denis Nunan, letter to mother, July 1, 1943.

7. As they trained: Denis Nunan, letter to mother, June 23, 1943; Nunan, letter to mother, September 20, 1943.

8. As the country's only: Denis Nunan, letter to mother, January 1, 1944.

9. Unbeknown to Nunan: Garfield, *The Thousand Mile War*, 273–277.

10. Now, in addition: Ibid., 278–284.

11. The day the battle began: Denis Nunan, letter from mother to Nunan, August 15, 1943.

12. "I'm carrying this letter": Denis Nunan, letter to his family, August 13, 1943.

13. Once the sun: Garfield, *The Thousand Mile War*, 288; Flint Whitlock, *Soldiers on Skis: A Pictorial Memoir of the 10th Mountain Division* (Boulder, Colo.: Paladin Press, 1992), 25.

14. Making his way: Denis Nunan, letter to mother, January 1, 1944.

15. "They had us terrified": Burton, *The Ski Troops*, 115–116.

16. Major Robert Works: Whitlock, *Soldiers on Skis*, 26.

17. Art Delaney's platoon: Author's interview with Art Delaney, May 30, 2001.

18. Over on Ranger Hill: Whitlock, *Soldiers on Skis*, 29.

19. "Every time a helmet": Burton, *The Ski Troops*, 114; Chandonnet, *Alaska at War*, 106.

20. In all, 24 men: Author's interview with John Imbrie, April 26, 2002; author's interview with Art Delaney, May 30, 2001.

21. After the debacle: Author's interview with Art Delaney, May 30, 2001.

22. Domestic life on Kiska: Denis Nunan, letters to mother, September 9, September 30, October 16, and November 7, 1943.

23. Predictably, the Kiska blues: Burton, *The Ski Troops*, 118–119.

24. Life got so dull: Denis Nunan, letter to mother, September 30, 1943.

25. Eventually, the remaining members: Denis Nunan, letter to mother, January 1, 1944.

26. Later it dawned: Denis Nunan, letter to mother, December 1943.

27. Just before arriving: Denis Nunan, letter to Mim, January 31, 1944.

CHAPTER 7: THE MARCH UP THE BOOT

1. As the mountain troops: Mark Clark, *Calculated Risk* (New York: Harper & Brothers, 1950), 50.

2. In December 1942: Ibid., 313.

3. Anticipating a series: Carlo D'Este, *World War II in the Mediterranean, 1942–1945* (Chapel Hill, N.C.: Algonquin Books, 1990), 127; George F. Botjer, *Sideshow War: The Italian Campaign, 1943–1945* (College Station, Tex.: Texas A&M University Press, 1996), 67.

4. Two days later: Ernie Pyle, "The Italian Campaign: Slow Progress," in *Reporting World War Two. Part One: American Journalism 1938–1944*, ed. Samuel Hynes et al. (New York: Library of America, 1995), 728–729; D'Este, *World War II*, 149; Botjer, *Sideshow War*, 76.

5. The Germans relied: Frido von Senger und Etterlin, *Neither Fear nor Hope: The Wartime Career of General Frido von Senger und Etterlin*, trans. George Malcolm (New York: E. P. Dutton, 1964), 228–229, 231.

6. To Mark Clark: Clark, *Calculated Risk*, 311.

7. "If they could ignore": Daniel J. Petruzzi, *My War Against the Land of My Ancestors* (Irving, Tex.: Fusion Press, 2000), 216.

8. After threatening to pull: Homer Bigart, "Cassino, Once Thriving, Is Turned into a Scene of Unrelieved Grimness," in *Reporting World War Two. Part Two: American Journalism 1938–1944*, ed. Samuel Hynes et al. (New York: Library of America, 1995), 72.

9. Holding aloft a large crucifix: Clark, *Calculated Risk*, 323; Petruzzi, *My War*, 219.

10. From January 16: Eric Sevareid, "The Price We Pay in Italy," in Hynes et al., *Part Two*, 569–570; Clark, *Calculated Risk*, 333.

11. If there was one man: George P. Hays, "Personal Memoirs, 1892–1978," unpublished manuscript, 26, DPL.

12. News of the fighting: Anders Lund, letter to Minnie Dole, December 8, 1943.

13. While the camp veterans seethed: Stuart Abbott, field journal, DPL.

14. "While I think of it": Stuart Abbott, letter to mother, February 23, 1944.

15. Thankfully, Abbott had recently met: Stuart Abbott, letters to grandmother, July 4, December 13, and December 18, 1943.

16. As another Christmas: "Christmas Bells and Carols Fill Camp Hale Air," *The Denver Post*, December 23, 1943; *The Denver Post*, January 16, 1944.

17. Nonetheless, for many in camp: Denis Nunan, letter to mother, January 1, 1944; Nunan, letter to Mim, January 31, 1944; Nunan, letter to mother, March 6, 1944.

18. Like any soldier: Denis Nunan, letters to mother, February 15, and February 22, 1944.

19. Despite a camp: Dan Kennerly, Tape 1.

20. Kennerly had grown up: Kennerly, Tape 1.

21. As Kennerly grew: Kennerly, Tape 1.

22. Back in camp: Denis Nunan, letter to mother, January 1, 1944.

23. To make matters worse: E. J. Kahn, Jr., "The Philologist," a four-part series published in *The New Yorker*, March 11–April 1, 1950; "Camp Hale Soldier Is Caught in Mexico with 2 Escaped Nazis," *Rocky Mountain News*, February 20, 1944.

CHAPTER 8: THE D SERIES

1. Dale Maple's case: Stuart Abbott, letter to grandmother, February 29, 1944.

2. It was a remarkable sight: Robert Ellis, *See Naples and Die: A World War Two Memoir of a United States Army Ski Trooper in the Mountains of Italy* (Jefferson, N.C.: McFarland, 1996), 72–73.

3. From the outset: Stuart Abbott, letter to aunt and uncle, October 29, 1944.

4. Given a year's training: "Check List for Small Unit Leaders," March 23, 1944, DPL.

5. Increasingly disgusted: Denis Nunan, letter to Mim, April 1, 1944.

6. After a couple of days: Hugh Evans, letter to mother, April 19, 1944; author's interview with Hugh Evans, August 19, 2001.

7. The blizzard continued: Hugh Evans, letter to mother, undated (May 1944).

8.   High up on the ridges: Author's interview with Earl Clark, May 30, 2001.

9.   Men continued to fall out: Stuart Abbott, letter to mother, April 7, 1944; Hugh Evans, letter to mother, April 24, 1944.

10.   For virtually every soldier: Denis Nunan, letter to mother, April 16, 1944.

11.   Stuart Abbott and his crew: Stuart Abbott, letter to aunt and uncle, May 3, 1944.

12.   When the umpires: Hugh Evans, letters to mother, April 19, 1944; undated (May 1944); Dick Wilson, letter to family, April 17, 1944.

13.   When it was all over: Lloyd Jones, letter to Charles Minot Dole, May 29, 1944.

14.   Around the same time: Author's interview with Conrad Brown, April 22, 2001.

15.   Dole and John Morgan: Charles Minot Dole, letter to George Marshall, April 19, 1944.

16.   Dole pressed Marshall: Charles Minot Dole, letter to General Frank R. McCoy, June 13, 1944; John Morgan, letter to Charles Minot Dole, April 20, 1944.

17.   Marshall reiterated: John Morgan, letter to Charles Minot Dole, April 20, 1944; Hal Burton, *The Ski Troops* (New York: Simon and Schuster, 1971), 147.

18.   When it came to the war: George Marshall, *Biennial Report of the Chief of Staff of the United States Army, July 1, 1943 to June 30, 1945* (Washington, D.C.: U.S. Government Printing Office, 1945), 20–22; Mark Clark, *Calculated Risk* (New York: Harper & Brothers, 1950), 2; George F. Botjer, *Sideshow War: The Italian Campaign, 1943–1945* (College Station, Tex.: Texas A&M University Press, 1996), 103–106.

19.   On June 20: Carl Stenersen, letter to Charles Minot Dole, June 29, 1944.

20.   Everywhere they looked: Author's interview with Gene Hames, May 31, 2001; Hugh Evans, letter to mother, July 3, 1944.

21.   Others were not so fortunate: Denis Nunan, letter to mother, July 2, 1944.

22.   Stuart Abbott, the naturalist: Stuart Abbott, undated letter to family (June 1944).

23.   Soon after settling: *Ski Zette—Texas Edition* 1, no. 1 (July 26, 1944), DPL.

24.   In early November: Camp Hale *Ski Zette*, September 30, 1944, DPL.

25.   But with all the excitement: Stuart Abbott, letter to aunt and uncle, November 22, 1944.

26. In addition to new gear: Ellis, *See Naples and Die*, 89–90.

27. Jones had finally succumbed: Lloyd Jones, letter to Charles Minot Dole, February 20, 1945.

28. About this time: Charles Minot Dole, *Adventures in Skiing* (New York: Franklin and Watts, 1965), 150; George P. Hays, "Personal Memoirs, 1892–1978," unpublished manuscript, 11, DPL.

29. During their initial meeting: Charles Minot Dole, letter to George Hays, November 24, 1944.

30. Two days after arriving: Hays, "Personal Memoirs," 32.

31. Hays's speech marked: Dick Wilson, letter to family, November 27, 1944.

32. If Hays made: Stuart Abbott, letter to mother, November 18, 1944; Ellis, *See Naples and Die*, 94.

33. On Christmas Eve: Kennerly, Tape 1.

34. Although they would not: Dick Wilson, letters to family, November 12, November 19, and November 27, 1944.

CHAPTER 9: SEE NAPLES AND DIE

1. Throughout the summer: Douglas Orgill, *The Gothic Line* (New York: Zebra Books, 1986), 39–41, 81; Carlo D'Este, *World War II in the Mediterranean, 1942–1945* (Chapel Hill, N.C.: Algonquin Books, 1990), 178–181.

2. The most important ally: Orgill, *The Gothic Line*, 57–60; D'Este, *World War II*, 182–184.

3. Kesselring was not without: Daniel J. Petruzzi, *My War Against the Land of My Ancestors* (Irving, Tex.: Fusion Press, 2000), 277; Albert Kesselring, *A Soldier's Record* (Westport, Conn.: Greenwood Press, 1953), 272.

4. By the end of August: Orgill, *The Gothic Line*, 160; George F. Botjer, *Sideshow War: The Italian Campaign, 1943–1945* (College Station, Tex.: Texas A&M University Press, 1996), 175–181.

5. The mood at the front: D'Este, *World War II*, 182.

6. The troubles with furthering: Orgill, 283.

7. On the front lines: Mark Clark, *Calculated Risk* (New York: Harper & Brothers, 1950), 396–397.

8. When a group: "The Italian Ordeal Surprises Members of Congress,"

by Anne O'Hare McCormick, *The New York Times*, December 23, 1944; Kesselring, *A Soldier's Record*, 258.

9. On October 23: Lucien K. Truscott, *Command Missions: A Personal Story* (New York: E. P. Dutton, 1954), 457; Botjer, *Sideshow War*, 181–185.

10. On November 24: Imbrie chronology; Clark, *Calculated Risk*, 404–406.

11. By the end of 1944: Truscott, *Command Missions*, 451; Thomas R. Brooks, *The War North of Rome, June 1944–May 1945* (New York: Sarpedon, 1996), 332.

12. The end of the year: Truscott, *Command Missions*, 459–460.

13. Within the ranks: Clark, *Calculated Risk*, 368–370; Dan Kennerly, Tape 6; Imbrie chronology; George Marshall, *Biennial Report of the Chief of Staff of the United States Army, July 1, 1943 to June 30, 1945* (Washington, D.C.: U.S. Government Printing Office, 1945), 22–24.

14. On December 11: Robert Ellis, *See Naples and Die: A World War Two Memoir of a United States Army Ski Trooper in the Mountains of Italy* (Jefferson, N.C.: McFarland, 1996), 98; Kennerly, Tape 2; Stuart Abbott, letter to family, December 13, 1944; Dick Wilson, letter to family, undated (December 1944–January 1945); Denis Nunan, letter to mother, February 28, 1945.

15. Winter weather: Captain George F. Earle, *History of the 87th Mountain Infantry Regiment, Italy, 1945* (Denver: Bradford-Robinson Printing Co., 1945), 9.

16. The departure of the troops: Charles Minot Dole, letter to George Hays, January 30, 1945.

17. As the men embarked: George P. Hays, "Personal Memoirs, 1892–1978," unpublished manuscript, DPL.

18. The *West Point* moved: Dick Wilson, letter to family, January 19, 1945.

19. On January 13: Botjer, *Sideshow War*, 61–62.

20. When the mountain troops: Ellis, *See Naples and Die*, 96.

21. Not far from Pisa: Kennerly, Tape 2.

CHAPTER 10: RIVA RIDGE

1. By mid-January: Author's interview with Gene Hames, May 31, 2001; *The Blizzard*, March 7, 1945.

2. However arduous: Edward Nickerson, "Paragraphs About War," unpublished manuscript.

3. To combat late-winter rain: Stuart Abbott, letter to grandmother, January 5, 1945.

4. Getting to the villages: Denis Nunan, letter to family, February 28, 1945.

5. As Dick Wilson's company: Dick Wilson, letters to family, January 19, January 30, and February 8, 1945.

6. On duty near: Hugh Evans, letter to mother, February 6, 1945.

7. But the men's rest: Denis Nunan, letter to family, February 28, 1945; undated letter from Chaplain Thomas Cannon; letter to Nunan's family, March 2, 1945.

8. The division moved: Author's interview with Bruno Bartholomei, April 1, 2002.

9. If the men were ready: Charles Minot Dole, letter to George Marshall, December 6, 1944.

10. The prospect of going: "Rock Climbers Lead Assault Up Sheer Cliff," *The Blizzard*, February 27, 1945.

11. Given its arrival: Captain George F. Earle, *History of the 87th Mountain Infantry Regiment, Italy, 1945* (Denver: Bradford-Robinson Printing Co., 1945), 12–13.

12. Another night: Timothy Nunan, letter to author, October 29, 2001.

13. A soldier in the 85th: Author's interview with Edward Nickerson, May 3, 2001.

14. Stuart Abbott shuttled: Stuart Abbott, letter to family, February 6, 1945.

15. As the days went by: Stuart Abbott, letter to grandmother, February 12, 1945.

16. In mid-January: Dan Kennerly, Tape 2; George P. Hays, "Personal Memoirs, 1892–1978," unpublished manuscript, 33–34, DPL.

17. Tomlinson left: Wilson Ware, "The Riva Ridge," *American Alpine Journal* 6, no. 2 (1946), 216.

18. The first thing: Henry Hampton, "The Riva Ridge Operation: Report of Lt. Col. Henry J. Hampton, Headquarters, 86th Mountain Infantry," 1, DPL.

19. In fact, the lull: Frido von Senger und Etterlin, *War Diary of the Italian Campaign: The Destruction of Army Group C*, trans. R. D. Young, Historical Division Headquarters, U.S. Army, Europe, 10, DPL; First Lieutenant Ian Francis, "The Assault of Riva Ridge: 1st Battalion, 86th Mountain

Infantry Regiment, 19 February 1945. A Battle Analysis Submitted to the Infantry School Faculty for Completion of the Infantry Captain's Career Course in Military History, April 10, 1999," 3, DPL; Frido von Senger und Etterlin, *Neither Fear nor Hope: The Wartime Career of General Frido von Senger und Etterlin*, trans. George Malcolm (New York: E. P. Dutton, 1964), 281.

20.   One afternoon: Author's interview with Bob Frauson, April 23, 2002.

21.   On January 15: Ware, "The Riva Ridge," 214.

22.   Finally, with the help: Hampton, "The Riva Ridge Operation," 3.

23.   With two routes: Ibid., 4.

24.   As the final routes: Hays, "Personal Memoirs," 36.

25.   The men were told: Albert H. Meinke, Jr., *Mountain Troops and Medics: Wartime Stories of a Frontline Surgeon in the U.S. Ski Troops* (Kewadin, Mich.: Rucksack Publishing Company, 1993), 96.

26.   As the time for: Author's interview with Howard Koch, November 2001.

27.   On February 15: Hampton, "The Riva Ridge Operation," 5.

28.   The most difficult: *The Blizzard*, February 27, 1945.

29.   Each assault platoon: Hampton, "The Riva Ridge Operation," 8; Ware, "The Riva Ridge," 218.

30.   By far the best thing: Hampton, "The Riva Ridge Operation," 7; Captain William E. Neidner, "The Operations of Company A (Less One Platoon) 86th Mountain Infantry Regiment (10th Mountain Division) in Attack on Mancinello-Campiano Ridge, Italy, 18–22 February (North Apennines Campaign); Personal Experience of a Company Commander," 5, DPL.

31.   These final days: Kennerly, Tape 2.

32.   Hays began: Imbrie chronology.

33.   Then Hays paused: Kennerly, Tape 2.

34.   On the morning: Kennerly, Tape 2; Neidner, "The Operations of Company A," 8–9.

35.   At 7:30 P.M.: Author's interview with Bob Frauson, April 23, 2002; Neidner, "The Operations of Company A," 9.

36.   When the bulk: Ware, "The Riva Ridge," 219.

37.   Once again, the assault platoon: Author's interview with Howard Koch, November 2001.

38.   Heavily armed: Author's interview with Bob Frauson, April 23, 2002.

39.   At 4:15 A.M.: Neidner, "The Operations of Company A," 10.

40. As dawn spread: Battalion journal, 1st Battalion, 86th Mountain Infantry, Riva Ridge Operation, Lizzano in Belvedere, February 18–22, 1945, DPL.

41. Almost as soon: Neidner, "The Operations of Company A," 11–12.

42. With all objectives: Hampton, "The Riva Ridge Operation," 10.

43. The climb was: Author's interview with Harry Reinig, May 9, 2002.

44. By 6:30: Flint Whitlock, *Soldiers on Skis: A Pictorial Memoir of the 10th Mountain Division* (Boulder, Colo.: Paladin Press, 1992), 82–83.

45. As the sun rose higher: Hampton, "The Riva Ridge Operation," 10; Neidner, "The Operations of Company A," 14; Whitlock, *Soldiers on Skis*, 81; Battalion journal, 1st Battalion; author's interview with Howard Koch, November 2002; author's interview with Bob Frauson, April 23, 2002.

46. The importance of Riva Ridge: Author's interview with Harry Reinig, May 9, 2002.

47. As the second night: "Rock Climbers Lead Assault Up Sheer Cliff," *The Blizzard*, February 27, 1945.

48. Finally the shells: Battalion journal, 1st Battalion; Francis, "The Assault," 10–11; Hampton, "The Riva Ridge Operation," 9–11; "Mountaineers Push Nazis off 3 Peaks in Week of Fighting," *The Blizzard*, February 27, 1945; *The Blizzard*, June 7, 1945; Whitlock, *Soldiers on Skis*, 85.

49. Getting the dead: Charles Minot Dole, *Adventures in Skiing* (New York: Franklin and Watts, 1965), 131.

50. On the first day: Hampton, "The Riva Ridge Operation," 9, 12; Imbrie chronology; Ware, "The Riva Ridge," 220.

51. Even with the fighting: Neidner, "The Operations of Company A," 13.

CHAPTER 11: MOUNT BELVEDERE

1. Several hours: Dan Kennerly, Tape 2.

2. Hugh Evans: Hugh Evans, "Baptism on Belvedere," in *Good Times and Bad Times: A History of C Company 85th Mountain Infantry Regiment, 10th Mountain Division, July 1943–November 1945*, ed. John Imbrie and Hugh W. Evans (Quechee, Vt.: Vermont Heritage Press, 1995), 46; author's interview with Hugh Evans, August 19, 2001.

3. At 4 P.M.: Kennerly, Tape 2.

4. Uphill from Kennerly: Evans, "Baptism on Belvedere," 48.

5. After quietly picking: Dick Wilson, letter to family, March 20, 1945; author's interview with Dick Wilson, June 27, 2001.

6. Moving up behind: Kennerly, Tape 2.

7. Hugh Evans: Evans, "Baptism on Belvedere," 48–50.

8. As the sun's rays: Kennerly, Tape 2.

9. As the blackness: Author's interview with Hugh Evans, August 19, 2001.

10. For much of the night: Staff Sergeant Paul Anderson, letter to Abbott's family, October 10, 1945, Abbott file, DPL; Mollie Abbott, letter to grandmother, n.d., Abbott file, DPL; Staff Sergeant Paul Anderson, letter to Abbott's family, August 27, 1945, Abbott file, DPL.

11. Staff Sergeant Ben Duke: Staff Sergeant Ben Duke, letter to Abbott's family, March 30, 1945; Abbott file, DPL; Henry Brendemihl, regimental chaplain, letter to Abbott's family, March 7, 1945.

12. As the day wore on: Kennerly, Tape 2.

13. As American planes reappeared: Ibid.

14. Finally word came: Commendation of division signed by Major General George P. Hays, February 25, 1945.

15. On Wednesday, February 21: Kennerly, Tape 2.

16. With the Allied tanks: Author's interview with Edward Nickerson, May 9, 2002.

17. As the attack: Kennerly, Tape 2.

18. Finally, late in the day: *The Blizzard*, March 15, 1945.

19. As the men: *The Blizzard*, March 15, 1945; Imbrie chronology; Dan Kennerly, Tape 3.

CHAPTER 12: MOUNTAIN OF HOPE

1. The division's astonishing: Lucien K. Truscott, *Command Missions: A Personal Story* (New York: E. P. Dutton, 1954), 468; George P. Hays, "Personal Memoirs, 1892–1978," unpublished manuscript, 44.

2. General Hays laid out the plan: *The Blizzard*, March 24, 1945.

3. Art Delaney's battalion: Author's interview with Art Delaney, May 30, 2001; Captain George F. Earle, *History of the 87th Mountain Infantry Regiment, Italy, 1945* (Denver: Bradford-Robinson Printing Co., 1945), 39.

4. Not far from: Flint Whitlock, *Soldiers on Skis: A Pictorial Memoir of the*

10th Mountain Division (Boulder, Colo.: Paladin Press, 1992), 112; Frank Harper, *Night Climb: The Story of the Skiing 10th* (New York: Longmans, Green, 1946), 196; author's interview with Bob Franson, April 23, 2002.

5.   Tokle's death: Author's interview with Bob Franson, April 23, 2002.

6.   Over on della Spe: Dan Kennerly, Tape 3.

7.   Along the road: Dan Kennerly, Tape 4.

8.   Once della Spe: William Lowell Putnam, *Green Cognac: The Education of a Mountain Fighter* (New York: American Alpine Club Press, 1991), 109–110.

9.   Other booty had less: *The Blizzard*, March 15, 1945.

10. Over near Castel d'Aiano: Denis Nunan, letter to parents, March 23, 1945; Timothy Nunan, letter to author, April 1, 2002.

11. After the initial: *The Blizzard*, March 15, 1945.

12. To the American public: "Clare Luce Drops Shells on Jerries During Visit to 10th Division Front," *The Blizzard*, March 24, 1945.

13. With the fighting: *The Blizzard*, April 6, 1945.

14. By the end of March: Denis Nunan, letter to mother, March 18, 1945; Nunan, letter to parents, March 23, 1945.

CHAPTER 13: THE CRUELEST MONTH

1.   On April 13: Denis Nunan, letter to parents, May 2, 1945.

2.   Dan Kennerly could see: Dan Kennerly, Tapes 5 and 6; "10th Paces Central Offensive: 85th, 87th Spearhead Drive," *The Blizzard*, April 19, 1945.

3.   Stepping gingerly: Kennerly, Tapes 5 and 6; author's interviews with Edward (Nick) Nickerson, May 3, 2001; John Imbrie and Conrad Brown, April 22, 2001; "Red Cross's Debby Dishes Out Doughnuts, Skiing Chatter, and Feminine Charm," *The Blizzard*, February 17, 1945.

4.   As the troops advanced: Jake H. Thompson, *Bob Dole: The Republicans' Man for All Seasons* (New York: Donald I. Fine, 1994), 29.

5.   If many of the German: Nick Nickerson, letter to Mr. and Mrs. Elgin Nickerson, May 13, 1945.

6.   To Denis Nunan: Denis Nunan, letter to parents, May 2, 1945; Timothy Nunan, letter to author, October 29, 2001.

7.   Flying over all this: Author's interview with Conrad Brown, April 22, 2001.

8. As the day wore on: Captain George F. Earle, *History of the 87th Mountain Infantry Regiment, Italy, 1945* (Denver: Bradford-Robinson Printing Co., 1945), 68.

9. Evans, who had: Evans letter to family, May 16, 1945; author's interview with Hugh Evans, August 19, 2001; J. A. Ulio, telegram, May 5, 1945.

10. This time, from his perch: Author's interview with Hugh Evans, August 19, 2001.

11. Edward Nickerson: Edward Nickerson, unpublished essay on John Magrath; author's interview with Edward Nickerson, May 14, 2002.

12. Just two weeks after: William Lowell Putnam, *Green Cognac: The Education of a Mountain Fighter* (New York: American Alpine Club Press, 1991), 119–124.

13. Down in a deep valley: Richard Ben Cramer, *Bob Dole* (New York: Vintage Books, 1995), 30.

14. As a Kansas native: Thompson, *Bob Dole*, 28.

15. Dole was gray: Cramer, *Bob Dole*, 36–42; Thompson, *Bob Dole*, 32–36.

16. By the second day: Imbrie chronology; Kennerly, Tape 6.

17. But the victory: Frido von Senger und Etterlin, *War Diary of the Italian Campaign: The Destruction of Army Group C*, trans. R. D. Young, unpublished manuscript, 16, DPL; George P. Hays, "Personal Memoirs, 1892–1978," unpublished manuscript, 48, DPL.

18. As the worst of the fighting: Author's interview with Conrad Brown, April 22, 2001.

19. Marching their way north: Kennerly, Tape 6.

CHAPTER 14: ACROSS THE PO AND INTO THE ALPS

1. Their work in the mountains: George P. Hays, letter to Donald Douglas, May 14, 1945; Mark Clark, *Calculated Risk* (New York: Harper & Brothers, 1950), 441; Frido von Senger und Etterlin, *War Diary of the Italian Campaign: The Destruction of Army Group C*, trans. R. D. Young, unpublished manuscript, 18, 21–22; George P. Hays, "Personal Memoirs, 1892–1978," unpublished manuscript, 49, DPL.

2. Fast in pursuit: Dan Kennerly, Tape 7.

3. For meals: Kennerly, Tape 7; Hays, "Personal Memoirs," 50.

4. General Robinson Duff's: Hays, "Personal Memoirs," 52.

5. Given more time: Captain George F. Earle, *History of the 87th Mountain Infantry Regiment, Italy, 1945* (Denver: Bradford-Robinson Printing Co., 1945), 122, DPL; Hays, "Personal Memoirs," 53.

6. The night before: Kennerly, Tape 7.

7. As the 87th loaded: Denis Nunan, letter to parents, May 2, 1945; Timothy P. Nunan, letter to author, October 29, 2001.

8. As Dan Kennerly: Kennerly, Tape 7; Hays, "Personal Memoirs," 54.

9. What the men: Senger, *War Diary*, 21.

10. With the war in Europe: "Let's Be Friends," unsigned editorial, *The Blizzard*, May 22, 1945.

11. Even with the Germans: Kennerly, Tape 7.

CHAPTER 15: SLEEPING IN MUSSOLINI'S BED

1. With only flatland remaining: Author's interview with Gene Hames, May 31, 2001; Kennerly, Tape 7.

2. On April 26: Captain George F. Earle, *History of the 87th Mountain Infantry Regiment, Italy, 1945* (Denver: Bradford-Robinson Printing Co., 1945), 135–138, DPL; author's interview with Edward (Nick) Nickerson, May 14, 2002.

3. The next day: Dan Kennerly, Tape 8; George P. Hays, letter to Donald Douglas, May 14, 1945; George P. Hays, "Personal Memoirs, 1892–1978," unpublished manuscript, 58–59, DPL.

4. "The shells were coming": Merrill Pollack, "Battlefield Notebook," *The Blizzard*, May 22, 1945; Flint Whitlock, *Soldiers on Skis: A Pictorial Memoir of the 10th Mountain Division* (Boulder, Colo.: Paladin Press, 1992), 170.

5. Not long after this: Author's interview with John Imbrie, May 9, 2002.

6. As the mountain troops: Daniel J. Petruzzi, *My War Against the Land of My Ancestors* (Irving, Tex.: Fusion Press, 2000), 309.

7. Indeed, rumors of: Whitlock, *Soldiers on Skis*, 173; Mark Clark, *Calculated Risk* (New York: Harper & Brothers, 1950), 435–436; Lucien K. Truscott, *Command Missions: A Personal Story* (New York: E. P. Dutton, 1954), 493.

8. On May 4: Clark, *Calculated Risk*, 439; Carlo D'Este, *World War II in the Mediterranean, 1942–1945* (Chapel Hill, N.C.: Algonquin Books, 1990), 196.

9. By the end: George Marshall, *Biennial Report of the Chief of Staff of the United States Army, July 1, 1943 to June 30, 1945* (Washington, D.C.: U.S. Government Printing Office, 1945), 24; Truscott, *Command Missions*, 553; Samuel Hynes et al., eds., *Reporting World War Two. Part Two: American Journalism 1938–1944* (New York: Library of America, 1995), 892; Clark, *Calculated Risk*, 438; Imbrie chronology; George P. Hays, letter to Donald Douglas, May 14, 1945.

10. Praise streamed into Italy: Earle, *History of the 87th*, 146.

11. For the men: "And the Tenth Shall Be First," *The Blizzard*, May 22, 1945.

12. Hays ended the campaign: Hays, "Personal Memoirs," 64.

13. Dan Kennerly: Kennerly, Tapes 7 and 8; Hugh Evans, letter to family, May 11, 1945.

14. For Dick Wilson: Dick Wilson, letters to family, March 20 and April 11, 1945; author's interview with Dick Wilson, June 27, 2001.

15. Denis Nunan rediscovered: Denis Nunan, letter to parents, May 23, 1945.

16. Perhaps no one: Author's interview with Gene Hames, May 31, 2001.

EPILOGUE

1. In late March: Clyde Hyssong, letter to Charles Minot Dole, March 21, 1945; Charles Minot Dole, letter to George P. Hays, April 6, 1945; George Marshall, letter to Charles Minot Dole, May 17, 1945.

2. Minnie Dole had spent: Charles Minot Dole, *Adventures in Skiing* (New York: Franklin and Watts, 1965), 26; Morten Lund, "Minot Dole, the Man Who . . . ," *Ski*, January 1966.

3. To be sure: Author's interview with John Imbrie, September 22, 2002.

Bates, Robert. *The Love of Mountains Is Best: Climbs and Travels from K2 to Kathmandu.* Portsmouth, N.H.: Peter E. Randall, Publisher, 1994.

———. "Mount McKinley in Wartime." Unpublished manuscript, DPL.

———. "Mt. McKinley, 1942." *The American Alpine Journal* 5, no. 1 (1943): 1–13.

Bates, Robert, and Charles Houston. *K2: The Savage Mountain.* Seattle: The Mountaineers, 1979.

Battalion journal, 1st Battalion, 86th Mountain Infantry, Riva Ridge Operation, Lizzano in Belvedere, February 18–22, 1945. DPL.

Botjer, George F. *Sideshow War: The Italian Campaign, 1943–1945.* College Station: Texas A&M University Press, 1996.

Brooks, Thomas R. *Tenth Mountain Division.* Paducah, Ky.: Turner Publishing Company, 1998.

———. *The War North of Rome, June 1944–May 1945.* New York: Sarpedon, 1996.

Brower, David. *For Earth's Sake: The Life and Times of David Brower.* Salt Lake City: Peregrine Smith Books, 1990.

Burton, Hal. *The Ski Troops.* New York: Simon and Schuster, 1971.

Casewit, Curtis. *Mountain Troopers: The Story of the Tenth Mountain Division.* New York: Thomas Y. Crowell, 1972.

Chandonnet, Fern, ed. *Alaska at War, 1941–1945: The Forgotten War Remembered: Papers from the Alaska at War Symposium, Anchorage, Alaska, November 11–13, 1993.* Anchorage: Alaska at War Committee, 1995.

Clark, Mark. *Calculated Risk.* New York: Harper & Brothers, 1950.

Cowley, Robert, et al., eds. *No End Save Victory: Perspectives on World War II.* New York: Putnam, 2001.

Cramer, Richard Ben. *Bob Dole.* New York: Vintage Books, 1995.

D'Este, Carlo. *World War II in the Mediterranean, 1942–1945.* Chapel Hill, N.C.: Algonquin Books, 1990.

Dole, Charles Minot. *Adventures in Skiing.* New York: Franklin and Watts, 1965.

Dusenbery, Harris, and Wilson P. Ware. *The North Apennines and Beyond with the 10th Mountain Division.* Portland, Oreg.: Binford and Mort, 1998.

Earle, Captain George F. *History of the 87th Mountain Infantry Regiment, Italy, 1945.* Denver: Bradford-Robinson Printing Co., 1945. DPL.

87th Mountain Infantry Mountaineering School Training Schedule. DPL.

Ellis, Robert. *See Naples and Die: A World War Two Memoir of a United States Army Ski Trooper in the Mountains of Italy.* Jefferson, N.C.: McFarland, 1996.

Ford, Corey. *Short Cut to Tokyo: The Battle for the Aleutians.* New York: Charles Scribner's Sons, 1943.

Francis, First Lieutenant Ian. "The Assault of Riva Ridge: 1st Battalion, 86th Mountain Infantry Regiment, 19 February 1945. A Battle Analysis Submitted to the Infantry School Faculty for Completion of the Infantry Captain's Career Course in Military History, April 10, 1999." DPL.

Fussell, Paul. *Wartime: Understanding and Behavior in the Second World War.* New York: Oxford University Press, 1989.

Garfield, Brian. *The Thousand Mile War: World War Two in Alaska and the Aleutians.* New York: Doubleday, 1969.

Hackett, Major William D. "87th Mountain Infantry Regiment Detachment Field Testing of Prototype Experimental Military Oversnow Vehicles, Columbia Icefield Expedition, Alberta, Canada, 5 July 1942–7 November 1942. DPL.

Hames, Eugene. "From Gyppo to Topkick: A Rapid Transition." Unpublished manuscript, May 1998.

Hampton, Henry. "The Riva Ridge Operation: Report of Lt. Col. Henry J. Hampton, Headquarters, 86th Mountain Infantry." DPL.

Hapgood, David, and David Richardson. *Monte Cassino.* New York: Congdon and Weed, 1984.

Harper, Frank. *Military Skiing: A Handbook for Ski and Mountain Troops.* Harrisburg, Pa.: Military Service Publishing Company, 1943.

———. *Night Climb: The Story of the Skiing 10th.* New York: Longmans, Green, 1946.

Hays, George P. "Personal Memoirs, 1892–1978." Unpublished manuscript. DPL.

Houston, Charles, and Robert Bates. *K2: The Savage Mountain.* Seattle: The Mountaineers, 1954.

Hynes, Samuel, et al., eds. *Reporting World War Two. Part One: American Journalism 1938–1944.* New York: Library of America, 1995.

————. *Reporting World War Two. Part Two: American Journalism 1938–1944.* New York: Library of America, 1995.

Imbrie, John, and Hugh W. Evans, eds. *Good Times and Bad Times: A History of C Company 85th Mountain Infantry Regiment, 10th Mountain Division, July 1943–November 1945.* Quechee, Vt.: Vermont Heritage Press, 1995.

Johnson, William. "Phantoms of the Snow." *Sports Illustrated,* February 8, 1971, 55–67.

Kahn, E. J., Jr. "The Philologist." A four-part series published in *The New Yorker,* March 11–April 1, 1950.

Keegan, John. *The Face of Battle.* New York: Penguin Books, 1976.

Kennerly, Dan. "Oral History and Mule Stories," a series of ten cassettes, DPL.

Kesselring, Albert. *A Soldier's Record.* Westport, Conn.: Greenwood Press, 1953.

Lamb, Richard. *War in Italy, 1943–1945.* London: John Murray, 1993.

Leseur, Larry. *Twelve Months That Changed the World.* New York: Alfred A. Knopf, 1943.

Majdalany, Fred. *Cassino: Portrait of a Battle.* London: Longmans, Green, 1957.

Marshall, George. *Biennial Report of the Chief of Staff of the United States Army, July 1, 1943 to June 30, 1945.* Washington, D.C.: U.S. Government Printing Office, 1945.

Meinke, Albert H., Jr. *Mountain Troops and Medics: Wartime Stories of a Frontline Surgeon in the U.S. Ski Troops.* Kewadin, Mich.: Rucksack Publishing Company, 1993.

Neidner, Captain William E. "The Operations of Company A (Less One Platoon) 86th Mountain Infantry Regiment (10th Mountain Division) in Attack on Mancinello–Campiano Ridge, Italy, 18–22 February (North Apennines Campaign); Personal Experience of a Company Commander." Advanced Infantry Officers Course, The Infantry School, Fort Benning, Georgia. DPL.

Nickerson, Edward. "John Magrath." Paper presented at Eastern Regional Reunion of the 10th Mountain Division, Valley Forge, Pa., November 11, 2000.

————. "Paragraphs About War." Unpublished manuscript.

Orgill, Douglas. *The Gothic Line.* New York: Zebra Books, 1986.

Peters, Ed, ed. *Mountaineering: The Freedom of the Hills.* Seattle: The Mountaineers, 1982.

Petruzzi, Daniel J. *My War Against the Land of My Ancestors.* Irving, Tex.: Fusion Press, 2000.

Pote, Winston. *Mountain Troops.* Camden, Maine: Down East Books, 1982.

Putnam, William Lowell. *Green Cognac: The Education of a Mountain Fighter.* New York: American Alpine Club Press, 1991.

"Report of the Mount Rainier Test Expedition," May 8 to 20, 1942. DPL.

Ringholz, Raye C. *On Belay! The Life of Legendary Mountaineer Paul Petzoldt.* Seattle: The Mountaineers, 1997.

Rossi, Andrea. "On the Other Side of the Gothic Line." Unpublished manuscript delivered at the meeting "Una Montagna di Pace," Fanano, Italy, June 5, 2002.

Senger und Etterlin, Frido von. *Neither Fear nor Hope: The Wartime Career of General Frido von Senger und Etterlin.* Translated by George Malcolm. New York: E. P. Dutton, 1964.

———. *War Diary of the Italian Campaign: The Destruction of Army Group C.* Translated by R. D. Young. Historical Division Headquarters, U.S. Army, Europe. DPL.

Starr, Lieutenant Colonel Chester G. *From Salerno to the Alps: A History of the Fifth Army, 1943–1945.* Washington, D.C.: Infantry Journal Press, 1948.

Thomas, Lowell. Transcript from radio broadcast of 13 October 1942. DPL.

Thompson, Jake H. *Bob Dole: The Republicans' Man for All Seasons.* New York: Donald I. Fine, 1994.

Truscott, Lucien K. *Command Missions: A Personal Story.* New York: E. P. Dutton, 1954.

Ware, Wilson. "The Riva Ridge," *American Alpine Journal* 6, no. 2 (1946): 208–220.

Waterman, Jonathan. *Cloud Dancers: Portraits of North American Mountaineers.* Golden, Colo.: American Alpine Club Press, 1993.

Whitlock, Flint. *Soldiers on Skis: A Pictorial Memoir of the 10th Mountain Division.* Boulder, Colo.: Paladin Press, 1992.

Wood, Tom. "A Historical Study of Camp Hale, Colorado." Unpublished thesis, 1974. DPL.

ABOUT THE TYPE

This book was set in Photina, a typeface designed by José Mendoza in 1971. It is a very elegant design with high legibility, and its close character fit has made it a popular choice for use in quality magazines and art gallery publications.

BLOODY FALLS

of the COPPERMINE

McKAY JENKINS

In the winter of 1913, high in the Canadian Arctic, two Catholic priests set out on a dangerous mission: to reach a group of Eskimos and convert them. Upon their arrival, the priests were murdered, their livers removed and eaten.

Over the next three years, a remarkable 3,000-mile search was conducted for the bodies and the killers. During the astonishing murder trial that followed, the Eskimos were acquitted of the charges, despite the seating of an all-white jury. The outraged judge demanded a retrial—predictably, the Eskimos were then convicted of murder.

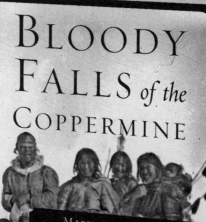

An almost perfect parable of late colonialism, combining the intensity of true crime with the romance of wilderness adventure, *Bloody Falls of the Coppermine* is a clear-eyed look at what results when two utterly different cultures come together in violent conflict.